Florida Real Estate 45-Hour Course Companion

PAMELA S. KEMPER,

With Content and Editorial Contribution by Regina A. Brubaker

Copyright © 2017 Pamela Kemper
Revised and updated as of February 2024.
All rights reserved.
ISBN: 172265497X
ISBN-13: 978-1722654979

DEDICATION

To all of our great students who have successfully become Florida Real Estate Agents.
Enjoy this next educational adventure!

CONTENTS

	Acknowledgments	i
	Course Introduction	3

SECTION 1 BUSINESS BUILDING

1	Business Planning	6
2	Prospecting	19
3	Managing Listings	34
4	Managing Buyers	49
5	Objection Handling	63

SECTION 2 THE DEAL

6	Financing Considerations	75
7	Condos/H.O. A's/C.D. D's	88
8	Contracts	102
9	Inspections	114
10	Closings	124

SECTION 3 LEGAL ISSUES

11	Licensing Law – Maintaining Compliance	140
12	Ethics and Business Practices	156
13	Fair Housing Applied	169
14	ECOA /TILA / RESPA – in Practice	181
15	Agency in Practice	191

SECTION 4 PROPERTY MANAGEMENT

16	Property Management	210
	Sources and Resources	219
	About the Authors	222

ACKNOWLEDGMENTS

The content of this book is original and was written to comply with The Florida Real Estate Post-Licensing Education 45-Hour requirements. See Sources and Resources at the end of the book for clarification of content credit and for further resource material.

For advice regarding real estate, legal, and accounting issues, always consult a professional.

COURSE INTRODUCTION

Every real estate sales licensee in the state of Florida is required to take an approved 45-hour post-licensing sales course prior to the first renewal of the licensee's license. Should the licensee fail to do so, the licensee's real estate license would become null and void. The only recourse that an individual would have in that situation is to take the pre-license course all over again and once again pass the state exam.

This course, Florida Real Estate Sales Associates Post-Licensing Excellence, is divided into 4 sections with a total of 16 chapters.

SECTION 1 BUSINESS BUILDING, focuses on building a thriving real estate business.
SECTION 2 THE DEAL, focuses on successfully taking a deal from contract to closing.
SECTION 3 LEGAL ISSUES, focuses on legal issues affecting the practice of real estate.
SECTION 4 PROPERTY MANAGEMENT, focuses on providing property management services.

Students of the 45-hour post-license sales course must pass an end-of-course 100 question multiple choice exam at 75%. There is not a state exam that must be passed. Upon successful completion, the real estate school must report the completion to the state of Department of Business and Professional Regulation. Be sure to allow for time for such reporting prior to the sales associate's license expiring!

It is in the licensee's best interest to take the 45-hour post-licensing course as soon as possible. This not only avoids any reporting time issues prior to the licensee losing his or her license, but due to the content of the course, it positions the licensee in best being able to develop a successful real estate career.

Licensees who have earned a 4-year degree specifically in real estate are exempt from the post-license education requirements.

475.17 (3)(a) The commission may prescribe a post-licensure education requirement in order for a person to maintain a valid sales associate's license, which shall not exceed 45 classroom hours of 50 minutes each, inclusive of examination, prior to the first renewal following initial licensure. If prescribed, this shall consist of one or more commission-approved courses which total at least 45 classroom hours on one or more subjects which include, **but are not limited to, property management, appraisal, real estate finance, the economics of real estate management, marketing, technology, sales and listing of properties, business office management, courses teaching practical real estate skills, development of business plans, marketing of property, and time management.**

Required post-licensure education courses must be provided by an accredited college, university, or community college, by a career center, by a registered real estate school, or by a commission-approved sponsor.

Administrative Code: Following is the provision regarding post-education requirements

61J2-3.020 Post-licensing Education for Active and Inactive Broker and Sales Associate Licensees.

(1) All applicants for licensure who pass a broker or sales associate licensure examination must satisfactorily complete a Commission-prescribed post-licensing course prior to the first renewal following initial licensure. The licensee must take the post-licensing course or courses at an accredited university, college, community college, area technical center in this state, real estate school registered, pursuant to Section 475.451, F.S., or Commission-approved sponsor ("provider").

(a) For a licensed sales associate, the post-licensing education requirement shall consist of one or more Commission-approved courses which shall not exceed 45-hours of 50 minutes each, inclusive of examination, in subjects as provided for in Section 475.17(3)(a), F.S. Post-licensing courses shall consist of a minimum of 15 hours of instruction of 50 minutes each.

(4) A grade of 75% or higher on the Commission-prescribed end-of-course examination constitutes satisfactory course completion. The provider shall develop at least 2 unique forms of the end-of-course examinations and submit them for approval with a detailed course syllabus. The answer key must be unique for each form of the examination and reference the page number(s) containing the information on which each question and correct answer is based. Examinations must test the material. At least 70% of the questions on each form of the test shall be application oriented. Application level means the ability to use the learned material in a completely new and concrete situation. It usually involves the application of rules, policies, methods, computations, laws, theories, or any other relevant and available information. No more than 10% of the questions on each form of the test shall be at the knowledge level. Knowledge level means the recall of specific facts, patterns, methods, terms, rules, dates, formulas, names or other information that should be committed to memory. A provider offering the Commission-prescribed courses must maintain a sufficient bank of questions to assure examination validity. End-of-course examinations shall contain at least 100 items. A course that is thirty-hours or less shall contain a minimum of 50 items. All questions shall be multiple choice with 4 answer choices each. The order of the examination questions may not follow the sequence of the course content. The overall time to complete the end-of-course examination must not exceed the equivalent of 1.8 minutes per item.

(8)(a) Students failing a Commission-prescribed end-of-course examination must wait at least 30 days from the date of the original examination to retest. Within one year of the original examination, a student may retest a maximum of one time. Otherwise, students failing the Commission-prescribed end-of-course examination must repeat the course prior to being eligible to again take the end-of-course examination. Providers shall administer a different form of the end-of-course examination to a student that is retaking the exam or repeating the course.

(10) Any licensee who has received a 4-year degree in real estate from an accredited institution of higher education is exempt from the post-license education requirements.

October 2016. https://www.flrules.org/gateway/RuleNo.asp?title=MINIMUM EDUCATIONAL REQUIREMENTS&ID=61J2-3.020

SECTION 1 BUSINESS BUILDING

SECTION 1 BUSINESS BUILDING, of this course, focuses on building a thriving real estate business. Chapters include:
1. Business Planning
2. Prospecting
3. Managing Listings
4. Managing Buyers
5. Objection Handling

Upon completion of this section, licensees should have a good grasp of how to launch and manage a real estate career, the importance of consistent prospecting, how to work with listings, how to work with buyers, and how to successfully handle objections.

1 BUSINESS PLANNING

<u>Learning Terms and Phrases</u>
- Intentional Action
- Pareto's Principle
- Production Goals
- Transactions Closed
- Clients to Leads Conversion
- Leads to Clients Conversion
- Prospects to Leads Conversion
- Action Plan
- Support Activities
- Lead Generation
- Time Management
- Communication Skills
- Technical Knowledge
- Product Knowledge
- Marketing Knowledge
- Assistants
- Spending Traps
- Branding
- MLS Brokerage
- Non-MLS Brokerage

Learning Objectives

- Licensees will be able to determine how many transactions are required to meet earning goals based on local averages.
- Licensees will be able to determine how many clients are required to meet transaction goals based on closing averages.
- Licensees will be able to determine how many leads are required to produce the client number goal based on conversion averages.
- Licensees will be able to determine how many prospects are required to produce the lead number goal based on conversion averages.
- Licensees will have developed an action plan designed to meet prospecting goals.
- Licensees will have increased skill in listening to apply to real estate activities.
- Licensees will have an understanding of what product knowledge is and developed a plan to increase product knowledge.
- Licensees will have an understanding of what technical knowledge is and developed a plan to increase product knowledge.
- Licensees will have an understanding of what marketing knowledge is and developed a plan to increase product knowledge.
- Licensees will have an understanding of what product knowledge is and developed a plan to increase product knowledge.
- Licensees will have developed a schedule to accommodate prospecting, knowledge building and administrative tasks based on either a part-time or full-time commitment.

Intentional Action

Success does not *just happen* in real estate. It is not just a matter of "build it and they will come." Instead, a successful career in real estate is the direct result of intentional action. This chapter addresses how to set goals in real estate, how to manage time for positive results, how to manage real estate expenses, and how to juggle a part-time versus full-time real estate career – all aspects of success.

80/20 Rule

Regardless of whether a licensee is working in a real estate market where the agent is competing with 500 or 5,000 agents, Pareto's Principle applies:

20% of the real estate licensees are producing 80% of the real estate sales.

Pareto's Principle

Vilfredo Pareto was an Italian economist from the early 1900s. He created a formula which analyzed the distribution of wealth. His calculations determined that 20% of the population owned 80% of the wealth. Others began documenting similar findings in various fields. In the 1930s, Dr. Joseph Juran looked to this phenomenon and promoted a universal principle that 20% of any group always produced 80% of results. Since Juran's publications, Pareto's Principle became an accepted truth.

Parato's Principle – The 80-20 Rule. By F. John Reh. November 2016.
https://www.thebalance.com/pareto-s-principle-the-80-20-rule-2275148

Happy with Less

The fact that 20% of licensees are producing 80% of the sales is not a bad thing for the licensees who are among the 20%! Actually, though, for many – being among the 80% producing the rest of the sales in real estate might also be a good place. Consider a semi-retired real estate licensee who only works part-time in real estate. This licensee may commit minimal time to the business of real estate producing only one sale every three months. In a market averaging $250,000 in home values, this licensee would potentially earn $30,000 in one year based on an average of 3% commission paid on each sale. (All commissions are negotiable between agents and clients.)

Becoming One of the 20%

Although some licensees are satisfied with lower levels of production, it is the goal of many licensees to become a top producing real estate agent. The key to breaking through to becoming one of the 20% producing 80% of the production relies on an understanding that the 80/20 rule applies not just to who is producing what – but to why. The "why" is that out of all the tasks that an average person engages in throughout a day, only 20% of the tasks actually produce desired results. In fact, 20% of all tasks engaged in produce 80% of the desired outcome. But because people only spend 20% of their time doing activities that produce success, success is limited.

Success, then, is tied directly to time management! Successful people flip the equation. They spend 80% of their time on the 20% of activities that actually produce results.

Put in plainer language:
- Successful people spend the majority of their time doing things that produce direct results.

Parato's Principle – The 80-20 Rule. By F. John Reh. November 2016.
https://www.thebalance.com/pareto-s-principle-the-80-20-rule-2275148

Measuring Success

A successful career for any one person may look quite different than another's successful career. This is due to the fact that what one person plans to gain from a career can vary dramatically from what another person plans to gain. So measuring success is a very personal process.

As such, a real estate licensee should have a clear vision for what the licensee wishes to gain from a career in real estate.

Is it a flexible schedule that pulls in a modest income?

Or is it a disciplined commitment to work that produces high levels of income?

The amount of money earned then, as compared from one licensee to another, is a flawed measurement of a successful career.

But for an individual licensee, having a monetary goal for production becomes a personal and reliable measure to gauge success.

Production Goals

A licensee can develop a reliable and successful action plan by answering this basic question:
- "How much money do I want to make?"

By knowing this income goal, the licensee can work industry standards backwards to determine how many deals have to be closed, how many clients have to be secured, how many leads have to be generated, and how many people have to be "touched." Once a licensee has a proven track record, the "industry standards" will be replaced with actual results to work this formula for each new year.

Long Term Vs. Short Term Goals

A new licensee should set clear, concise, measurable, and realistic goals. Although there are success stories of licensees starting their career with a bang creating large earnings from day one, this is simply an unrealistic expectation for most new agents. It's fine to think big. In fact, thinking with a large goal in mind helps to create success. But the best strategy is to break down the goals into smaller increments working toward the larger end goal.

For example, should a licensee desire to produce $250,000 in commissionable gross income in a year, the licensee might set out a goal to produce $75,000 in the first year, $125,000 in the second year, $180,000 the third year, and $250,000 in the fourth year.

From Yearly to Monthly Goals

A licensee who is looking to produce $75,000 in the first year, may also set the shorter goal of producing $10,000 within the first three months. Then, between months three and six, producing another $20,000. Then another $45,000 in the last six months. The idea is to set goals in workable increments.

Transactions Required to Reach Income Goals

Once an income goal has been set, the licensee must then determine, how many deals would be necessary to produce the expected income?

To measure this, take into account the agreed upon commission split between the licensee and his or her employing broker by taking the income goal and dividing by the percent you will keep in commission.

Then divide by the average commission percentage in the area. This gives the total in gross sales that must be made to produce the commissionable income.

Then take the total in gross sales and divide by the average sale price of real estate in the licensee's area. The result will be the number of transactions required to produce the income.

- Income goal ÷ % You Keep of Commission = Total Income Goal
- Total Income Goal ÷ Average Commission % = Total Gross Sales Required
- Total Gross Sales Required ÷ Average Sale Price = Total Transactions Required

Transactions Required Example

If per the employment agreement with the licensee's broker, the licensee keeps 75% of each commissionable deal and the licensee is looking to make $55,000 in the first year while working in an area with an average sale price of $250,000 and an average commission of 3%; then the number of transactions required to meet this income would be calculated as:
- Income goal ÷ % You Keep of Commission = Total Income Goal
    - $55,000 ÷ .75 = $73,333 Total Income Goal
- Total Income Goal ÷ Average Commission % = Total Gross Sales Required
    - $73,333 ÷ .03 = $2,444,433 Total Gross Sales Required
- Total Gross Sales Required ÷ Average Sale Price = Total Transactions Required
    - $2,444,433 ÷ $250,000 = 10 Total Transactions Required (9.7 rounded up)

In summary, to earn $55,000, 10 homes averaging $250,000 each for a total of $2,444,433 in sales must take place to meet the goal.

Percentage of Clients Closed

The reality of real estate is such that, if ten transactions are required, then approximately 13 to 16 buyers and sellers would be needed to be worked to account for deals that fail to come together or fail to close.

The exact numbers vary by area and licensee.
- A 75% successful deal rate would result in 13 clients needed to produce 10 closings.

- $10 \div .75 = 13$
- A 60% success rate would require approximately 16 clients to produce 10 closings.
  - $10 \div .6 = 16$

Clients are defined as a buyer or seller who has agreed to work with the licensee.

Leads to Clients - Conversion

If 16 clients are required to reach sales goals, the question then becomes as to how many leads must be generated to produce the clients. Not all leads are successfully converted into clients.

Leads are defined as individuals that have been identified as being in the market to buy or sell real estate. Leads are people that a licensee may know or who has been referred to the licensee. A lead is not yet a client as there is not yet a commitment to work together.

If a licensee has a 75% lead to client conversion rate, then 22 leads would be required to produce 16 clients:

- Clients Required ÷ Conversion % = Leads Required
  - $16 \div .75 = 22$

Creating Leads

Creating leads stems from consistently communicating with people. These communications are in the form of phone calls, door knocks, emails, and mailings.

How many people would need to be communicated with to create 22 leads?

This number varies within areas and within agent experience.

Gary Keller, the author of <u>The Millionaire Real Estate Agent</u>, teaches that consistently "touching" 12 people should produce 2 leads a year.

This means that to produce 22 leads in a year, 132 people would need to be communicated with consistently.

- Leads Required ÷ 2 = Groups of 12 People Needed
  - $22 \div 2 = 11$
- Groups of 12 Needed x 12 = Total Number of People to "Touch"
  - $11 \times 12 = 132$

The quality of the relationships and the touches greatly affect the conversion from "touch" to lead!

Goal Conversion

Prospect → Lead
Lead → Client
Client → Deal
Deal → $

★ **Students of the post-licensing 45-hour course are instructed to do the following exercise:**

Determine Personal Earnings Goal
- Earning Goal for Next 12 Months: _____
- Divide Yearly Earning Goal by 12 for Monthly Goal: _____

Determine Transactions Required to Meet Income Goal
- Income goal ÷ % You Keep of Commission = Total Income Goal _____
- Total Income Goal ÷ Average Commission % = Total Gross Sales Required _____
- Total Gross Sales Required ÷ Average Sale Price = Total Transactions Required _____

Determine Client Closed Ratio
- Consult with Broker for expected % of Client Closed Ratio to Use _____
- Total Transactions Required ÷ % of Client Closed Ratio for # Clients Needed: _____

Determine the Number of Leads Required
- Consult with Broker for expected % of Lead Conversion to Use _____
- Clients Required ÷ Conversion % = Leads Required _____

Determine the Number of Prospects Required to Create a Lead
- Leads Required ÷ 2 = Groups of 12 People Needed _____
- Groups of 12 Needed x 12 = Total Number of People to "Touch" _____

From Goals to Action Plan

Once a licensee has a clear idea of how many leads need to be generated to meet income goals, the licensee can then design a monthly and weekly action plan. The action plan should focus primarily on lead-generating activities. This includes making phone calls, meeting with people face to face, sending emails and mailings.

Support Activities

At the outset of a real estate career, a licensee will find him or herself busy doing things to develop real estate skills and knowledge. This includes tasks such as becoming familiar with the multiple listing service, visiting homes for sale, and practicing pricing property. The licensee should be acutely aware, however, that as important as these tasks are, they are the 80% of tasks that do not directly produce real estate deals. These tasks support the ability to effectively manage a real estate deal. This means these tasks are important. However, real estate licensees who allow themselves to be dominated by these "important" tasks will find themselves lagging in the one task that produces income: *Lead Generation.*

The Office Trap
Many real estate licensees will start their career in a real estate office – literally. They set up an office space. They make sure that their computer, desk and chair are ergonomically correct. They set out their lead generating tips books. They set out their pens, note papers, etc. They attend office meetings. They get advice from other agents by chatting around the office coffee station. They even fire up their smartphones, their tablets and their computer with the goal of beginning the arduous task of setting up online profiles to generate leads. But therein lies the trap. As important as these activities are, if the bulk of their time is spent doing these things as a new agent, then the one task that is proven to lead to success is often avoided. Talking to potential clients.

Distracted by Technology
Today's real estate licensee has a multitude of technology to assist in the development of leads and the business management. They have smart phones, FaceTime, Skype, social media, texting, tablets, computers, fancy video and camera equipment…the list goes on and on and is ever evolving with the advancements in the technological world. However, these same sales tools that can help propel a licensee to success also many times ends up distracting a licensee into failure. The trap lies in thinking that just because the licensee is spending time engaged in "real estate activities" that the licensee is actively generating leads.

Social Media
There is no doubt that spending time on social media can be a huge help to drive leads and ultimate success. In transitioning to the Florida Real Estate Market from the Indiana/Michigan area, Pamela Kemper (author of this book and course) secured her first Florida listing through communicating on facebook.com. However, the posts and subsequent messaging on facebook.com reinforced a relationship that had been established face to face. First time connections can be made, however, through social media sites with a carefully constructed plan. So, establishing online profiles and working a consistent presence online is a valuable tool for success. The trick is to make it a part of a larger lead prospecting plan.

Tips for Remaining Focused
Once you have established your prospecting action task list, it is imperative that you stick to it. When working in an "office" situation, examine what distracts you and work to eliminate the distractions. Although phone calls are a huge part of any successful real estate business, many successful agents find that designating a set time to "take" and "return" phone calls are far more productive than the constant interruption of calls. It is important to recognize an individual's tendency to procrastinate. Not everyone procrastinates. Yet, many, many do. Working as a real estate agent requires that individuals be self-starters; able to hold themselves accountable to goals and schedules.

Flipping Your Schedule
Most licensees plan to start their day in the office. A schedule of good intentions lies ahead of them which includes exploring new listings online, expanding training, posting on social media sites, sending out emails and mailings, making phone calls, and visiting potential clients – and in that exact order. What happens to most agents, though, is that they get sucked into doing everything before the actual making of calls and visiting of potential clients. Picking up the phone and approaching people are the two acts that are most closely connected with successful lead generation. Yet, these two tasks are the two tasks that most agents dread the most. Consequently, procrastination often sets in rather than plunging forward.

For the procrastinators, success comes easier by flipping the workday. Instead of starting out at the office doing "busy work," start out by knocking on doors and meeting people face to face. Once the goal has been met of how many people to communicate with face to face, then phone calls are made. Only once these phone calls are made would the office then be "entered" to perform the other necessary tasks.

Too Many Meetings

It is exciting as a new licensee to be around other agents. There is a definite benefit to witnessing others' success. When joining a brokerage, licensees will find themselves either invited or required to attend office meetings. Upon joining the local association of realtors, licensees will again find themselves invited or required to attend a multitude of meetings. Yet, when choosing how to spend the bulk of his or her time, successful agents recognize that the main thrust of their business will not be generated by rubbing elbows with these other agents. Rather it will come from spending time with non-agents beyond the real estate community.

Too Much Training

The completion of a real estate deal requires knowledge and skill. A new licensee will be given ample opportunity to build his or her knowledge base. The licensee will be encouraged to study communication skills, build technological knowledge such as manipulating the multiple listing service online website, and product knowledge by visiting properties that are listed. Although, all this training is vital to a successful career, if it overshadows time available to do consistent lead generating activities – then the very training provided for success becomes cause for failure.

Put another way, a new licensee that has an opportunity to take a listing who has not yet mastered a listing presentation may easily pair up with an experienced agent to win the listing and earn a commission. Yet, a new agent that has mastered the listing presentation through training will have no commission earnings if adequate time hasn't been spent to find a listing lead! Lead generation should be priority from day one. It should not be put off until after the licensee has built "skills!"

Saying "no"

One of the things that attracts many people to a real estate career is the flexibility the work schedule affords. Yet it is this flexibility which can often lead to failure. Just because a licensee does not have to "punch a time clock" at the beginning and end of a work day, if priority is not given to the development of a real estate career as priority the career is likely to falter. Learn to say no to other people and to yourself!

"No, I am not free to have lunch today," when asked by a fellow real estate agent. Instead have lunch with a non-real estate licensee!

"No, I cannot stay home and do laundry today," instead do the laundry after the work day is done – just as you would when punching a clock.

"No, I can't go to the beach today." Instead host an open house even if it is someone else's listing!

Ask whether the task at hand will really advance a career in real estate. If it doesn't, then say no. If unable to say "No," then find a way to make the activity prospecting related, such as having a yearly medical physical – wear a real estate identification badge and give the receptionists, nurses, and doctors a business card!

⭐ **Students of the post-licensing 45-hour course are instructed to do the following exercise:**

> What would you do if…
> You are struggling to start your real estate career and your sibling demands that you take over mowing your mother's lawn twice a week (after all you don't work a real job anyway).
>
> A. Agree to mow the lawn twice a week. Good kids should always go out of their way for a parent in need.
> B. Insist that the sibling either split the lawn mowing task or split the cost of hiring someone to do the mowing.
>
> B is the best answer. It is easy for other people to see your flexible schedule as something to be taken advantage of. However, only by engaging in real estate activities will success be achieved.

Personal Time

Where many licensees fail in being disciplined enough to prevent personal time from sabotaging their work day, others with a sense of urgency can become a victim to "burn out" by failing to schedule and honoring a need for a personal life. There are truly so many tasks that a new licensee "should" engage in to foster success that it can easily push out any time for a personal life. It is important to remember why a licensee has launched a real estate career. For many, it is to make a better life for their family. The solution to this is to be proactive at working in personal time into each and every day, week, and month. Block the time in for personal activities. Treat it as an important task and honor it!

Education Goals

Despite the warning about not letting training get in the way of spending an adequate amount of time on lead prospecting, there is no doubt that successful agents must be involved in educational components. Both new and experienced licensees will find that dedication to gaining education and skills is a vital and ongoing aspect of skill development. At the outset of a real estate career, there are many areas of knowledge and skill that the new licensee needs to quickly master.

Communication Skills

It is imperative that real estate licensees have good communication skills. Communication skills include listening, verbalization, writing, and nonverbal/body language. Listening is listed first because a good real estate licensee, first and foremost, must be able to take in information and process what is important. Verbalizing thoughts and facts effectively means more than just "talking" to a prospect or client. It involves phrasing words and tone to lead the conversation to a satisfactory point of agreement. Writing skills assist in the prospecting role as letters and emails are sent. Plus, it becomes vital in preparing legally correct contracts. Remember to use correct grammar and do a spell check! Body language involves the way a person holds him or herself including how hands are positioned and eye contact is maintained. It is viewed as holding more weight in a conversation than the actual words spoken.

The 7% Rule: Fact, Fiction, Or Misunderstanding. February 2017.
http://ubiquity.acm.org/article.cfm?id=2043156

★ **Students of the post-licensing 45-hour course are instructed to do the following exercise:**

> Practice Listening Skills by Expressing Empathy
> Find a partner and practice rephrasing what your partner tells you in order to "reflect" the fact that you are listening and care about what is being said.
> *Note: This is not the same as parroting which is repeating exactly what is said.
>
> Be sure to give each other feedback on whether what is being rephrased matches what was being said!

Technical Knowledge

The "how to's" of being a real estate licensee makes up the technical side of a licensee's education. Learning how to compare the value of one property to another is a good example of gaining technical skills. Being able to calculate closing costs and reading a closing disclosure would be two other good examples. Filling out a listing agreement or a purchase contract are also examples of technical knowledge.

Product Knowledge

Every profession has a "product" that the business revolves around. The real estate professional revolves around the sale or lease of property and/or business opportunities. Thus, gaining product knowledge, then, is the act of understanding the real estate market. Is it a buyer's market or a seller's market? What is currently for sale? What is current pricing?

The best way to gain product knowledge is to look at listing details online and to visit the listings. Plan to visit scheduled open houses and broker tours. Also, request to "preview" the property. This will normally be approved as sellers equate exposure with a higher probability of a successful sale. However, always disclose when there is not an actual buyer lined up at the time of the preview.

★ **Students of the post-licensing 45-hour course are instructed to do the following exercise:**

> Develop Product Knowledge
> Schedule concrete ways to develop product knowledge.
>   Dedicate time each week to reviewing new listings.
>   Dedicate time biweekly to visit open houses.
>   Dedicate time each month to go on Broker Property Tours.

Marketing Knowledge

Whereas "knowledge of the market" means understanding what is selling and for how much, marketing knowledge is understanding how to get a property to sell! A well written property description or a quality photograph triggers buyers' interest in showings. See Chapter 3, "Managing Listings," for more information.

A successful real estate career involves more than marketing property. It involves marketing the licensee to attract potential buyers and sellers. See Chapter 2, "Prospecting," for more information.

Continuing Education

Even beyond initial knowledge and skill development, real estate licenses will be involved in education. Some of this will be required by the state. Florida Statutes require that all real estate licensees complete 14 hours of continuing education beyond the first licensing renewal period. Many brokerages offer or require ongoing education offered through on or off site training meetings. The local, state, and national REALTOR® associations offer educational opportunities, as well.

Scheduling for Success

Successful agents create a plan for their days, weeks, and months. They block time for the activities that directly generate leads and deals and make that the priority in the schedule. Time is then allowed for training and ongoing skill development and education.

Sample Full-Time Schedule

The schedule shown here would be typical of an established agent handling most real estate tasks on his or her own. The yellow items reflect items that, although important, do not directly create leads or deals. Also included in yellow are the "administrative" type of tasks. Administrative tasks include things like preparing listing paperwork and entering listings into the multiple listing service system. Administrative tasks are tasks that advanced agents usually hire assistants to do. The green items are activities that are directly tied to concrete money-making activities. Included would be showing buyer property, writing and managing offers, conducting listing appointments, and attending closings. The red items are lead generating activities. These activities should be a very high priority for all agents!

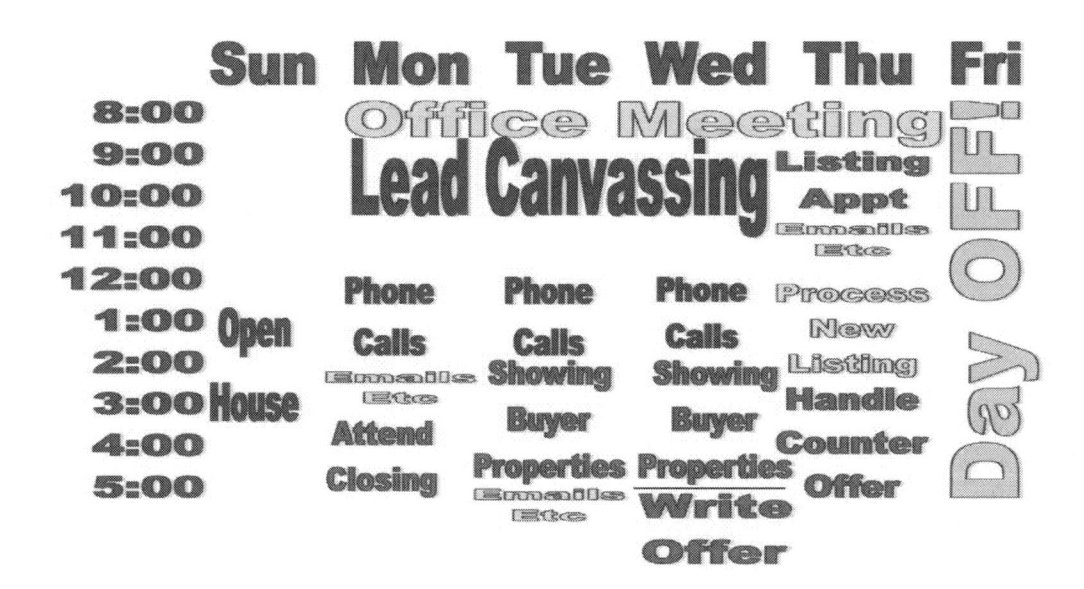

	Sun	Mon	Tue	Wed	Thu	Fri
8:00		Office Meeting				Day OFF!
9:00		Lead Canvassing			Listing Appt	
10:00						
11:00					Emails Etc	
12:00						
1:00	Open House	Phone Calls	Phone Calls	Phone Calls	Process New Listing Handle Counter Offer	
2:00		Emails Etc	Showing Buyer Properties	Showing Buyer Properties		
3:00		Attend Closing		Write Offer		
4:00			Emails Etc			
5:00						

Part-Time Agents

Not all successful real estate agents start out working full-time in the field. With careful planning, it is possible to juggle more than one job. It would be a mistake for a licensee to learn all that is involved in a real estate career and assume that a full-time commitment is necessary to get started. Success comes from being intentional in how time is used. Remember the 80/20 rule? The less time that is available to conduct real estate, means the more time that should be dedicated to the 20% of tasks that results in success!

Part-time agents should spend as much time as possible doing the red and green items from the schedule example! Where an experienced agent has lots of time spent directly working with clients, newer agents will more heavily focus on training and skill development.

★ **Students of the post-licensing 45-hour course are instructed to do the following exercise:**

> Develop A Work Schedule
> Using either a computer, phone, or a notebook, create a work schedule to follow to build your real estate business.
>
> Include time to do prospecting tasks.
> Include time to work directly with clients.
> Include time to do administrative tasks.
> Include time to build product knowledge.
> Include time to build technical knowledge.

Assistants

At the outset of a real estate career, it is common for a real estate licensee to do all tasks required as an agent. Sometimes, a real estate brokerage office will have assistants on hand to facilitate tasks such as inputting multiple listing data or processing pending deals. There comes a time, though, for most successful agents, when the licensee must consider hiring an assistant. Whether the assistant will also need to be a real estate licensee will depend upon the tasks performed.

> **FREC has issued the following specific guidelines as to the tasks which Unlicensed Assistants may perform under their broker's supervision:**
> - Answer the phone and forward calls
> - Fill out and submit listings and changes to any multiple listing service
> - Follow-up on loan commitments after a contract has been negotiated and generally secure the status reports on the loan progress
> - Assemble documents for closing
> - Secure documents (public information) from courthouse, utility district, etc.
> - Have keys made for company listings, order surveys, termite inspections, home inspections and home warranties with the licensed employer's approval
> - Write ads for approval of the licensee and the supervising broker, and place advertising (newspaper ads, update web sites, etc); prepare flyers and promotional information for approval by licensee and the supervising broker
> - Receive, record and deposit earnest money, security deposits and advance rents
> - Only type the contract forms for approval by licensee and supervising broker
> - Monitor licenses and personnel files
> - Compute commission checks
> - Place signs on property
> - Order items of repair as directed by licensee
> - Prepare flyers and promotional information for approval by licensee and supervising broker
> - Act as a courier service to deliver documents, pick-up keys
> - Place routine telephone calls on late rent payments
> - Schedule appointments for licensee to show a listed property
>
> http://www.myfloridalicense.com/dbpr/re/documents/Permissibleactivitiesrev092009.pdf

Expenses

An important word of warning to new real estate agents is to plan very carefully in regard to spending. It is easy to let spending get out of control. It seems that there is always an opportunity to spend money in real estate. There is signage, business cards and printing costs from the outset. Plus, many real estate licensees join the Realtor Associations and Multiple Listing Services which also costs money. Some brokerages require onboarding and/or monthly office fees. And then there are potential advertising costs.

Spending Traps

A rule of thumb for new agents is to make sure that any money spent on advertising should have concrete measurable results. For example, if a licensee pays an internet service to be included on a website resulting in a buyer contacting the agent through that site then there is a concrete measurable result.

Branding

Some advertising is said to contribute to the "branding" of an agent by bringing awareness to the public that the licensee is in the business of real estate. The hope is that someone will contact the agent when a real estate need arises. An aggressive agent might put his or her name on a park bench and on a billboard near a condominium development. This method usually has the best returns, especially when it is paired with door knocking in that neighborhood to meet the potential buyer and sellers!

Startup Costs

Each licensee must analyze their own startup funds and choose a broker that matches their financial resources. For example, not all brokers require that agents pay a fee when joining the firm. The licensee must analyze their own startup business funds as compared to the benefits that are being offered by the brokerage. For example, some brokers have opportunities for new agents to share in phone duty rotation – which can result in clients!

Choosing an MLS vs. Non-MLS broker

An initial fee that new agents often find challenging is paying the multiple listing service fee. Whenever a broker belongs to the MLS, then all the agents working within that brokerage must also join the MLS. Remember, though, that it is not a legal requirement to join the multiple listing service or the associations. Many licensees choose to join because of the advantages they see in doing so. However, licensees can legally sell real estate for others without joining either. It is easier to work with buyers than sellers without belonging to the MLS. Most sellers choose real estate agents specifically to see their property included on the MLS.

Licensees that choose to place their licenses under a non-MLS broker can work with buyers by taking advantage of property listing information that is shared all over the internet. Remember, though, that the listing broker is not required to pay a buyer's broker who isn't a member of the MLS unless a separate agreement is entered into for the employing broker to pay the buyer's agent broker. A licensee who is working with a non-MLS broker should look to their broker for assistance in securing an agreement for payment!

Brokerage Splits

How much a broker retains of the sales commission varies widely. It would seem common sense that the more a licensee gets to keep of a commission then the better the deal is. However, this is not necessarily true. 50% of a lot of deals may end up being a lot more money than 90% of hardly any deals!

The questions that an agent should ask him or herself when analyzing a brokerage commission split includes:

What are the benefits the agent is gaining from the relationship?
How much training and support is provided?
How many opportunities to work leads is provided?
Does the broker cover any of the startup or ongoing costs of the licensee?

With good planning, licensees can find success!

2 PROSPECTING

Learning Terms and Phrases
- Prospecting
- Specializing in Buyers
- Specializing in Sellers
- Office Duty
- Open Houses
- Sphere of Influence
- Referrals
- Phone Prospecting
- Community Involvement
- Prospecting to Professionals
- Farming
- Turnover Percentage
- Niche Market
- For Sale by Owners
- Expired Listings
- Email Marketing
- Door Knocking
- "Do Not Call"
- Paying for Leads
- Role Playing Script

Learning Objectives

- Licensees will have developed a sphere of influence prospecting list and plan.
- Licensees will have developed phone prospecting skills.
- Licensees will have developed a plan to expand sphere of influence by becoming involved with the community or a group.
- Licensees will have developed a plan to expand sphere of influence by developing relationships with business professionals and groups.
- Licensees will have developed a plan for farming.

LICENSEES WILL CUSTOMIZE PROSPECTING SCRIPTS AND DEVELOP SKILLS THROUGH ROLE PLAYING.

What is Prospecting?

Prospecting includes reaching out to people that a licensee knows or wants to get to know, in the hope that it will eventually generate business. Successful prospecting must be conducted in a systematic, consistent manner. As stated in Chapter 1, "Business Planning," creating leads stems from consistently communicating with people. Once a licensee has a clear idea of how many leads need to be generated to meet income goals, the licensee can then design a monthly and weekly action plan. The action plan should focus primarily on lead generating activities. This includes making phone calls, meeting with people face to face, sending emails and mailings. Other activities that contribute to lead generation include holding open houses, handling office and phone duty, and creating marketing pieces that are advertised online and in print media. This chapter describes these specific ways to prospect while emphasizing the different demographic groups to target when prospecting.

A Prospect vs. a Lead vs. a Client

Chapter 1, "Business Planning," noted that a prospect is different from a lead. A lead is when a licensee has a specific name for someone that is in the market to buy or sell real estate, whereas a prospect is someone who is not yet in the market. The whole point of prospecting is to create leads.

With a lead comes the opportunity to gain a client. A client is different from a lead in that the client has committed to working with the licensee to pursue the buying or selling of real estate.

Importance of Prospecting

The very essence of real estate success lies with successful prospecting. Without prospecting, a few real estate deals might come to the licensee, but it is doubtful that it would be enough to sustain a fruitful career. Every prospect that the licensee consistently communicates with creates an opportunity to work as an agent in real estate for that person at some point in the future and/or an opportunity to work with someone the prospects refer to the licensee.

Prospecting for Buyers

Prospecting for buyers is often a recommended focus for new licensees. According to the National Association of REALTORS®, buyers are easier to find than sellers. Plus, prospecting for sellers has a much lower return on the output of effort as compared to prospecting for buyers. In fact, it is estimated that even if a licensee spends 85% of his time or resources focused on prospecting for sellers, a good 50% of the licensee's business is apt to still be generated from buyers!

Prospecting Buyers. February 2017. http://realtormag.realtor.org/tool-kit/prospecting/article/prospecting-buyers

Prospecting for Sellers
Yet, as Chapter 3, "Managing Listings," details; although prospecting for sellers may be a bit more challenging, listings potentially generates not only other listings but buyers as well. So even agents that hope to work with many buyers will find that an emphasis on sellers is a productive way to attract buyers!

Specializing in Buyers or Sellers
A licensee, then, when developing marketing material and marketing campaigns may decide to focus on either attracting buyers or sellers. The licensee may even balance the marketing efforts to attract both buyers and sellers. Despite whether seeking to attract buyers, seller or both, the key is to engage in a well thought out and diverse array of activities that produces leads.

Office and Phone Duty
One of the most basic ways that a licensee can hope to come in contact with potential buyers and sellers is through taking duty at a brokerage office to handle "walk ins" and "phone calls." Buyers interested in specific property or sellers seeking a professional to list a property often call or walk into a brokerage for assistance. The opportunity to work office or phone duty is not provided by all brokerages, but when it is, it can be a very productive way to prospect and capture leads. This is even more true when signage and advertising puts the brokerage phone number and location front and center in the advertising. The quality of leads resulting from phone and office duty contacts tend to result in a high "lead-to-client" conversion.

Open Houses
Another common prospecting activity that new agents are encouraged to engage in is to host property open houses. Although a new licensee may not have any of his or her own listings, most dynamic offices will have veteran agents with an abundance of property listings available for new agents to host. Homeowners appreciate the opportunity to have the property exposed for a possible sale. The licensee has the opportunity to represent a buyer that walks in off the streets either in the sale of that home or in another that the licensee later shows the buyer. Plus, the licensee has an opportunity to schedule listing appointments with seller prospects that also visit the open house. The key is to actively gather contact information from everyone attending the open house. With contact information, the agent can individually follow up with attendees to ascertain the needs of each person.

The people that attend the open house are prospects. Individuals that profess a current desire to buy or sell real estate becomes a lead. Someone who agrees to work with the agent becomes a client. This all becomes a possibility from holding an open house and doing good ongoing follow-up!

Sphere of Influence
An important first step to developing a good prospecting plan is to reach out to family, friends, and co-workers (people that a licensee already knows) to let them know about the licensee's real estate services. The existing trust between the licensee in these individuals makes it easier for these individuals to use the licensee whenever they are in the market to buy or sell real estate. It's important to reach out to them on a regular basis to stay top of mind when a real estate need arises.

A key element to implementing this type of prospecting is to realize that people like to help other people. Thus, by reaching out and asking for help to build a licensee's business through referrals, the licensee taps into a whole network of people to drive business to the licensee.

Asking for Referrals
Successfully asking for and receiving referrals is the result of proper approach.
A licensee, for example, should never ask, "Do you know someone who is in the market to buy or sell real estate?" This question almost always results in the answer, "No, I don't."

Instead, the licensee should ask the POSITIVE question, "Who do you know that is the market to buy or sell real estate?" The assumption of the question is that, yes, the person does know someone. It is just a matter of recalling who that person is.

Once the question is asked, though, the licensee may have to prod to help the person recall who is in the market. Their mind may go blank with the initial question. So, follow up the question by pairing it with particular places the person associates with throughout the day. For example, "How about at work? Who do you know at work that is in the market to buy or sell real estate? How about at your child's school? How about at church?"

Walking a person mentally through different aspects of a person's life often roots out the referral the licensee is after!

See the *new agent prospecting script* included with the scripts at the end of this chapter.

★ **Students of the post-licensing 45-hour course are instructed to do the following exercise:**

> Sphere of Influence
> Make a list of friends, family, and acquaintances – people that you already know:
> - Include contact information
>   - Name
>   - Address
>   - Phone Number
>   - Email
>   - How you met
>   - How long you have known them
>   - Special Notes to make communications easier: name of kids, pets, where they work, etc.
> - Develop a plan to stay in contact with them starting with the *New Agent Prospecting Script*.
>   - Follow-Up Example:
>   - Week 1 New Agent Prospecting Script
>   - Week 2 Thank-you note in mail
>   - Week 3 Email
>   - Week 4 Phone call - Update
>   - Week 6 Lunch
>   - Week 8 Email
>   - Week 12 Drop off marketing brochure
>   - Etc…

★ **Students of the post-licensing 45-hour course are instructed to do the following exercise:**

> Practice Phone Prospecting
> Follow the New Agent Script presented at the end of this chapter and start contacting people listed in your Sphere of Influence:
> 1. Greeting
> 2. Quick Small Talk
> 3. Announcement of new business
> 4. Ask for business
> 5. Get commitment to make referrals
> 6. Ask "Who do you know that is in the market to buy or sell real estate?"
>   a. Ask specifically about 3 different areas of the person's life
>   b. Ask for contact information of person being referred
>   c. Ask for him or her to contact the person on your behalf – to let them know you are going to be calling.
> 7. Confirm permission to keep in touch.
>
> *Be sure to schedule a follow up contact!

Joining a Group or Club

As demonstrated in Chapter 1, "Business Planning," it can take a sizeable number of prospects to produce a licensee's business goals. Relying on someone's current sphere of influence can fall short of being able to produce the leads needed to produce clients and ultimately real estate deals. This forces the licensee to find ways to reach more prospects. As stated, working phones and office duty plus hosting open houses are opportunities to increase the number of prospects that a licensee can market.

Joining groups and clubs is another strategy. Joining these organizations puts a licensee in contact with more people. When the licensee purposely gathers contact information and consistently engages in a plan to stay in touch with these individuals, the licensee is increasing his or her prospects. However, true success at this type of prospecting comes from keeping the relationships made through the groups the primary focus with the prospecting efforts secondary. This is because the strongest leads come from prospects that are relationship based.

★ **Students of the post-licensing 45-hour course are instructed to do the following exercise:**

> Join a Group or Club
> Consider joining groups found at:
> - Church
> - Professional Networking Organizations
> - Hobby Clubs
> - Volunteering Groups
> - Local Business Chamber
>
> *Note that participating in local real estate groups does not count toward prospecting activities!

Prospecting to Professionals

Another source for referrals comes from building relationships with professionals in fields besides real estate. Interactions with these professionals will result in receiving referrals from them which helps to build the licensee's business. In turn, the licensee may also have the opportunity to refer people to these professionals. Many of these professionals will be tied directly to the real estate transaction such as inspectors, property insurance agents, and lenders. When the referral being made is tied directly to the real estate transaction, it is important to always refer the licensee's client to three professionals in the same field. By making three referrals, the licensee removes him or herself from liability in regard to the work that the other professional performs.

★ Students of the post-licensing 45-hour course are instructed to do the following exercise:

> Prospecting to Businesses
> Make a list of businesses and professionals to contact
> - Include contact information and special notes
> - Group the names by business type such as
>   - Hair Salons / Stylists
>   - Barber Shops / Barbers
>   - Bars / Bar Tenders
>   - Restaurants / Wait Staff
>   - Child Care / Care Givers
>   - Elderly Care / Care Givers
>   - Counseling Offices / Counselors
>   - School / Teachers and Coaches
>   - Police Station / Police Officers
>   - Fire Station / Firemen
>   - Bridal Shops / Clerks
>   - Wedding Planning / Wedding Planners
>   - Event Planning / Event Planners
>   - Attorney Offices / Attorneys
>   - Accounting Offices / Accountants
>   - Insurance Offices / Insurance Agents
>   - Banks / Bank Tellers and Bank Loan Officers
>   - Mortgage Brokerage Offices / Mortgage Brokers
> - Note the top 10 that know the most people and/or consistently come in contact with new people. These are people that are a priority to contact.
> - Use the Business to Business script found at the end of this chapter to create an initial referral relationship.
> - Institute a plan to make follow-up contacts.

Farming

Most licensees find that to reach a large enough prospect group, "farming" is required. In real estate, a farm area is an area/neighborhood picked by a licensee to market to on a very regular basis, thus cultivating buyers and sellers. This requires extensive and continued follow up by "touching" these individuals on a regular basis with mailings, emails, door hangers, etc.

By continuing to feed marketing material or making face to face or phone contacts with the individuals in these areas, top of mind awareness is created. The goal is for the individuals within the households in these locations to think of the licensee first when they have a need for a real estate agent – In many cases, even without ever having met the licensee!

"Touch" Schedule

- Week 1 Door Hang Introduction Brochure
- Week 3 Mail Post Card – Highlights of Brokerage Expertise
- Week 7 Mail Neighborhood Sales Update
- Week 11 Door Hang "Curb Appeal" Tips and Coupon for Free CMA
- Week 15 Mail Post Card – Benefits of Buyers Agent
- Week 19 Door Hang Personal Newsletter

Picking a Farm Area

A good farm area is based on four criteria. 1. An area with enough properties to make it large enough to handle being farmed; 2. The right price range; 3. Having enough sales to support farming; and 4. Isn't already dominated by one real estate agent. A starting farm area usually consists of between 125 to 175 homes. These homes should be clustered close together to make the process of "farming" simpler. When choosing a price range to farm, keep in mind that it will take just as much effort and expense to farm a neighborhood with an average sales price of $200,000 as one with $450,000 as the average selling price. Yet, it isn't just a matter of finding a higher priced neighborhood to farm. Instead, it is about finding the price range with enough demand in the area that it creates at least 7% turnover in the neighborhood – meaning that at least 7% of the homes sell every year. This means that if there are 150 homes in the farm area, at least 10 are selling every year. Although it is possible to crack a neighborhood already dominated by another agent there is usually another neighborhood nearby without the instant competition!

5 Criteria for Choosing a Neighborhood Farm. February 2017.
eroyhouserseminars.com/2012/06/04/5-criteria-for-choosing-a-neighborhood-farm/

★ **Students of the post-licensing 45-hour course are instructed to do the following exercise:**

> Neighborhood Farming
> Choose a neighborhood to Farm
> 1. Check for how many houses are in the area as defined by your farm. (Goal is between 125 and 175 for best results!)
>   a. Tip: The post office has route forecasting tools that makes it easy to gauge how many houses are in an area!
>   https://www.usps.com/business/every-door-direct-mail.htm
> 2. Determine how many houses have sold in the area in the last 12 months.
>   a. Pull data from multiple listing service and/or tax records.
> 3. Verify that the rate of turnover percentage is 7% or higher:
>
>   a. <u>Total Houses Sold in the past 12 months</u> ÷ total houses in the farm area = turnover percentage

Your Own Neighborhood

It may make sense to work a licensee's own neighborhood as a farm area. This is particularly true when the licensee has established relationships scattered throughout the area. However, keep in mind that although the proximity makes it convenient to farm, if there isn't enough turnover in the neighborhood, it may not be the best choice. Target marketing can also mean picking certain demographics and marketing regularly to a specific group of individuals based on demographic information rather than geographic area. *Note: Target marketing is not the same as working a group of people that you have met over the years.*

Niche Market

Niche Marketing forms from the licensee establishing a specialization in the field of real estate such as focusing on homes located around golf courses. The rules and approaches to niche marketing follow the same guidelines as farming.

For Sale by Owners and Expired Listings

Many new licensees (and experienced goal-oriented agents) focus on a plan to prospect For Sale by Owners and sellers that were previously listed but failed to sell their home. Expired listings can be found in the multiple listing service. It is acceptable to contact these sellers without breaking the code of ethics. For Sale by Owners can be found by driving through neighborhoods, through craigslist, and through for sale by owner websites. Although resources are available to find phone numbers for these sellers, licensees will avoid "Do Not Call" conflicts when visiting the seller in person rather than relying on phone calls.

Marketing Material

Regardless of the prospecting plan that the licensee engages in, the licensee will likely need to develop a combination of marketing material to distribute. This may include brochures, newsletter, market updates, postcards, print advertisements, and online marketing advertisements. Utilizing email services and social media sites, the licensee will find no cost or low-cost marketing options. Plus, licensees that are members of the MLS may find opportunities to develop online profiles on a multitude of sites such as realtor.com and Zillow.com.

Sample Emails

Subject: **Curious About How Much Your Home is Worth?**

Did you know that in the Manatee Sarasota County area, home values rose between 18 and 23% in 2015!

I'd be happy to do a free Comparative Market Analysis (CMA) to determine how much your home would sell for in today's market.

Visit _____ to find out what makes our brokerage different.

Find links to my profile here_____.
Contact me directly for all of your real estate needs.

And feel free to share my information with your friends and family. I appreciate referrals!

Subject: **A Killer Deal on a House!**

Are you interested in finding a Killer Deal on a House?

I have access to the best priced bank repos in the area. Just let me know the area, price range, rooms, baths and any other requirements and I'll get you into see the best priced homes before they sell to someone else!

Visit _____ to find out what makes our brokerage different.
Find a link to my profile here _____.
Contact me directly for all of your real estate needs.

And feel free to share my information with your friends and family. I appreciate referrals!

Subject: **Let's dream about your new home!**

Interested in finding your dream home?

Here's a link to my search site: _____

Even better, I can personalize a search for you directly from the MLS. To set up your search, I need to know a few things: Price range? What area(s) do you want to live in? Are you interested in a specific neighborhood? What kind of home do you want to buy? What syle of home do you want to buy? How many bedrooms? How many bathrooms? Specific features (e.g., waterfront, large lot, garage size, built-in vacuum, distance to school)?

© Pamela Kemper

Sample Postcards

Paying for Leads

Licensees may also find it beneficial to pay for leads. Opportunities for seller and buyer leads can be gained from contracting with sites such as Trulia.com, Realtor.com and Zillow.com. There are many more lead buying sites and opportunities available.

As with all expenditure, it is important to budget carefully when opting to pursue these opportunities.

Role Playing

A good prospecting plan executed with consistency is the key to success.

★ **Students of the post-licensing 45-hour course are instructed to do the following exercise:**

> Scripts
> **See Prospecting Scripts presented at the end of this chapter.**
> - Create your own scripts using the scripts provided as a guide
>   - alter them to fit the licensees own marketing plans.
> - Find someone to role play the scripts for practice.

A good prospecting plan executed with consistency is the key to success.

See Prospecting Scripts presented at the end of this chapter.

Licensees are encouraged to use these scripts and alter them to fit the licensees own marketing plans.

"Do Not Call", "Fax" and "Can Spam" Laws

Always adhere to applicable laws whenever prospecting for leads.

Prospecting Scripts
New Agent Script

New Agent Prospecting Script

1. "Hi, Carol, this is Henry Walton. It's been a while since we have spoken, I hope all is well?"

    2. "Henry, how nice to hear from you. Everything is going pretty good with me. How about with you?"

3. "Actually, that's why I am calling. Things are going pretty good for me, too. In fact, I wanted to let you know that I am working with Albright Realty as a real estate agent."

    4. "That's great, Henry."

5. "I am really enjoying it. I was hoping you would keep me in mind when you happen to be in the market to buy or sell real estate. You know, Carol, that I would do a good job for you, right?

    6. "Sure, Henry, you've always been good at what you do."

7. "I'm glad you would feel that way. I'm going to need all the help I can get and it's good to know that I have you on my side."

    8. I am, Henry, I really am!"

9. "Great, because I was also hoping you would be comfortable referring friends and family to me. I promise that I'll take great care of anyone you refer to me."

    10. "Sure! I'll definitely keep you in mind if I come across anyone."

11. "Wonderful, just let me ask you, though—who at your church might be ready to buy or sell a house?"

    12. "Sorry, no one that I can recall."

13. "How about at work?"

    14. "Sorry—no one!"

15. "How about your daughter's swim team?"

    16. "Now that I think about it—yes! One of the other mother's mentioned wanting to sell their home.

17. "Great, I'd really appreciate it if you could give me her contact number. But could you do me an even bigger favor? Would you please call her first and let her know that you gave me her number. That way she will be more comfortable with my calling."

    18. "No problem, Henry. I'll call her this evening!"

19. "It was good talking with you. If you don't mind, I'll check back every now and then to see if you have come across anyone else in the market.

    20. "I'll look forward to it."

Business to Business Scripts

Business to Business Script

1. "Hello, I'm Clara Barton with Cross Realty. I'm reaching out to find professionals that I can refer my clients to whenever they need services. Since they look to me for advice and guidance, I really need a good person to refer. Would you mind if I give out your information when someone is in need of your services."

    2. "Absolutely, I am always looking to expand my business!"

3. "Wonderful. I am as well. Would you mind giving out my contact information whenever you come across someone looking to buy or sell real estate."

    4. "I'd be happy to do that."

5. "That's great. It'll be good helping each other's business grow.

6. Exchange information.

Buyer Scripts
  Inquiry to Appointment

Inquiry to Appointment Script

1. Having answered a phone call about a house listed, the buyer responded by stating, "Never mind, then, I was hoping it had more bedrooms."

2. "That's no problem. There are plenty of other homes available. How about if we meet so I can find out exactly what you are looking for in a home. Plus, I can explain how you can take advantage of my services as a buyer's agent. The best part is that I'm paid by the seller—not the buyer! Would tomorrow at 10 am in the morning or 5:30 pm in the evening work better for you."

    3. "That's O.K., I've just started looking."

4. "I can certainly understand that you've just started looking and it may seem too early to meet with an agent. Whenever I start something new, I don't rush into anything too quickly either. Yet, I also want to make sure that I'm getting started on the right foot. Wouldn't it make sense to get together so that we can go over the many choices and decisions that you have ahead of you with the home buying process?

See Chapter 10, "Objection Handling."

Buyer Broker Agreement

Buyer Agent Prospecting Script

1. "Mr. and Mrs. Buyer, we've gone over in detail what you are looking for in a home. I've explained about what to expect with the current market and how the home buying process works. Plus, I've explained how working with a buyer's agent puts you at an advantage in the marketplace. So, now, I'd like to ask your commitment to work with me exclusively as your agent."

2. "I don't know. We've just started looking and this house hunting business is a new experience for us."

3. "I can certainly understand how making a commitment to someone you just met could be a bit overwhelming. Whenever I do something as important as buying a home, I always want to make sure that the person I'm working with really understands my needs. And with the thought of committing to a home purchase; it may seem a bit much to also commit to one agent, am I right?"

4. "Yes, it really does."

5. "I understand. I really do. Just as I am sure that you can also appreciate that whenever I make a commitment to work with someone, I give it my all. I put a lot of energy, time, and passion into making sure that my clients find the perfect home. So I am not just asking for a commitment from you. I'm offering to commit myself to you—to work hard on your behalf. With a decision as important as buying a home ahead of you, doesn't it make sense to team up with an agent that will be looking out for your best interests?"

6. "Now that you put it that way. It does make sense to agree to work together!"

See Chapter 10, "Objection Handling."

Seller Scripts
    Listing

Listing Agent Prospecting Script

1. "Mr. and Mrs. Seller, thank you for taking time to show me your lovely home. I've shared with you what sets my services apart from other companies and the strategies I will use to get your home sold with terms that meets your needs. And we have settled on a listing price that makes sense. So, now, I'd like to ask your commitment to work with me exclusively as your listing agent."

    2. "I need more time to make a decision."

3. "I can certainly understand how making a commitment to someone you just met could be a bit overwhelming. Whenever I do something as important as buying a home, I am always hesitant to commit. Let me ask you this, though, if I brought you a contract from a buyer which met your selling terms, would you be ready to accept it?"

    4. "At the price we talked about? Yes, of course."

5. Then let's go ahead and get the paperwork handled so I can make that happen. Doesn't that make sense?

See Chapter 8 "Listing Management," and Chapter 10, "Objection Handling."

FSBO

FSBO Prospecting Script

1. "Hello, I'm Garth Brooks with Record Realty. I noticed that you are selling your home as a for sale by owner. I was wondering if you could take a moment to show me your home. I work with buyers in this area and would like to know more about your property—in case I find a buyer that will be a good fit."

    2. "I'm not paying a real estate agent."

3. "I understand that. If I bring you a buyer, though, I'll be representing the buyer. I imagine that as a For Sale By Owner, you are interested in pocketing as much money as possible at closing. Is that true?

    4. "Yes, that's why I don't want to pay a commission."

5. "No worries. I'd love to see your home and then I can share with you my different buyer and seller services and how that can work to your advantage!

See Chapter 8 "Listing Management," and Chapter 10, "Objection Handling."

Expired

Expired Prospecting Script

1. "Hello, I'm Donna Reed with MGM Realty. I noticed that your property was listed previously with another agent yet failed to sell. If we could sit down for a few moments, I'd be happy to explain what I do differently as a real estate agent that will get your home sold.

2. "I don't think so. A lot of agents showed my home and none of you brought me a buyer."

3. "I can understand how frustrating it must have been to go to so much trouble only to have your property not sell. Whenever I make up my mind about something as important as selling a home, I expect to get results. Wouldn't it be great to actually have a contract to get this property sold so that you can move forward with your plans?

4. "That's what I kept telling my agent. Bring me a contract!"

5. "That's exactly why I am here. It's time to actually make it happen. Shall we get started?

3 MANAGING LISTINGS

Learning Terms and Phrases

- Open Listings
- Exclusive Right to Sell
- Exclusive Brokerage
- Limited Listing
- Seller Property Disclosure
- CMA
- Adjustments
- Comparable Properties
- Superior Property
- Inferior Property
- Alternative Square Footage Calculation
- Pricing Strategy
- Seller Net Proceeds
- 2 Step Listing Presentation
- 1 Step Listing Presentation
- Seller Feature Benefit
- Presentation Timeline
- Closing the Deal
- Listing Administration
- Marketing Plan

Learning Objectives

- Licensees will have practiced the determination of property value through CMA adjustments.
- Licensees will have an understanding of the alternative square footage calculation for property values.
- Licensees will be able to calculate average seller net proceeds to present to potential sellers.
- Licensees will develop a feature benefit list regarding their brokerages to present to sellers.
- Licensees will develop a feature benefit list regarding licensees' attributes to present to sellers.
- Licensees will customize a listing presentation script and develop skill of use through role playing.
- Licensees will develop a marketing plan for listings.
- Licenses will gain an understanding of the various types of listing agreements.
- Licensees will develop knowledge of how to stay compliant with fair housing laws while working with sellers.

Importance of Obtaining Seller Listings

In the world of real estate, it is said that to be truly successful, a licensee must be a strong listing agent. Why? Because listings are the basis of deals, not just for the property being sold, but for other deals as well. It can be expected that from one listing, a licensee will pick up another listing. Often this will come from a friend or a neighbor of the home listed. Or it may come from someone visiting an open house held at the property. Plus, the listing usually brings potential buyers. At least one buyer can be expected to come from buyers who contacted the agent to see the property but instead of buying that property uses the agent's real estate services to find another home to buy.

And from the sale of the listing itself, agents have the opportunity to represent both the seller and the buyer. This turns one sale into two sales or "sides."

So, one listing may easily turn into 3 or 4 deals!

Types of Seller Listing Agreements

Licensees may engage a property for sale either as an open listing, an exclusive right to sell listing, or an exclusive brokerage listing.

Open Listings

Although, open listings are legal, which allow for any number of brokerages to list the same property at the same time, this type of listing agreement is rarely used in the current real estate market. The point of the open listing is to allow a seller to get as much exposure to a property as possible. This stems back to when it was normal for brokerages to only show property that was listed by the brokerage company.

Today's agreement between brokers, which participate in the multiple listing services, fosters the environment of brokers showing property listed by other brokers. This has made the need for open listings to become obscure. In fact, open listings are now so rare that they are not offered as a prepared form accessed by licensees who are members of the Florida Realtor Association.

Exclusive Right to Sell

The process of obtaining, managing, and selling a listing is a rather arduous one that also carries marketing costs. It is for this reason that brokers prefer to work primarily with Exclusive Right to Sell Listings. This listing format ensures that the broker will receive a commission in the event that a property sells during the listing period.

Exclusive Brokerage Listings

With the exclusive brokerage agreement, the seller retains the right to sell the property without the help of the broker. This is a popular provision to convince owners who are attempting to sell the property without the use of an agent to go ahead and list with a brokerage. As with the open listing, a broker who utilizes an exclusive brokerage listing agreement may face not being paid if the property sells by the seller without the aid of the broker.

Because of this risk, it as a more popular method for agents to utilize the exclusive right to sell agreement and allowing for "exclusions" to specific individuals that the seller may have already created an interest in for the property.

Limited Listings

Becoming increasingly popular is the limited listing which is an exclusive brokerage listing agreement. Florida statutes allow for a broker to offer limited representation to sellers. This provision allows a broker to be paid for specific listing tasks rather than the agent being required to offer services that the client does not wish to pay the agent for providing.

Preparing Paperwork and Disclosures

When preparing listings, it is important to first gather all the paperwork that will be required to legally list the property. This includes any disclosures that need to be made by the seller.

The main disclosures include:
- Seller's Property Disclosure
- Condominium Property Disclosure
- Lead Based Paint Disclosure
- Homeowner Association Disclosures
- Over 55 Disclosure
- Mold Disclosure
- Community Development District Disclosure

Although it is not required to have these disclosures to list a property, they are required for a potential sale. It is good practice to gather these disclosures at the time of listing. They can be uploaded into the multiple listing service system to be available should another agent wish to write an offer on the property.

Listing Contracts and Disclosures

See Chapter 8, "Contracts", for details about working with various types of listing format contracts, disclosures, and addendums.

Tax Records

When preparing to list a property for sale, the licensee should pull tax records. This provides the legal description for the property. It reflects legally permitted improvements made to the property, it shows the tax assessment levied against the property, and whether the property has been homesteaded or lies in flood area.

(Note that a couple of years ago, flood areas were re-designated and that created a delay in the reliability of tax records regarding flood areas.)

Members of the multiple listing service will have links to tax records found easily within the system. Others will need to go to the local county websites to pull the information.

Comparative Market Analysis

Listing a property starts with being able to guide a seller to an appropriate asking price. The most common method that agents use is to conduct a comparative market analysis also referred to as a CMA. CMAs are not appraisal reports, but they do use some of the same processes. A CMA determines value based on recently sold properties, properties currently on the market, and properties expired unsold. Data is gathered from the Multiple Listing Service (MLS), Property Appraiser's Office, and Clerk of the Courts.

Select Similar Properties

The goal when determining a sale's value for a subject property is to pick comparable properties that are as similar as possible to the subject property. Just as an appraiser may have to adjust values for differences, adjustments are also made when doing a CMA.

Adjustments

Adjustments are made to account for differences in square footage, the number of rooms, existence of garages, pools, etc. Adjustments are also made based on appeal of location such as whether one property is waterfront, and one is not. If properties are chosen that were sold since the market changed in pricing levels, then an adjustment is also made for the market difference.

If the comparable property is better than the subject property, then you subtract value from the comparable property. If the comparable property is inferior to the subject property, then you add to the comparable property value. How much you add depends upon the value attributed to the difference.

Property Traits

Boat Slip	Interior Layout	Pool
Condition of Exterior	Kitchen Design	Shape of the Property
Condition of Interior	Lanai	Size of the Property
Construction Quality	Landscaping	Quality of View
Construction Style	Livable Square Footage	Water Access
Exterior Layout	Location	Water Frontage
Garage	Number of Bathrooms	
Golf Course Frontage	Number of Bedrooms	

Adjusting for Time Difference

The process is the same if you are making an adjustment for a time difference. Let's say that the market isn't as strong as what it was nine months ago. The comparable that is used would need to be adjusted down by the % of change in the market.

Assigning a Value to the Differences

One of the most challenging things for a new agent is to know how much value to assign to a difference such as an extra room. Ask an experienced agent how much they assign to these different traits and the answers will generally be vague and varying. It isn't that the agents are trying to "hold secret" information. The fact is that applying value is as much as an art as it is mathematical. It is something that agents develop a feel for as experience is gained. How much value a garage brings, for example, in one part of town may vary greatly from another part of town.

Performing CMA Adjustments

In the example presented here, three properties have been chosen. Before averaging their sold prices to use as a basis for the expected sales price of the subject property, additions and subtractions are made to each comparable for property traits that are notably different from the subject property.

Please understand that the values assigned to each difference may not apply to a property that you are evaluating!

	Subject Property	Comparable Properties					
		Address # 1		Address #2		Address #3	
Sold Price		$375,000		$265,000		$310,000	
Boat Slip	No	Yes	-20,000	No	0	No	0
Condition of Interior	Good	Upgraded	-25,000	Good	0	Good	0
Construction Style	Tile Roof	Tile Roof	0	Shingle	10,000	Tile Roof	0
Garage	Yes	Yes		No	15,000	No	15,000
Golf Course Frontage	Yes	Yes	0	No	15,000	No	15,000
Lanai	Yes	Yes	0	No	5,000	Yes	0
Number of Bathrooms	2 1/2	3	-3,000	2	2,000	2	2,000
Number of Bedrooms	4	5	-5000	3	5,000	3	5,000
Pool	Private	Private	0	No	20,000	Community	5,000
Total Adjustments			-53,000		72000		42,000
Adjusted Sales Price		$322,000		$337,000		$352,000	

Calculated Value of Subject Property:	$337,000

(Taken as an average of the 3 Adjusted Values)

Alternative Square Footage Comparison

Calculating value based on adjusting for property difference can be a time-consuming task that requires specific knowledge of a subject property's features and conditions. A quicker method that is often used by real estate agents is based on the average sales price per square foot of property in an area.

For agents working within the multiple listing service system, this approach can be particularly fruitful. There are functions within the program which allow the agent to choose a multitude of properties that have sold in an area. The program will then show the statistical average, high, and low selling prices and price per square foot for properties sold or still on the market.

Imagine then that a real estate licensee is door knocking trying to convert "for sale by owners" into listings. The agent, without knowing many details about the subject property or investing too much time preparing, can approach the seller knowing the average sale price in the area, plus the highs and the lows. Then based on the condition and features of the property, the agent can give the "for sale by owner" instant feedback about property pricing.

The following example shows that this method will many times produce results that aren't too skewed from the more labor-intensive process of adding and subtracting for specific values. The closer the comparable are to the subject property, the better quality the results are. Fortunately, many neighborhoods are built in Florida where features are fairly consistent from property to property.

	Sold Price	Livable Square Feet	Sold Price Per Sq. Ft
Address #1	$375,000	2,500	$150
Address #2	$265,000	2,300	$115
Address #3	$310,000	2,250	$138

Average Square Footage in area: $134

Livable Square Footage of Subject Property: 2,275

If subject is of average condition with average features:
2,275 × $134 $305,605

If subject is superior than the average:
2,275 × $150 $341,250

If subject is inferior than the average:

2,275 × $115 $262,119.57

> **Students of the post-licensing 45-hour course are instructed to do the following exercise:**

> Study Property Differences
> Pick an area of town that you would like to list property. Pull listing data showing property that has sold and is currently on the market.
> - Make note of the average selling price based on square footage.
> - Make note of properties selling above the average square footage.
> - Make note of properties selling below the average square footage.
> - Notice property traits that seem to raise or lower the square footage value.
> - Using this information, pick a property based on tax records and assign a probable sales value.
> - Have an experienced agent or your broker review your assigned value!

Pricing Strategy

Keep buyer behavior in mind while guiding a seller toward pricing a property. With the example used, the CMA adjustments resulted in an expected sales price of $337,000. By using the simpler square footage method, $341,250 might seem like a reasonable price.

However, it would be best to back off of that price for two reasons. One reason is that subject property is not the best of the best – just "better." Two is that the although the two prices are only $4,000 apart, $337,000 SEEMS a lot lower than $341,250. Again, this is not a mathematical truth. Just more of a feeling that agents keep in mind.

Room for Negotiations

Advising a seller on an expected sales price is a bit different than choosing a listing price. It is important to analyze sales in an area and compare list prices to actual selling price. When listing in an area where the buyers are expecting to be able to "negotiate" a better price, it may be best to cushion the asking price by increasing it to allow for this.

Be aware that this can backfire by the seller setting his or her sights on that list price. It is best to get written acknowledgement from the seller that the seller understands that the list price is not the expected sale price and that no guarantees are given regarding sales price. However, sellers can be comforted to know that they always have a right to refuse a deal!

Buyer Property Searches

Buyer's spend hours searching for property on their own using the internet. The internet searches are based on parameters of highs and lows in property sales prices. More than likely, the same buyer would see a property priced at $341,250 the same as if it was priced at $337,000. But what if it was priced at $351,000? Buyers that use $350,000 as the top price would not see a property listed at $351,000 in a property search. For this reason, a $349,999 selling price would have a lot more eyes on it through searches!

Seller Net Proceeds

It is also extremely important that the sellers are told their expected costs of selling when choosing to list a home. It is a good strategy to get a seller to focus on how much they can expect to walk away from the sale with as net proceeds rather than the actual selling price.

SELLER'S CLOSING COST ESTIMATE						
SALE PRICE					$337,000	
CLOSING DATE					September	
TITLE EXPENSE PAID					*100%*	
2,275	**SQUARE FEET (Living Area)**				$148.13	/Sq. Ft
	Costs Related to Sale of Home					
	Title Insurance	(>100k*.005375; *.00575)		$1,811.38	Based on Sale Price	
	Closing Fee			$450.00		
	Search Fee (includes lien search)			$150.00		
	Documentary Stamps on Deed (.70/$100)			$2,359.00	Based on Sale Price	
	Municipal Lien Search			$150.00		
	Brokerage Listing Fees		6%	$20,220		
	Real Estate Taxes Prorated			$1,100.00		
	1st Mortgage Pay-Off			$155,000.00		
	Other Mortgage(s) Pay-Off					
	Liens and/or Assessments					
	#1 Homeowner Fees (prorated)			$550.00	*Subtract from total	
	Homeowners Association Estoppel Fee			$150.00	Average if applies	
	Notary Fees			$100.00	Average if applies	
	Overnight Wire Fees, FedEx, etc.			$150.00	Average if applies	
	Repairs of Warranted Items					
	WDO Repairs/Treatment					

Home Protection Plan	
Sellers contribution to buyer	
Total Estimated Expenditures	**$181,090.38**
Seller's Estimated Net Proceeds	**$155,909.62**

This is an estimate ONLY and is not a guarantee of total expenses

★ Students of the post-licensing 45-hour course are instructed to do the following exercise:

Seller Net Proceeds
Using a spreadsheet, set up a form to calculate Expected Seller Costs and Seller Net Proceeds
- Consult with an experienced agent, your broker, or a title company to determine the figures that should be entered in as expenses
- Keep in mind that commissions are negotiable
- Property Taxes are prorated and paid in arrears, so entered as a debit.
- Homeowner Association fees are prorated and paid ahead, so entered as a credit.

*Some title companies offer apps to help calculate expected title expenses.

The 2 Step Listing Presentation

A 2 Step Listing Approach involves the agent meeting briefly with the homeowner to first tour the property. Then, after researching the area with first-hand information gained from the property tour, the agent prepares a pricing strategy to present to the seller at a second meeting.

Some agents prefer this strategy as the agent believes it better enables the agent to build rapport with the seller. By using this strategy, the seller is left with an increased impression that the seller's property is important and has been carefully considered. The downside of this approach is that it takes longer and delays "asking for the listing." While the agent is spending time "researching" the property pricing, another agent may be at the property getting the seller to sign.

1 Step or 2 Step Presentation

By going into a listing presentation completely prepared, agents can accomplish a 1 Step Listing Approach. This means that the agent is prepared to meet with the homeowner and take the listing on the spot.

This generally requires a good phone interview about property features to be successful. It also requires understanding and being able to apply the concept of average, high, and low selling prices based on square footage. The agent is then prepared to make a determination of how the seller's property compares to other properties without going back to the office for more research. When using this strategy, the agent will normally have multiple seller net sheets prepared to present to the seller to match various pricing possibilities.

Preparing for a Listing Presentation

Preparing for a listing presentation involves a lot more than just being prepared with paperwork and pricing. Most sellers meet with several real estate agents before picking one to list their property. Although the licensee's goal when going into a listing presentation is to have the opportunity to represent the seller in the sale of the seller's home, the licensee must first be successful at selling him or herself!

What Makes You Stand Apart from Your Competition as a Company – for Sellers

It is important to be able to verbalize why the licensee has chosen to work with the real estate brokerage the licensee is representing. The same features that attracted the agent to the company can also be highlighted as important benefits to attract a seller.

Feature Benefits Emphasis

When listing features, always pair the features with how it benefits the seller.

For example, if the licensee chose a small brokerage to work with due to desiring personal attention, this can be presented as, "The broker at XYZ Realty gets involved with every deal. That means that you don't just have me looking out for your interests, but the broker as well!"

On the other hand, if the licensee chose a large brokerage because of formalized training, this can be presented as, "I work for one of the largest brokerages in town. This means that not only am I working to sell your property, but you have more than a hundred top trained agents making the sale of your property a priority!"

What Makes You Stand Apart from Your Competition as an Individual – for Sellers

Even new agents must be able to verbalize the benefits of listing with him or her as an individual. Don't be afraid of admitting to the fact that you are new to the field. Highlight the benefits of the company and then highlight accomplishments made in other areas of life and other professions. For example, a licensee who is transitioning from being a teacher could emphasize the years spent aiding students in reaching educational goals and the agent is now using that same dedication to helping owners reach their selling goals.

★ **Students of the post-licensing 45-hour course are instructed to do the following exercise:**

> Feature Benefit
> Develop a list of feature benefits to present to a seller
> - What makes your company stand apart?
> - What makes you as an individual stand apart?
>
> *Be sure to emphasize EXACTLY what the benefits are to the seller!

Conducting a Listing Appointment

A trick to putting sellers at ease and to take control of the listing appointment, is to follow up your greeting with sharing a timeline of the meeting. For example:

"Mr. and Mrs. Seller, thank you for allowing me to discuss listing your wonderful home. This process will only take about an hour to an hour and a half. If it's okay with you, first I'd like to take a look around. It would really help me out if you point out features that you believe sets your home apart.

Then, we will sit down together. I'll share information with you about what strategies I can use to help you reach your selling goals. Then together, based on information I have about properties that have sold and are currently for sale. Together, we can come up with a pricing and marketing strategy that makes the most sense. How does that sound?"

Seller Presentation Practice

Students of the post-licensing 45-hour course are instructed to do the following exercise:

> Listing Presentation Role Playing – 1 Step Listing Approach
> After laying out the feature benefits of working with you, practice conducting a listing presentation.
> 1. Start with a formal greeting and set the time-line that the "seller" can expect for the appointment
> 2. Walk through the home and take notes about features
> 3. Sit down with the "seller" and take a moment to establish rapport by mentioning something personal that you noticed that you can relate to with the seller.
>   a. For example, if you noticed team memorabilia; ask if they watched a particular game
> 4. Present the benefits of working with you and your brokerage
>   a. "Mr. and Mrs. Seller, let me assure you that if you choose my services you are in the best of hands and this is why…."
> 5. Summarize the strengths you noticed about the seller's property…
>   a. "Mr. and Mrs. Seller, one of the reasons I am excited to represent your property is the care you have taken in keeping the kitchen and bathrooms updated. This is something that buyers will certainly find desirable!
> 6. Present market information about similar properties on the market, properties that have sold, and properties that have failed to sale.
> 7. Suggest a sales price range
> 8. Get an agreement from the seller based on pricing strategy
> 9. Present a marketing summary to get the property sold
> 10. Ask the seller to list the property with you!

Closing the Deal

Don't forget to ask for the listing! One of the things that attracts individuals to the field of real estate is thinking that the act of selling a home requires less traditional "hard sales" approaches than selling something like a car. However, selling real estate is selling. Yes, working as an agent involves as much "counseling and guidance" as it does selling, but being successful requires the same ability to "close the deal" as any other type of sales. Closing the deal requires asking for the sale. In the case of listings, it requires asking for the listing!

Objection Handling with Sellers

Not every seller will immediately agree to list a property with an agent. That's where "selling" skills come into play. The agent will be required to understand and handle objections that sellers have to keep the seller from immediately listing. Don't be discouraged by objections. This is a normal part of the process.
See Chapter 5, "Objection Handling."

Following Fair Housing when Listing Property

Remember when listing property to follow fair housing laws. See Chapter 13, "Fair Housing Applied."

Seller Listing Management

Once the listing has been obtained, it is time to go to work. Listing management is a combination of administrative tasks such as inputting listings into the multiple listing service system while also developing and facilitating a great marketing plan. The result of this hard work comes through contract negotiations and closings.

Listing Administration

Each brokerage is designed differently in regard to how much support exists for listing administrative. Some brokerages are very hands off where the agent is expected to do everything. Others are very hands on where the agent has a lot of support and assistance. It is important to be working with a brokerage that matches a licensee's needs in this area. Remember that when choosing a brokerage to work with, it may be worth working with one that has higher fees if these types of tasks are being handled.

On the other hand, if a licensee has his or her own routine and systems in place to handle listing administration, then paying a brokerage to manage these issues would be redundant and unnecessary.

Developing a Marketing Plan

The listing presentation should outline an action plan for marketing a property. Once the listing has been taken, it is time to put the plan into action. Components of a good marketing plan may include signage, pictures and videos of the property, marketing online, flyers, open houses, mailings, email campaigns, advertising in magazines and home magazines.

Signage

Despite all the time that buyers spend online looking for property, For Sale signs placed in front of a property and directing people to the property is a major marketing component. Be sure to follow license law when designing signs. All signs must identify the broker. Most agents that pay for their own signs place their own phone number on the signs to ensure that the agent captures as many leads as possible from buyers interested in the property.

It is also common to add selling points to sign rides such as "POOL." Not all neighborhoods and associations allow For Sale signage. Some allow signage but dictate size and style that is allowed. Be sure to check for guidelines.

Pictures

A picture is worth a thousand words. This is definitely true when presenting a property for sale through photographs. Photographing a home should be done with care and skill. If a licensee is choosing to do his or her own pictures, then be sure to use a good camera. Take time to make sure the lighting is correct. Take shots from areas of the room that show the room at the best perspective emphasizing the space.

Take time to edit photos before uploading them into the MLS or marketing spots. However, be careful not to misrepresent a home by doctoring photographs. This would include things like blotting out a crack in the wall. The pictures will also be used to create virtual tours of the property by the MLS or through other means.

Videos

Buyers look for property videos now as much as they do still photographs or virtual tours. Many buyers are looking to move to Florida from across the country. A well-produced video can provide a buyer with the confidence to purchase a home that the buyer has never visited.

A well-produced video does not require a paid video photographer. Although paying a photographer or video photographer may be appropriate for luxury properties, it is possible for agents to create videos that bring results by making sure the video gives a good presentation of the property.

MLS Inclusion

The Multiple Listing Service provides mass exposure of property not only to other agents, but to the public. The MLS uses data exchange agreements to send listing information to numerous websites such as realtor.com, trulia.com, Zillow.com – just to name a few.

Be sure to make certain that the property description and photographs in the MLS is designed to honestly and effectively promote the property. Take time to make sure that all the fields are property filled out as this will affect whether the property is found through specific buyer searches.

Websites

Taking time to feature the property on the agent's own and brokerage websites is a great marketing tool. Furthermore, most of the major sites such as trulia.com and Zillow.com allow for agents to access the listing information and customize on those sites. With so many buyers searching for property online, it is important to realize that reviewing the property online is as important as a first showing!

Social Media

Highlighting the property on social media is also a selling tool. Remember, though, that others are on these sites to foster "relationships" not "sales." So, the best strategy to take is to find a feature about the property that the licensee is excited about and share that with their social media friends. Doing this will draw interest to the property without appearing to infringe upon the online relationships.

★ **Students of the post-licensing 45-hour course are instructed to do the following exercise:**

> Which is the better choice…
> You just listed a home for $650,000 that has a private elevator and a pool.
>
> A. Post on your regular facebook.com an announcement about the listing and include the price plus a link to the listing.
> B. Post an announcement with listing details on your business facebook.com page. Plus, on your regular facebook.com post pictures of you riding the elevator and standing by the pool with the following statement, "I have the best job in the world. Today a seller took me on a ride in a private elevator in his beautiful home! Thank you, Mr. Johnson, for trusting me to sell your amazing property. Can't wait find a buyer for this lovely pool home!" -Plus, invite people to visit your business page to find out more about the home.
>
> B is the better choice. The style of the facebook.com post draws attention to the property in a fun way.

Flyers

Having property information available for the taking can also be viewed as an asset. These flyers can be kept in the home for open houses and showings and/or placed in an information box by the For-Sale sign.

Consider working with a mortgage broker to also provide payment information on the flyers. Doing this can be beneficial to create buyer interest. Furthermore, the lender will usually share in the cost of the printing.

Open Houses

There is much debate about how effective open houses are in getting a home sold. The fact is though, whether it is a low percentage or not, open houses do occasionally sell homes. Therefore, sellers will generally want agents to hold open houses. Most agents are eager to hold open houses as a way to meet potential buyers. Even when these buyers do not buy the home being held open, the buyers will often work exclusively with the agent to find another home that is a good fit.

How to Hold an Open House

Advance preparation makes the difference between a good turnout and not-so-good turnout for an open house. Be sure to use the internet, print media, and signage to give advance notice for open houses. Many agents will take time to personally invite the neighbors in hopes of making contact with someone else who is in the market to sell a home. Be sure to have supplies on hand to make the open house more comfortable and enjoyable. This includes things like chocolate chip cookies and toilet paper.

Safety First

It's best to avoid holding open houses alone. Having someone with the agent provides protection both to the agent and to the home. When people are touring the home, someone should be escorting them to monitor that the seller's personal possessions are not being touched. Once an open house has ended, be sure to go around and check that the windows are all still locked.

Postcards

Just listed, pending, and sold postcards are commonly sent to neighbors around a listing. The seller views this as a way to drum up interest from a neighbor wanting to move someone they know closer to where they live. Agents like these, though, more from the perspective also hoping to find a neighbor who is interested in also selling their home.

Email Campaigns

Emailing property information is a cost-free way to promote a property. However, anyone sending these types of emails must follow Can Spam laws. The law requires that an unsubscribe mechanism be included in the email and opt-out requests must be honored within 10 business days.
Can Spam Act of 2003. February 2017. https://en.wikipedia.org/wiki/CAN-SPAM_Act_of_2003

Newspapers and Home Magazines

With the rise of online marketing, print marketing has become less of a main component of marketing.

A licensee should study buyer behavior in the area the agent is working to measure the cost benefit of utilizing print media.

Managing Showings

Successful marketing efforts should produce showings. It is the job of the listing agent to coordinate showings. The agent may need to go as far as to be present at all showings. The agent may only be responsible to coordinate the showings between buyer's agents and clearing that the date and time is acceptable for the seller. Lockboxes make access to the property easier, but also opens up liability issues to the licensee that must be considered. Electronic supra lockboxes track all agents that have opened the lock boxes.

Pricing Updates

It is important to monitor showing feedback, how long the property has been on the market without an offer, and changes within the market since listing. All this information may point to a need to get a price reduction. If this situation applies, be sure to lay out the information factually while also updating the seller of specific activity that the marketing has produced. This will reassure the seller that the licensee is working hard for the seller and will make the seller more agreeable to a price adjustment.

Dealing with the Overpriced Listing

Be careful about taking a listing on a property that is obviously overpriced from the outset. Many a new agent will be so anxious to get a listing that it is tempting to take listings even when the price isn't suited to the market. When taking an overpriced listing, one strategy to use is to have the seller sign a piece of paper acknowledging what the recommended price was as compared to the actual listing price. Then after an agreed period of time meet again with the seller. During the meeting, pull out the piece of paper and remind the seller what the recommended price was and ask if the seller is ready to list at that price. By having the recommended price in writing the seller will be unable to claim that agent is failing to deliver on a price that was promised – which is how the seller will remember it!

Presenting Offers

The goal of listing a property for sale is to secure an offer. Presenting an offer to a seller may involve a bit of finesse. Remember that emotions often run high when it comes to selling a home. If the offer is quite a ways from the list price, a seller may react with emotion including being angry and offended by the offer. Much of this reaction can be muted and coaxed by the phrasing used to set the stage for presenting the offer.

See Chapter 5, "Objection Handling," for strategies to deal with upset sellers during negotiations.

Negotiating the Best Terms for a Seller

It is important for a licensee to remember agency responsibility when representing a seller. It is the agent's job to get the best deal possible for the seller. See Chapter 15, "Agency in Practice," for more on this topic.

Record Keeping

Records of executed listing agreements and purchase contracts should be kept for five years.

Successfully managing listings is key to agents' success and is definitely obtainable!

4 MANAGING BUYERS

Learning Terms and Phrases
- Buyer Broker Agreements
- Establishment of Agency
- Procuring Cause
- Unbroken Chain of Events
- Compensation
- Courting Period
- Buyer Presentation
- Buyer Feature Benefits
- Needs Assessment
- Prequalifying the Buyer
- Realistic Expectations
- Counselor
- Partnering with Buyers
- Buyer Drive-By's
- Buyer Rebates
- MLS
- Property Search
- Staggered Showings
- Offers
- Counteroffers

<u>Learning Objectives</u>

> - Licensees will develop an understanding of how to establish formal agency relationships with buyers.
> - Licensees will understand how procuring cause develops.
> - Licensees will develop a feature benefit list regarding their brokerages to present to buyers.
> - Licensees will develop a feature benefit list regarding licensees' attributes to present to buyers.
> - Licensees will customize a buyer presentation script and develop skill of use through role playing.
> - Licensees will gain knowledge of how to conduct a buyer's needs assessment.
> - Licensees will gain knowledge about how to assist buyers in property selection and showings.
> - Licensees will develop knowledge of how to stay compliant with fair housing laws while working with buyers.

Importance of Working with Buyers

Buyers are the lifeblood of a successful real estate career. Every real estate purchase transaction requires a buyer. Successful real estate agents must understand how to work with buyers. This includes being able to ascertain buyer's must-haves in property, how to fairly represent buyers, and how to assist buyers in accomplishing homeownership goals.

Specializing as a Buyer's Agent

Many licensees specialize in working with buyers. Often this specialization develops from joining a real estate team. Established real estate agents often do not have time to work with all the buyer leads being cultivated. Therefore, teams are established with buyer's agents brought on board specifically to work with buyers.

Being Prepared

Buyer needs are different from sellers. Therefore, an agent's marketing emphasis in promotional material will be different than when marketing to sellers. Plus, there are different forms that will be used with buyers such as buyer agent contracts. It is important that licensees prepare themselves to work with buyers with the same forethought that the licensee prepared to work with sellers.

Buyer Broker Agreements

When a licensee gains an agreement to sell a house, without hesitation, the licensee will ask the seller to sign a formal listing agreement. Yet, the same licensee will often invest hours working with a buyer without ever getting a formal commitment from the buyer officially engaging the licensee as the buyer's agent. Buyer Broker Agreements are a formal contract that secures a commitment from a buyer not to purchase a home through some other agent. Use of a buyer broker agreement increases the likelihood that an agent will be adequately compensated for all of his or her hard work.

Creation of a Relationship

In this technological age, it is not unusual for buyers and licensees to connect without meeting. First contact is made through the internet. Phone conversations are initiated. And emails are exchanged. Recognizing that a buyer is in pursuit of a home, the licensee begins putting time into finding the right property for the buyer. The licensee sets up automatic searches for the buyer. The licensee personally reviews the searches. The licensee may even personally visit the property to preview the property. Until finally, the licensee meets personally with the buyer to actually show property to the buyer. And a buyer client relationship has been established! Or has it?

Multiple Agents

It is not unusual for a buyer to communicate online with several agents at the same time! When the buyer first begins searching the internet for a home, the buyer will find several properties of interest and send inquiries about the property.

Depending upon the website, these inquiries will be intercepted by the listing agents of each individual property being inquired about or by agents that have paid the websites for buyer leads. Sometimes inquiries on one property will be sent to multiple agents. As a result, the buyer will find him or herself being contacted by a multitude of agents. Some buyers respond to this by latching onto the first agent that successfully makes contact. Other buyers will take advantage of the situation and accept the offer from multiple agents to "find the buyer the perfect property!"

Pertinent Questions

Despite whether a buyer is working with only one licensee or several, because of the scenario that was described, there are four pertinent questions:
1. Has an agency relationship been established?
2. Does the licensee deserve compensation if the buyer purchases a home not shown by that licensee?
3. Does the licensee deserve compensation if the buyer purchases a home the licensee personally showed the buyer?
4. If compensation is due, who is obligated to pay the licensee?

Has an Agency Relationship Been Established?

The establishment of an "agency" relationship is not necessarily tied to compensation. Yet, once the licensee began acting on behalf of the buyer, the licensee was automatically obligated, under Florida statute, to uphold duties to the buyer in the capacity of a Transaction Broker. This is the presumption unless the licensee establishes a different form of relationship with a written disclosure.

This means that the licensee is obligated to the seven duties detailed in Chapter 15, "Agency in Practice." This includes dealing honestly and fairly with the buyer, disclosing all known facts that materially affect the value of residential property that are not readily observable to the buyer, accounting for all funds entrusted to the licensee, using skill, care, and diligence, presenting all offers and counteroffers in a timely manner, exercising limited confidentiality, unless waived in writing by a party, and performing additional duties mutually agreed to with a party. Despite the establishment of obligation from the licensee to the buyer, in no way has the buyer become obligated to the licensee to ensure that the licensee is paid.

Does the Licensee Deserve Compensation if the Buyer Purchases a Home NOT Shown by That Licensee?

So even though the licensee is working hard for the buyer and legally obligated to the buyer, the buyer has no actual obligation to the licensee. This means that if the buyer chooses to work with another licensee and purchase a different home, there is no compensation due to the licensee. The licensee, who was working hard to secure a home for the buyer, is left having wasted his or her valuable time. It is tempting for new agents to blow off this time lost by stating, "I didn't have any other clients anyway." The fact is, though, that any time spent with a buyer that is not loyal to the licensee, is time lost working to find a different client.

Does the Licensee Deserve Compensation if the Buyer Purchases a Home the Licensee Personally Showed the Buyer?

Also, if the buyer did not sign a buyer broker agreement, the buyer is still not obligated to ensure that the licensee gets paid -- this is true even if the licensee personally showed the buyer the property that the buyer later decides to purchase! If, however, the licensee is a member of the multiple listing service and REALTOR® association, the licensee may be entitled to compensation if the property purchased was advertised as offering a commission within the multiple listing service.

Procuring Cause would need to be proven, though, to ensure compensation. See commission disputes in Chapter 12, "Ethics and Business Practices."

If Compensation is Due, who is Obligated to Pay the Licensee?

The point of a buyer broker agreement is that it formally obligates the licensee to work for the buyer and the buyer to compensate the licensee. Within the buyer broker agreement, though, compensation is shifted from being paid by the buyer to being paid by the seller as compensation is normally offered to buyer's agents through the Multiple Listing Service. Although ultimately paid by the seller, through the buyer broker agreement, the buyer is making a formal commitment to see that the agent is paid. Plus, the agreement may even commit the buyer to making up the difference in commission if the seller isn't paying the amount of commission agreed upon in the buyer broker agreement.

With the agreement in place, if the buyer chose to close a transaction without seeing that the licensee is paid, the licensee's broker may sue the buyer for compensation. This is true even if the home purchased was never actually shown by the licensee. Without the agreement in place, a broker may claim procuring cause and demand payment through the listing broker – but only for a home shown by the licensee to the buyer.

Unbroken Chain of Events

Winning a procuring cause case is difficult to do. The broker must prove that the licensee initiated an unbroken chain of events that led to the sale of the property. One faltering in this chain, and the broker would likely lose a procuring cause claim.

Compensation

- Neither Sales associates or broker associates can sue either a seller, buyer, or another broker for compensation.
- Suits have to be brought forth by the employing broker.

⭐ **Students of the post-licensing 45-hour course are instructed to do the following exercise:**

> Does Procuring Cause Exist?
> Several months ago, you met with a buyer and showed him several homes. He stated that none of the homes met his needs. You set him up on an automatic property search with the MLS so that other properties would be emailed to him on a regular basis. When a particular property seemed extremely well suited for the buyer, you phoned him. In doing so, you discovered that earlier that week, the buyer entered into a purchase agreement on one of the properties you had shown him. The contract was written by the listing agent. You had never asked the buyer to sign a buyer broker agreement.
>
> Your broker contacted the other broker about the situation and discovers: The buyer had contacted the listing agent about a 2nd property that the agent had listed. Upon doing so the agent met with the buyer at the agent's office. At the office, the agent and the buyer selected several properties to view – which included the one that the you had already shown the buyer. Because the other agent demonstrated how the hurricane shutters worked, the buyer decided that the home was a good choice after all.
>
> Which is the likely outcome?
>
> A. Your broker insists that commission must be paid to your brokerage under Procuring Cause siting that you had originally shown the property to the buyer in addition to keeping up communications with the buyer
> B. Your broker drops the matter explaining to you that you were not directly responsible for creating a chain of events that led to the sale.
>
> B is the more likely outcome. Showing a buyer property is not enough to prove procuring cause. The other agent would argue that the desire for the property was created not by the showing that you made, but rather by showing the features of the house by the other agent.

Courting Period

If a licensee is unable to secure a buyer broker agreement from the outset of a relationship with the buyer, the licensee may employ a "courting period." By doing so the licensee lets the buyer know that the licensee needs a formal commitment to maintain the relationship long term. However, the licensee offers to work with the buyer for a short period to make sure that the buyer and the licensee are a good "fit." It is important when utilizing this strategy to follow through with asking for the formal agreement once the allotted time period has passed.

Formally Asking for a Buyer Agency Agreement

Asking a buyer to enter into a buyer agency agreement is easier when included as part of a "Buyer Listing Presentation." The phrase "listing" here is used more broadly than just "listing homes." It is about "listing clients." Sometimes the listing of clients is as sellers and sometimes as buyers. From the outset of working with a buyer, the licensee should take an opportunity to do a buyer presentation with the buyer where the benefits of working with the licensee as the buyer's agent is explained. As with the end of a seller listing presentation concludes with the goal of listing the seller's home, the buyer presentation concludes with the goal of listing the buyer as an official client.

Preparing for a Buyer Presentation
When a buyer calls the licensee for the first time and asks to see a property, it is tempting for the licensee to drop everything and rush to meet the buyer at the property. However, it's best to meet a buyer for the first time at the licensee's office to facilitate the presentation. If not at the office, then at some other location not connected to the property in question. By conducting a formal meeting at a location other than the property, the licensee can go through a presentation about the licensee's services as a buyer's agent. The licensee is also better able to formally establish the value of the licensee's time. The licensee should have any marketing material on hand to share with the buyer as well as the buyer broker agreement to work through. Part of the time will be used as an assessment of what the buyer is looking for in property.

What Makes You Stand Apart from Your Competition as a Company – for Buyers
Just as it is important to verbalize to sellers why the licensee has chosen to work with his or her real estate brokerage, the licensee must also verbalize this to buyers. The features that attracted the agent to the company would now be emphasized as benefits to the buyer.

For example, if the licensee chose a small brokerage to work with due to desiring personal attention, this can be presented as, "The broker at XYZ Realty reviews every contract that I write. That means that you have the best of the best making sure that your interests are being well represented!"

Or if the licensee chose a large brokerage because of formalized training, this can be presented as, "I work for one of the largest brokerages in town. This means that I have undergone the best training possible to make sure that I am looking out for your best interests!"

What Makes You Stand Apart from Your Competition as an Individual – for Buyers
Primarily buyers want licensees that are dedicated to helping them find the home of their dreams. Being able to write an effective contract and negotiating the best deal is of utmost importance. One of the primary factors that causes a buyer to commit to an agent comes from the rapport and sense of connection that is established early in the relationship. It is important then, when selling a licensee's skills, to include things that will cause the buyer to connect personally with the licensee.

Admirable Qualities

- Confidence
- Commitment
- Honesty
- Dedication
- Gratitude
- Compassion

★ **Students of the post-licensing 45-hour course are instructed to do the following exercise:**

> Feature Benefit
> Develop a list of feature benefits to present to a buyer
> - What makes your company stand apart?
> - What makes you as an individual stand apart?
>
> *Be sure to emphasize EXACTLY what the benefit are to the buyer!

Conducting the Buyer Listing Presentation

Take control of the appointment by following up a greeting with sharing a timeline of the meeting. For example:

"Mr. and Mrs. Buyer, thank you for meeting with me to discuss your home search. This meeting will only take about an hour. If it's okay with you, first I'll share with you information about what strategies I can offer to ensure that you not only find the perfect property, but that you purchase it at the best price and the best terms. Then I will ask you some questions to make sure that I fully understand your homeownership goals. And then, together, we can come up with a plan that makes the most sense. How does that sound?"

Buyer Presentation Practice

★ **Students of the post-licensing 45-hour course are instructed to do the following exercise:**

> Buyer Presentation Role Playing
> After laying out the feature benefits of working with you, practice conducting a listing presentation.
> 1. Start with a formal greeting and set the time-line that the "buyer" can expect for the appointment
> 2. Take a moment to establish rapport
>   a. For example, if you notice that one of the buyers is wearing team memorabilia; state something about the sport.
> 3. Present the benefits of working with you and your brokerage
>   a. "Mr. and Mrs. Buyer, let me assure you that if you choose my services you are in the best of hands and this is why…."
> 4. Conduct a Buyer's Home Needs Assessment
> 5. Provide summary of the market
> 6. Layout a plan to start looking for property
> 7. Get an agreement from the buyer to enter into a formal buyer brokerage relationship

Buyer Needs Assessment

Working with a buyer means understanding what a buyer is looking for in a property. This is best accomplished through a formal needs questionnaire.

Buyer Assessment

1. When is your buying goal?
2. How long have you been looking?
3. What price range?
4. What areas are you considering?
5. Have you been preapproved for a mortgage?
6. Do you have a home to sell before you can make a purchase?
7. Single family home? Town Home? Condominium? High Rise? Other?
8. Garage?
9. Storage?
10. Style?
11. Pool?
12. Yard?
13. # of Bedroom?
14. # of Bathrooms?
15. Den?
16. Square footage?
17. What else is important to you?

Objection Handling with Buyers

Not every buyer will immediately agree to work exclusively with an agent. Sometimes true "selling" skills come into play to get this commitment. Once working with a buyer, it may be difficult to get a buyer to commit to a home. Don't be discouraged by buyer objections. This is a normal part of the process.

See Chapter 5, "Objection Handling."

Prequalifying the Buyer

Working with a buyer is time consuming. It only makes sense to invest time with a buyer that is not only willing to purchase a home, but is able to purchase a home. If the buyer needs to secure a mortgage to purchase then it is vital that the buyer be pre-qualified before showing the buyer property. In Florida, this is particularly true as a good percentage of the property sold is subject to either homeowner association fees or flood insurance. Both factors greatly impact how much home a buyer would qualify to buy. When a buyer has not yet been prequalified, the licensee should refer the buyer to several lenders. It is important never to refer the buyer to only one lender as this will construe that the licensee is responsible for the lenders actions!

For cash buyers, it is just as important to your own "prequalifying process" by discussing how the buyer plans to secure the funds for the purchase. Many sellers will only accept an offer accompanied by proof of funds.

Communicate Directly with the Lender

A good lender will explain carefully to the buyer what funds the buyer needs to close. It is heartbreaking for a buyer to pick out a home only to find out that the buyer can't purchase it due to loan restrictions. This can be avoided by asking for permission from the buyer to communicate directly with the lender. This will enable to you to clearly understand the parameters needed to meet with the property search. The lender should provide the buyer and the agent a copy of a preapproval letter that can used to accompany an offer on a home. Not only does this put the deal in a stronger negotiating position, it is usually required if an offer is being made on a bank owned property.

See Chapter 6, "Financing Considerations," for more about how a loan affects a real estate deal.

Following Fair Housing with Buyers

Remember when working with buyers to always follow fair housing laws. "There is good housing everywhere and only you can decide where you want to live," is the mantra that every licensee should say. When a buyer specifically requests that the buyer only be shown property within a certain area it is good practice to get this in writing from the buyer. This proves that the licensee is not "steering" the buyer to or away from property but is instead only following instructions.

Out of town buyers can make the process more difficult as those buyers will look to their agent to sell them property that the buyers consider "safe." To avoid conflicts with fair housing laws, it is best to provide ALL BUYERS links to crime and school statistics of areas that the licensee shows property. This way the licensee can put it upon the buyer to always pick and choose the areas to see property rather than the agent.

See Chapter 13, "Fair Housing Applied," for more information.

> **Fair Housing**
>
> **Avoid Common Fair Housing Mistakes**
> - Whatever processes you use for one client, use for all.
> - If you ask clients to obtain a prequalification letter from a lender before showing them homes, apply that standard to <u>everyone</u>.
> - Avoid verbiage that makes a judgment about the type of buyer who would be most interested in the home.
>   - For example, saying a home is "within walking distance to the beach" could be seen as excluding people with certain disabilities.
> - Avoid steering by letting buyers state whether they want to live near certain amenities, such as a church, school, etc.
>
> Fair Housing is in Your Hands. February 2017. http://realtormag.realtor.org/law-and-ethics/feature/article/2016/03/fair-housing-in-your-hands

Buyer Management

Once a buyer broker relationship has officially been established, it is time to go to work. Buyer management is a combination of administrative tasks such as setting up auto searches for properties and buyer representation tasks such as buyer showings. The result culminates in the writing of an offer and an eventual property closing.

Setting Up Realistic Expectations

There is a big difference between a buyer's want list and a buyer's must have list. It is the licensee's job to separate the two. This can be particularly difficult when the buyers' must have lists don't quite match up. It is not unusual for spouses to have a different version of a dream home in mind.

Working through this process is like acting as a counselor. Buyers must come to some type of agreement as to what they are looking for in a home. Otherwise, the licensee will find him or herself spinning wheels trying to find a property that meets conflicting expectations. Add in the reality of the market and the home buying process may suddenly turn from exciting to daunting for the buyer.

As a Counselor

Licensees must gauge the emotional reactions of the buyers to know how to move forward. Emotional buyers are best handled by first acknowledging the emotions. When excitement turns to frustration, the licensee should make statement such as "I understand that you are frustrated. I would be as well in your situation. Doing something like buying a home is such an important task and I know you want everything to be perfect…"

Assure the buyers that the licensee is on their side, and that together they will solve their home buying issues will give the buyers the confidence to keep moving forward.

See Chapter 5, "Objection Handling" for more tips.

The Extra Needy Buyer

Occasionally licensees will find themselves working with the extra needy buyer. These are buyers that want to contact the licensee constantly without regard to the licensee's personal time and needs. Often these buyers are apprehensive about the home buying decision and will demand that they see nearly every home in the county before making a decision!

Safeguarding Your Time

The licensee, from the outset of the relationship, should lay out clear expectations of the market and how the home buying experience should unfold. The licensee should establish communication guidelines plus establish when the agent is and isn't available. Of utmost importance is that the licensee should establish an expectation of decision making on the part of the buyer. Buyers are able to eliminate much of the property options if the buyer is realistic about what they are looking for. This can even be done without having to visit the property.

Partnering with Buyers

It is a good idea to signal to the buyer that the buyer is a crucial partner in the home search and elimination process. This can be accomplished by giving the buyer "homework" to participate in the home selection process. It is the buyer's job to review listings that the licensee sends to the buyer by email to determine whether the property seems to fit the buyer's needs. Often buyers can tell by looking at a photo or a video that they do not like the house. This may be true even though the property seems to match what the buyer is looking for on paper. Buyer preference is not always about checking off boxes about how many bedrooms and baths a home has!

Importance of "Drive-Bys"

Another homework assignment to give a buyer before showing the buyer property is to have the buyer drive by the property. Often the buyer will eliminate property based on the feel of the neighborhood or some other external factor that the buyer may judge without ever seeing the home. This can be accomplished even when the timeline is tight in a competitive market place. For example, if a showing is being set up for the next day, the buyers should drive by the property that evening. This is also an effective strategy as it takes the buyer into the neighborhood at different times of the day, which helps the buyer to get a better feel for the property choice.

Buyer Visits to Open Houses

Many buyers enjoy visiting open houses. If a buyer is determined to visit property without the licensee, the licensee should arm the buyer with the licensee's business cards. Upon entering a property, the buyer should immediately disclose to the listing agent that the buyer is being represented by another agent. The buyer should give that agent one of the licensee's cards. This process should help eliminate the listing agent claiming procuring cause if the buyer decides that the property seen during an open house is the right one for the buyer.

Buyer Rebates

Becoming more popular in the national real estate marketplace is the offering of "rebates" or "commission sharing" to the buyer. This is legal and allowed under RESPA and TILA if handled properly – including being disclosed to all parties. The idea is that since the seller is offering to pay a buyer's agent a commission, the buyer can put part of that money in the buyer's pocket. Anyone working with a buyer wanting a rebate who is also using a loan to finance the purchase should consult with the buyer's lender to make sure the lender does not object to the rebate being given.

Using the MLS to find Property to Show

Licensees that become members of the multiple listing service should take advantage of the property search tools when working with buyers. The MLS systems will also allow agents to set up automatic searches that email buyers property updates. It's best in these situations to encourage buyers to STOP using other websites to look for property. The reason for this is that the buyer will constantly be asking you about property that is not really available. For example, some websites will make it look as though property is for sale that is not. Others that pull from the MLS may not be as timely in updating as the information as you are providing. For example, a buyer will ask why the licensee didn't include a certain property and the licensee will take valuable time to look the property up only to find out that it wasn't included because it was already pending. Assuring buyers that the licensee is providing the best most updated information directly from the MLS will help to curb these frustrations.

★ **Students of the post-licensing 45-hour course are instructed to do the following exercise:**

Property Search Practice
Licensees that are members of a multiple listing service should practice looking for property in the North-West side of their town that meets the following criteria:
- 3 to 4 bedrooms
- At least 2 full baths
- Single Family detached home
- 2 car garage
- Private pool

What is the average selling price?

Scheduling Property Showings

Scheduling property showings as a new licensee can be nerve wracking. Here is a process that has been successful for many licensees:

1. Print out all the MLS listing sheets of properties to schedule
2. Place the properties in the order for driving
3. Make note of any vacant properties as these are more flexible for showing; Put a V on the top left of your MLS printout for vacant properties.
4. Place a number at the top left of each listing sheet noting the showing order 1, 2, 3…
5. If the properties are close together by driving, then schedule the first showing for a full hour. But

then stage the next showing by starting that showing a half hour from the first with access for an hour. Keep staggering. Write the time at the top left of the listing sheet next to the numbered position for showing.

6. Then look at the showing directions.
    - Some will direct you to use the showing button on the computer
    - Some will have you call a Showing Center or a Brokerage office.
    - Put any duplicates together so that you can request all at the same time.
7. Call to set up showings.
8. Put a star next to confirmed showing next to the time on the MLS listing sheet.

Staggered Showings

1.	2472 Waldo Street	9:00 a.m. to 10:00 a.m.
2.	5678 Emerson Rd	9:30 a.m. to 10:30 a.m.
3.	5459 Whitman Ct	10:00 a.m. to 11:00 a.m.
4.	7634 Poe Ave	10:30 a.m. to 11:30 a.m.

Comparative Market Analysis for Buyers

When a buyer is writing an offer for a property, the buyer will look to the agent for guidance on how much to offer. The licensee should employ the same comparative market analysis process that is used to assist a seller with pricing. By doing so, the licensee will be acting in the best interest of the buyer. At the end of the day, though, true market value is what a buyer is willing to pay for a property and the price that the seller is willing to accept. It is the licensee's job to direct, not to decide for a buyer, in how much should be offered.

Writing an Offer

Licensees who are members of the Florida Association of Realtors® will have access to several versions of purchase contracts that can be used to write an offer. Plus, these offers can be written and signed electronically. The important thing in preparing an offer is to be very careful that it matches the actual desires of the buyer!

Managing Counteroffers

Many offers are met with counteroffers. It is a good idea to prepare a buyer to expect a counter. It is the licensee's job to help keep the buyer's emotions in check throughout this process. Again, when presented with a counter, review the new contract in detail to make sure that you can clearly communicate what has changed from the original offer. If the buyer would like to counter the counter, a new "clean" offer should be written.

Negotiating the Best Terms for a Buyer

Licensees should keep in mind when constructing a deal for the buyer that it is not always the best price that makes it the best deal. Negotiating a deal involves analyzing the buyer and seller needs and to bring them together with some type of offer that both will find satisfactory. This is true even when the licensee is only working as an agent for one of the parties.

See Chapter 8, "Contracts," for more about contracts.

★ **Students of the post-licensing 45-hour course are instructed to do the following exercise:**

> Negotiating the Best Deal
> You have been working hard to find a buyer the best home to suit the buyer's particular housing needs. It has been difficult, but finally you have found one that the buyer wants to purchase. It has come to your attention from the seller's agent that the seller needs to sell the home before the seller can afford to move.
>
> Which would be the best approach to take in writing an offer?
>
> A. Advise the client what you were told by the seller's agent. Suggest that the buyer might want to consider pairing a lower purchase price with allowing the seller to remain in the home for 10 days after closing to give the seller time to transition.
> B. Because finding a home for the buyer has been so difficult, encourage the buyer to pay asking price before someone else purchases it instead.
>
> A is the better answer. By meeting a need of the seller, the buyer may be able to purchase the property at a lower price than if the seller had to move out before closing.

Successfully managing buyers can be a rewarding and obtainable part of a licensee's real estate career!

5 OBJECTION HANDLING

Learning Terms and Phrases

- Objection Handling
- Life Experiences
- Five Step Method
- Recognize the Problem
- "Heard and Understood"
- Identify with the Person
- Armor
- Isolate the Objection
- The "One Thing"
- Propose an Answer
- Confirm Agreement
- Hidden Objection
- Negotiating
- Series of Objections
- New Agent Objections
- General Listing Objections
- For Sale by Owner Listing Objections
- Expired Listing Objections
- Price Reduction Objections
- Buyer Objections

Learning Objectives

- Licensees will gain an understanding about the importance of objection handling.
- Licensees will develop knowledge about the five-step method to handling objections.
- Licensees will develop skill and using the five-step method with buyers and sellers through role playing for
    - New Agent Objections
    - General Listing Objections
    - For Sale by Owner Listing Objections
    - Expired Listing Objections
    - Price Reduction Objections
    - Buyer Objections
    - Contract Negotiations

Importance of Mastering Objection Handling

Selling real estate is a sales job. On the surface, this would seem like a redundant statement. The truth, though, is that many individuals are lured to the field of real estate because they love houses. Furthermore, they love the prospect of assisting others in finding their dream homes. But many of these same individuals hate the idea of "pressuring someone into making a decision." They hate selling. Furthermore, they hate selling because they confuse "pressuring" with "assisting" someone into making a decision.

What is Objection Handling?

All sales, even the sale of real estate, involves the skill of objection handling. Objection handling is working with an individual to figure out why the person really doesn't want to move forward and then helping them to decide. If the goal is to sell a home, then the decision that the licensee is aiming for is to agree to move forward with a real estate deal. Objection handling starts with the agreement to work with the licensee as an agent, and proceeds through closing.

Pulling from Life Experience

Despite the reluctance to "sell," most licensees have been involved with "objection handling" throughout the course of their life. Even a child that wants another cookie and is told "no" will go into "objection handling" mode to try to convince the adult that the child really should have another cookie! As grownups, personal relationships still involve objection handling. When one spouse wants to make a major financial expenditure and the other one doesn't, for example, the spouse will need to handle objections to reach the goal of the expenditure.

Pulling from Business Transactions

All sales jobs involve some type of objection handling. The most obvious, of course, is the business of car sales. If a car salesperson takes a buyer on a test drive, the salesperson has the goal of selling the car. At the end of the test drive, the salesperson will ask the buyer to buy the car. When the buyer refuses, the salesperson will then start asking questions – trying to ascertain why the buyer isn't buying the car. By knowing what the buyer is "objecting" to, the salesperson can then propose a solution that will encourage the buyer to move forward with the deal.

A bad salesperson will seem obvious and clumsy with this process and will get poor results. A good salesperson will seem helpful and be appreciated. After all, the buyer really is wanting to buy a car. It is just a matter of being guided to make a decision.

Five Step Method

Objection handling can be broken down into five easy steps. These steps apply whether trying to get another cookie, trying to convince a spouse to spend money, trying to convince someone to buy a car, or trying to have a successful career in real estate!
1. Recognize the Problem
2. Identify with the Person
3. Isolate the Objection
4. Propose an Answer
5. Confirm Agreement

Recognize the Problem

Sometimes situations can be somewhat heated and adversarial. Thus, the best way to start the objection handling process is to "recognize the problem." When it comes down to it, everyone wants to be "heard and understood." So, before someone will be open to listening to a way to resolve the issue, first that person must know that the other person really hears and understands him or her. This is done by making statements such as, "I understand not getting your offer accepted is frustrating."

Identify with the Person

Recognizing the problem works to start softening someone's resistance. But it usually isn't enough to really get that person to put down his or her resistant "armor." To do that, it is important to "identify with the person." This is done by identifying with the emotion and the situation. It involves using statements such as, "Whenever I am in a situation like this, I too always want …." It helps even more to be very specific about a situation, such as, "When I bought my last house, I too wanted…."

Isolate the Objection

Once the problem has been recognized and the person has been identified within the situation, it is time to "isolate the objection." This means trying to find out what really is keeping the person from moving forward - the ONE thing. It may also be a bit of a guessing process as the one thing that is holding up the deal is prodded out. This is accomplished by making statements such as, "So although the house seems like a great choice, you are not happy with the amount of the seller's counteroffer."

Propose an Answer

The next step is to offer a solution to the problem. Sometimes this is easy. Sometimes this takes a more creative solution. Either way the person will usually be open to hearing an answer to the problem.

This can be accomplished by making statements such as, "We could write another offer meeting the seller midway between what you had originally offered and the seller's counteroffer."

Confirm Agreement

The final step is to ask for an agreement to the proposal. This step finalizes the "close." It gets a commitment from the person. This can be accomplished by making statements such as, "How does that sound? Shall I write it up?"

The Five Steps Together

The five steps should flow together without the other person even realizing that they are being taken through a series of closing steps.

"I understand not getting your offer accepted is frustrating. When I bought my last house, I too wanted to get the home at a lower price than what the house was listed at. So, although the house seems like a great choice, you are not happy with the amount of the seller's counteroffer. We could write another offer meeting the seller midway between what you had originally offered and the seller's counteroffer. How does that sound? Shall I write it up?"

> **Objection Handling**
> 1. Recognize the Problem
> 2. Identify with the Person
> 3. Isolate the Objection
> 4. Propose an Answer
> 5. Confirm Agreement

The Hidden Objection

If a confirmed agreement isn't given at the end of step five, then either the solution isn't acceptable or the true "objection" hasn't been uncovered. The latter happens more than people realize. Many licensees will spend an enormous amount of time trying to come up with a solution to the wrong problem. It doesn't matter how creative or clever a solution may be, if it doesn't address the real issue then it will never move the deal forward! The true objection remains hidden until a good salesperson uncovers it.

Negotiating the Best Deal – Revisiting Chapter 4

Recall the last exercise in Chapter 4, "Buyer Management". In that lesson, it was demonstrated that constructing a deal not always about price. Yet, price is what most buyers and sellers voice as being the objection – even when it really isn't the biggest issue. With a little digging, the licensee often finds that the price is not actually the main objection. By dealing with the other objection, the objection of price will often fall away. In the exercise, it was discovered that the seller's objection was more about convenience than price. So, the deal was crafted specifically to overcome the seller's objection, solve the problem, and to come to an agreement.

Series of Objection Handling

At times, working with a client may mean handling a series of objections. Different objections may crop up throughout different stages of a deal. Each one will have to be handled in order to keep moving forward. Whether at the beginning of a deal (or conversation), the five-step process always applies.

Multiple Objections

1. Recognize the Problem
2. Identify with the Person
3. Isolate the Objection
4. Propose an Answer
5. Confirm Agreement
6. "Rinse and Repeat!"

*Different objections may crop up throughout different stages of a deal. Each objection will have to be handled in order to keep moving forward.

★ **Students of the post-licensing 45-hour course are instructed to do the following exercise:**

Objection Handling Scenario 1
You are meeting in your office with two buyers, Steve and Donna Clark.
You have been working together for months and have finally written an offer on a house.
"Steve, and Donna, thank-you for meeting with me at my office today. We have a counteroffer from the seller and I wanted to go over the terms with you."
"That's wonderful," Donna immediately reacted.
"Not so fast," Steve cautioned. "I already told you that I am not paying a penny more than what was written in the offer."

Which would be the best response to Steve's objection?

A. "Steve, we have been looking for the right home for months. Donna has her heart set on this house. You are going to disappoint her if you don't at least consider the counteroffer!"

B. "I understand that the phrase counteroffer can be a bit distressing. When I bought my last home, I didn't want a counter either. We do have a counter, though, so how about if I share with you the terms. Would that be alright?"

B is the better answer. It takes Steve through the 5 steps of objection handling and will more than likely produce a better result than A.

Objections as a New Agent

Not only does the inexperience of being a new real estate licensee make handling objections more difficult, but often being a new agent becomes the objection. As explained in Chapter 3, "Listing Management," and Chapter 4, "Buyer Management;" these objections can be avoided through a well-prepared presentation. The presentation will counter the new agent objection before that objection is put forth by the seller or the buyer. Despite, the licensee's best efforts to avoid it, sometimes the agent may have to deal head-on with the "new agent objection."

★ **Students of the post-licensing 45-hour course are instructed to do the following exercise:**

> Objection Handling Scenario 2
> You are meeting in your office with two buyers, Steve and Donna Clark. You have been working together for months and have finally written an offer on a house. "Steve, and Donna, thank you for meeting with me at my office today. We have a counteroffer from the seller and I wanted to go over the terms with you."
> "That's wonderful," Donna immediately reacted.
> "Not so fast," Steve cautioned. "I already told you that I didn't want a counter. I knew we needed a more experienced agent to handle our deal. If we had one, we wouldn't be sitting here right now!"
>
> Which would be the best response to Steve's objection?
>
> A. "I understand that the idea of a counteroffer is disappointing. When I bought my last home, I also wanted to make sure that I had the best person looking out for my interests and getting me the best deal. We do have a counter, though, and I can assure you that my broker is on hand and is prepared to step in to assist us if necessary. How about if I share with you what the seller is proposing and then we can discuss your options? How does that sound?"
> B. "I am really hurt that after working so hard for you all these months that you still don't trust me!"
>
> A is the better answer. Although Steve is siting the issue of you being a new agent, he is most probably just concerned about the terms of the counteroffer and is taking it out on you. However, both objections are handled together in this response which is designed to keep the buyer moving forward by utilizing the 5 steps of objection handling.
>
> B gets off track by playing defense about being a new agent and would not be nearly as effective.

Handling Listing Objections

Deciding to sell a home and choosing a real estate agent, is a huge decision for sellers. Even when the decision to sell is based on practical reasons it often evokes high emotions. When a licensee is conducting a seller listing appointment, the licensee may have to deal with objections around the actual decision to sell, plus the decision of which agent to hire.

As explained in Chapter 3, "Listing Management", it is important for the licensee to follow through with a well laid out listing presentation. Apprehension that sellers feel is often calmed by the sense that the agent is well-prepared and knows what he or she is doing to best represent the seller. Despite, the licensee's best efforts, though, many times the agent finds the seller hesitating to agree to go forward. In these situations, the licensee should use the 5-step method to overcome the seller's objections.

Students of the post-licensing 45-hour course are instructed to do the following exercise:

> Objection Handling Scenario 3
> You have spent the past hour with sellers, George and Kay Smith, discussing the possible listing of their home for sale. You have been feeling very confident throughout the presentation. The sellers seemed to like you and smiled and nodded often.
> "Mr. and Mrs. Smith, now that we have decided on the best listing price, how about if you go ahead and sign the listing agreement so I can get to work finding a buyer for your lovely home?"
> "Sorry, but Kay and I agreed beforehand that we are going to meet with at least three agents before making a decision."
>
> Which would be the best response to George's objection?
>
> A. "I understand that choosing a real estate agent is an important decision. Whenever I must do something as important as selling a home, I also want to make sure that I have the best person representing me. Interviewing multiple agents probably seemed like the best way to make that happen. I could share with you, though, how my sales results and the sales results of my office compares to some of these other agents you may be interviewing. Wouldn't you agree that results are really what it's all about?"
>
> B. "I understand that choosing a real estate agent is an important decision. Whenever I must do something as important as selling a home, I also want to make sure that I have the best person representing me. I respect your desire to meet with more than one agent. How about if we agree to meet again when you are ready?"
>
> A is the better answer. It shows respect for the sellers while getting to the heart of the matter. The fact is that the sellers have no actual desire to "meet" three agents. The real objection is that they want to make sure they are hiring the best agent.
>
> Honestly, most licensees give an answer similar to B in these situations. It may even look like the 5-step method was used. After all, it proposes a solution of getting together after the sellers have interviewed the other agents. But the reality is that 99.9% of the time "later" will never come because instead the sellers will have signed with an agent who "pushed" them a little harder as in choice A.

Handling FSBO Objections

As discussed in Chapter 2, "Prospecting", licensees often find great success by approaching "For Sale by Owners" to list their property. Mastering this process involves learning how to apply the 5-step approach to objection handling. "For Sale by Owners" have already ruled out using a real estate agent, so the licensee will need to be prepared to "isolate" each of the reasons that the seller does not want to use an agent and be prepared to offer a counter narrative to provide solutions to the objections.

A well laid out listing presentation will still apply, but the first objection to handle may very well be just getting the seller willing to sit down with the licensee. Regardless of whether dealing with the seller on the telephone, at the seller's front step, or in the seller's living room, the licensee will experience the best success by employing the 5-step method. If carried out effectively, the seller will not notice the redundancy of the approach. Rather the seller will appreciate the solutions being provided.

★ **Students of the post-licensing 45-hour course are instructed to do the following exercise:**

> Objection Handling Scenario 4
> You have knocked on the door of a "For Sale by Owner" in hopes of convincing the seller to consider listing the home for sale with you as the real estate agent. You prepared for the opportunity by pulling tax records on the property and running comparable sales in the MLS.
>
> After you introduce yourself, the seller immediately states, "I have already decided not to list my home with an agent!"
>
> Which would be the best response to the seller's objection?
>
> A. "Mr. Seller, I wouldn't have bothered you except that I have a buyer very interested in seeing your home. If only you would take a few minutes to meet with me, I think that together we can make sure that you are able to pocket the amount that you are looking for in selling your property. After all, wouldn't it be great to actually have your home sold?"
> B. "I'm sure that having real estate agents knocking on your door must seem like a waste of your time. Whenever I have made such an important decision as you have in deciding to sell your home on your own, I also just want other people to respect the choice that I have made. I'm also sure that in coming to that decision, you must want to save money. Let me ask you this, if I could show you how you could pocket the most money by using me as an agent, wouldn't it make sense to take a couple of minutes to find out how?"
>
> B is the better answer. It takes the seller through the 5 steps by first recognizing the problem and identifying with the seller. It then goes after the heart of the true objection by focusing on the seller's desire to save money. (This is the most common motivation of FSBOs.) Steps 4 and 5 are rolled together with the ending question designed to give the seller a reason to agree to meet with the licensee.
> A would NEVER be the correct or ETHICAL answer UNLESS you have a ready, willing, and able buyer that has expressed interest in that home. Unfortunately, pretending to have a buyer lined up is the #1 line used on "For Sale by Owners!"

Handling Expired Listing Objections

Also discussed in Chapter 2, "Prospecting", is the process of securing listings by approaching home sellers whose listings in the multiple listing service has expired. These home sellers are usually armed with just as many objections as "For Sale by Owners" are – having just had what was probably a disappointing experience in the previous listing of the property. Just as with the "For Sale by Owners," success for the agent in getting these properties back in the market comes by mastering the 5-step approach to objection handling.

⭐ **Students of the post-licensing 45-hour course are instructed to do the following exercise:**

> Objection Handling Scenario 5
> You have knocked on the door of a property that has expired in the MLS. You hope to convince the homeowner to use you as his next real estate agent by getting the property relisted. You prepared for the opportunity by pulling tax records on the property, printing the previous listing, and running comparable sales in the MLS.
>
> After you introduce yourself, the seller immediately states, "I have decided to wait until the market is stronger before selling."
>
> Which would be the best response to the seller's objection?
>
> A. "Mr. Seller, I wouldn't have bothered you except that I have a buyer very interested in seeing your home. It only would take a few minutes to meet with me, I think that together we can make sure that this time you won't be disappointed by having your home go unsold. After all, you wouldn't want to lose out on a possible deal, would you?
> B. "I'm sure that going to the trouble of listing your home only to have it not sell must have been a frustrating experience for you. And I'm sure that if I was in your situation, I, too, would be tempted to wait before relisting. But if I was able to bring you a buyer today that met your selling goals, wouldn't it still be the right time to sell? How about if we sit down together so I can explain what I can do different to make this happen for you?"
>
> B is the better answer. It takes the seller through the 5 steps by first recognizing the problem and identifying with the seller. It then sorts out the fact that the seller doesn't really want to wait – he just doesn't want to be disappointed again! Steps 4 and 5 are rolled together with the ending question designed to give the seller a proposed answer so that the seller would agree to meet with the licensee.
>
> A again is the wrong approach to take unless there is an actual buyer waiting to see the house!

Handling Objections to Price Reductions

Chapter 3, "Listing Management," provided tips and warnings about working with overpriced listings. Yet, sometimes despite an agent's best efforts, a property sits on the market without securing a buyer. After exhausting other solutions, the only prudent step remaining may very well be a price reduction. Approaching a seller and suggesting that the seller needs to drop the price is often aligned with the old adage "Don't shoot the messenger!" An agent in this situation can take heart when having kept the seller fully informed about the conditions of the sales market and having kept the seller informed of all marketing steps taken to sell the property. Feedback from property showings provided to the seller is also an important component to securing a price reduction. And finally, the licensee can rely on the 5-step approach to handling the seller's objections when working through this issue.

★ **Students of the post-licensing 45-hour course are instructed to do the following exercise:**

> Objection Handling Scenario 6
> You are meeting with a seller of a property that you have listed. Despite your best marketing efforts and multiple showings, you have decided that the property is overpriced.
>
> After sharing updated information with the seller and suggesting the reduction, the seller responds by stating, "If I have to take a reduction in my price then you have to take a reduction in your commission!"
>
> Which would be the best response to the seller's objection?
>
> A. "Mr. Seller, I have been working so hard for you. I have even been spending my own money on advertising. It really isn't fair that after all this time, effort, and expense that I have invested that you would punish me by expecting me to drop my commission! After all, I am already going to make less money when we drop the asking price!
> B. "I'm sure that it is very disappointing not to have gotten an offer yet for your wonderful home. I know that whenever I set out to do something as important as selling my own home, I want to make sure that I have done everything possible to ensure that I get the best price. And I'm sure that I, too, would be trying to figure out to save every penny I could. But I think that we can both agree that the real issue boils down to securing a buyer for your home. How about if we take some time to develop a pricing strategy that will really work?"
>
> B is the better answer. It takes the seller through the 5 steps by first recognizing the problem of seller frustration and disappointment. It takes time to identify with the seller putting you back on the seller's side rather than being viewed as the problem. It then redirects the issue away from the fake problem of the commission issue to the real problem of the listing price. Steps 4 and 5 are rolled together asking for agreement to the proposed solution.
>
> A is a defensive response that focuses on the agent rather the solving the seller's actual problem.

Handling Buyer Objections

As pointed out in Chapter 4, "Buyer Management," the first objection a licensee may encounter with a buyer is to object to signing a buyer broker agreement. Then once working with a buyer, the buyer may have difficulty making a decision to actually put an offer in on a property. Then once the negotiating process has begun, the buyer may have objections while dealing with counteroffers. There may be other objections through the inspection process. Sometimes buyers get right up to end of the deal but suddenly "object" to closing – out of fear! At each one of these stages, the licensee can use the 5-step process to help guide the buyer forward.

★ **Students of the post-licensing 45-hour course are instructed to do the following exercise:**

> Role Playing Assignment
> Practice makes perfect! Find a partner to work with to practice handling the following objections:
> - "But I don't want to go to bed at 8:30. I want to stay up until 10!"
> - "I cleaned my room last week. Why should I have to clean it again?"
> - "I don't think we can afford a new washer and dryer!"
> - "But what if the next house to come on the market is finally the house of my dreams (said after you have shown the buyer 30 properties matching her criteria)?
> - "How dare the buyer offer such a low price? I'm not even going to counter such an insulting offer!"
> - "But how can I commit to you as my buyer's agent when I don't really know you yet?"
> - "I don't want to pay that much in commission!"
> - "All real estate agents are thieves!"
> - "When my brother sold his house, he didn't have to pay any of the buyer's expenses so why should I!?"
> - "I want to wait until after the holidays before I list my home!"
>
> *Check each other's responses for following the 5 steps! This process isn't about memorizing what to say. It is about memorizing the 5 steps and being able to use them in any situation.

Success Through Objection Handling

It doesn't matter how extreme or out of a blue a seller or buyer statement may be, success in dealing with objections and moving someone forward lies in mastering the 5-step approach!

SECTION 2 THE DEAL

SECTION 2 THE DEAL, of this course, focuses on taking a deal from contract to closing. Chapters include:
6. Financing Considerations
7. Condos/H.O. A's/C.D. D's
8. Contracts
9. Inspections
10. Closings

Upon completion of this section, licensees should have a good grasp of how financing affects the real estate deal, the differences between real estate contracts, issues specific to selling condominiums, properties with homeowner associations and/or community development districts, how to manage inspections, and how to facilitate a successful closing.

6 FINANCING CONSIDERATIONS

<u>Learning Terms and Phrases</u>
- Financing Contingency
- Appraisal
- Estimate of Value
- Short Appraisals
- Prequalified
- Preapproved
- Loan Application
- Conventional Loans
- Down Payment Calculation
- PITI
- PMI
- Total Obligation Ratio
- FHA Loans
- Housing Expense Ratio
- 203K
- VA Loans
- USDA Loans
- Homebuyer Assistance Programs
- Mortgage Fraud
- Red Flags

<u>Learning Objectives</u>

- ➢ Licensees will gain an understanding about how to work with a financing contingency.
- ➢ Licensees will gain an understanding about how to deal with a short appraisal.
- ➢ Licensees will understand how to evaluate buyer loan pre-approvals
- ➢ Licensees will have an understanding of the loan approval process.
- ➢ Licensees will have an understanding about matching buyers' loan approval amount to property.
- ➢ Licensees will understand how different loan types affect deal management.

LICENSEES WILL UNDERSTAND HOW TO RECOGNIZE AND AVOID MORTGAGE FRAUD.

Financing Can Make or Break a Deal

Florida real estate agents have the advantage of closing a high percentage of real estate deals with the buyers using cash to make the purchase. That said, licensees must acquire expertise in managing deals that utilize loans to fund the closing. If a deal is contingent upon financing, the loan being successfully funded will literally make or break the deal. This chapter guides licensees through the ins and outs of managing deals that involve loans. This is an important consideration regardless of whether working with the seller, the buyer, or both.

Financing Contingency

When a buyer requires a loan to purchase property, the contract is normally written to include a contingency, which states that the buyer may cancel the deal if the loan fails to fund. This provision allows the buyer to reclaim any earnest money paid. With this provision in place, it is a big concession for a seller to accept an offer which relies on a loan. The seller will look to his or her agent's expertise to guide the seller in whether accepting the deal is a good risk. The buyer will look to his or her agent's expertise to help navigate the loan process ensuring that the buyer is able to close on his or her chosen home.

See Chapter 8 "Contracts," for more information about writing contracts.

Appraisal

Whenever there is a loan involved, a property appraisal will be ordered by the lender. The appraisal will ascertain an estimate of a property's value. Since the property is being used as collateral for the loan, the appraisal is required before the lender will approve the loan. The point of the appraisal is to ensure that the property's value will cover the loan in the event that the borrower defaults. So, although market value is determined by how much a particular buyer is willing to pay and how much a particular seller is willing to sell, the appraisal value must be supported by the actual sales history of similar properties.

Agent's Estimate of Value

The licensee will be the first line of defense to ensure that a property appraises. A seller that is asking substantially more than any other property has sold for may be ecstatic when the seller secures an offer on the home, but if the offer is tied to an appraisal, the licensee will be obligated to warn his or her client that the property may not appraise.

Rising Market Value

When licensees work in a market where home values are on the rise, it is common to have issues with short appraisals. Appraisal values are based on three recent comparable sales.

> **Rising Market**
>
> | Comp 1 | Comp 2 | Comp 3 |
> |---|---|---|
> | Sold | Sold | Sold |
> | April 2017 | June 2017 | Aug 2017 |
> | $275,000 | $289,000 | $305,000 |
> | | Increased 5% | Increased 5.5% |
>
> Based on the above trend, a home seller could expect to find a buyer willing to pay $320,250 in October 2017.
>
> (305,000 x 1.05)
>
> Yet appraised value would only be $289,667!
>
> ($275,000 + $289,000 + $305,000)/3
>
> **If financing is involved, there would be a shortfall of over $30,000!**

Short Appraisals

If an appraisal falls short of the needed value to close the deal, one of four outcomes would result.
1. The seller would need to drop the selling price.
2. The buyer would need to bring more cash to the deal to make up the shortfall.
3. The seller would drop some on the selling price and the buyer would bring more cash – a combination of #1 and #2.
4. The deal would fail to close.

Disputing Appraisals

Often when an appraisal fails to support the selling price, either the seller or buyer will request to challenge the appraisal value. It is possible to challenge an appraisal. Yet, unless the appraiser made a blatant mistake, it is unlikely to change the results. Start by obtaining a copy of the appraisal. Included in the appraisal is a list of homes used as comparisons. Cross reference facts for accuracy including square footage, lot size, condition, age, amenities and improvements. Property located within the same neighborhood will hold the most weight – even "better" than matched properties located outside of the immediate area.

Double check that the comparisons used were for property located within the same school district. Schools can affect buying behavior. Even though two properties may be located only a block apart, if it changes school district – it may no longer be a valid comparison. Also check to see if any "unpermitted" improvements were struck out which created less value than expected. This can be countered by correcting the situation with the local building permit department. If factual discrepancies are found, the information should be compiled to present to the bank. Include factual details about the property being appraised that helps to substantiate value.

12 Steps to Fight a Low Appraisal. February 2017. https://www.trulia.com/blog/12-steps-fight-low-appraisal/#sthash.PDnMJSjq.dpuf

Structuring a Deal Based on Expected Appraisals

As previously noted, both the seller and the buyer will be looking to his or her agents for guidance on whether a property is likely to appraise.

When a listing agent puts a property on the market based on a market that is bringing higher and higher sales prices, the agent must educate the seller on the fact that a cash buyer (or a buyer making up the value difference in cash) would be necessary to close a deal at the higher expected price. When a seller is selling property in a market where there are a lot of cash deals, this increases the likelihood of attracting a cash buyer and successfully closing at the higher increasing price. If the seller is selling property in a market where there are a lot of financed deals, then the seller is less likely to attract a cash buyer. In this situation, the seller may be forced to sell at a lower price.

Gambling on the Odds

Buyers who are looking to finance a home in a market with increasing home values (seller's market) will have better luck in areas that attract less cash buyers. Yet, the very fact that the area attracts more buyers using financing than cash will in itself slow the increase in home values - working to the buyer's advantage. Still, licensees will find success writing deals in a seller's market with a bit of perseverance. The trick is to find the "motivated" seller that doesn't have time to wait for the cash buyer.

Students of the post-licensing 45-hour course are instructed to do the following exercise:

Sellers' Market
You have been working diligently with a nice couple to help them purchase a home. It is a sellers' market with rising values and about 65% of the deals closing with cash buyers. Over the weekend you looked at several homes and narrowed it down to two properties.
Based on the following information, on which property would you guide your buyers to make an offer?

- Home A where the list agent disclosed that the seller has already turned down 3 other offers and is not in a hurry to sell the property.
- Home B where the list agent disclosed that the sellers are getting a divorce and must sell the property in order to each purchase new homes.

* Home B is clearly the better choice. The unfortunate situation of the divorcing sellers is actually an advantage to the buyers since it motivates them to sell quickly.

Qualifying Buyers

Most sellers will not consider accepting an offer contingent upon financing unless the buyer is already pre-approved. This is absolutely true if the property being sold is owned by a bank as a repossessed property. Therefore, any licensee working with a buyer should advise the buyer to get pre-approved prior to officially starting a home search. In the event that a buyer is not pre-approved prior to making an offer, contracts may be written to allow time for the buyer to initiate the loan approval process.

Prequalified or Preapproved

If a loan officer has done a brief interview with a buyer without verifying documentation such as income, the loan officer may deem that the buyer is "Pre-qualified." This means that if everything the buyer has told the loan officer is true, then the buyer is likely to be able to purchase a home matching the pre-qualified terms. Being "Pre-approved" is generally more reliable than being "Prequalified." It means that the loan officer has already verified needed documentation. Anything that hasn't been verified will be listed on the preapproval as "contingencies."

When representing the seller, a licensee should examine the preapproval carefully in order to advise the seller on how much of the approval process is left in order for the buyer to close on the home purchase. When representing the buyer, a licensee should examine the preapproval carefully in order to advise the buyer on what the buyer still needs to do to qualify for the loan.

★ **Students of the post-licensing 45-hour course are instructed to do the following exercise:**

Comparing Preapproval Letters

You have been working hard to sell a home for a seller. You listed the home for $345,000. Your hard work has finally paid off with two competing offers.

Based on the following information, which offer would you guide your buyers to make an offer?

- Offer A is $340,000 with the buyer securing a 96.5% loan for the property. Attached to the offer is a letter from a loan officer stating that the buyer has been preapproved. The approval is contingent upon the following:
    o An appraisal supporting the value of the purchase
    o The buyer supplying proof that he has been employed for 2 years and is currently employed at closing
    o Documentation verifying income that the buyer reported on the loan application
    o Documentation verifying income that the buyer has the assets reported on the loan application
    o Verification that the buyer has at least a 680 credit score

- Offer B is for $335,000 with the buyer paying cash. No financing involved. Proof of funds was attached to the offer.

* Although Offer A is for more money than Offer B, it appears from the contingencies included within the "preapproval" that the buyer has not actually been vetted. It would be your duty to explain this risk to the seller. Although every seller has to make up his or her own mind, in many cases the cash offer would be accepted over the financing offer even though it is for less money.

Applying for a Loan

Lenders use the Uniform Residential Loan Application to collect information needed to qualify borrowers. However, the information collected on the loan application is then verified by the borrower providing documentation. Things like verification of employment will come from the lender contacting the employer directly. Plus, the lender will check the buyer's credit by pulling the buyer's score from the three major credit bureaus: TransUnion, Experian, and Equifax. All the information gathered will be used along with the property appraisal to determine whether the loan will be approved.

Applying for a Loan

Information Required by Lenders

Income: A buyer should be prepared to provide information about employment history. Lenders will document the information from W2s, pay stubs and federal tax returns (1040's) and Year-to-Date Profit and Loss Statements if self-employed.

Assets: A buyer should be prepared to provide Bank statements on all accounts, stocks, mutual funds, bonds, and 401K statements. The buyer will need to explain any large deposits and sources of those funds. And the copy of the closing disclosure if the buyer recently sold a home.

Credit Verification: A buyer should be prepared to provide the Landlord's name, address, and phone number (if renting), an explanation for any credit report Late payments, inquiries, Charge-offs, Collections, Judgments, and Liens. And a copy of bankruptcy papers if filed bankruptcy within the last seven years.

*If the lender verifies the majority of this information at the outset, a Credit Pre-Approval will be provided to the buyer

*If the lender takes verbal information from the buyer without enough documentation; then a Pre-Qualification is provided.

Income and Credit Guidelines

Lenders verify borrowers' income to ensure that buyers have income stability as well as enough income to satisfy a payment schedule. Debt to income requirements as well as credit requirements change depending upon the type of loan being sought as well as the lender providing the loan.

Licensees are best served by relying on mortgage professionals to determine whether a buyer qualifies for a mortgage. Loan officers provide licensees with guidelines to help match buyers to homes that meet requirements.

How Much Home Does a Buyer Qualify to Buy?

Whether a buyer qualifies to buy a particular property relies not only on the strength of the buyer financially, but other factors such as mandatory insurance, fees, and taxes required to pay along with the repayment of the mortgage itself. To qualify for a loan, a borrower's income will be measured against the amount of existing debt the buyer has, the monthly principal and interest required to repay the mortgage, and the costs associated with owning the home including taxes, homeowner's insurance, flood insurance and if applies – flood insurance, homeowner's insurance, and/or condominium fees. (Community Developments fees are paid as part of taxes.)

★ **Students of the post-licensing 45-hour course are instructed to do the following exercise:**

> Qualifying Payment Amount
> You were told by a lender that a buyer would qualify for a loan for home of up to $275,000. The lender advised you that this was based on the house being located in an area not located in a flood zone and with a homeowner association fee of no more than $150 a month.
>
> The buyer was searching online himself and found a house located in a popular neighborhood. When you pull the listing information you discover that the house is only $255,000 but is located in a Flood Zone "A" and that the homeowner association fees are $300 a month.
>
> Which is the best course of action to take?
>
> A. Since the buyer is already determined to see the property, schedule the showing and immediately write an offer if the buyer wants to move forward.
> B. Contact the buyer's lender to review the information about the property and schedule a showing to coincide immediately after the expected response time from the lender.
>
>> B is the better choice. Not all buyers will be patient enough to wait. In a competitive seller's market, waiting may risk losing out on the property. It is important, however, to stay within the limitations that the lender has provided. Although the property is selling for less than the approval amount, the fact that it will probably require flood insurance along with the elevated homeowner association fee makes it less probable that the buyer will qualify to buy the property.
>
> *It is important to work with a lender that is as quick to respond to loan questions as you are quick to respond to a buyer's request for showings!

Referring Buyers to a Lender

Buyers can work directly with a bank, a savings and loan, or a credit union to obtain a loan. Or borrowers can work with a mortgage broker who acts as an intermediary to broker loans for borrowers that are funded by either a bank, a savings and loan, a credit union or a mortgage lender. Mortgage lenders do not provide the public with savings or checking accounts. Instead mortgage lenders are only in the business to lend money.

Mortgage loan origination is the actual process of working with a buyer to process loan applications and to negotiate the terms and conditions of the loan between the borrower and the lender. The Secure and Fair Enforcement for Mortgage Licensing Act (SAVE Act) of 2008 created minimum standards for the licensing and registering of Mortgage Loan Originators. The act requires all mortgage loan originators to register with the Nationwide Mortgage Licensing System (NMLS). If the mortgage loan originators are not employed by federally chartered and regulated institutions, he or she must also be state licensed to work as a mortgage loan originator.

Licensees are advised to network with a number of lenders to have a wide variety of lender options to refer the buyer to who need help obtaining a loan. To avoid liability for the work provided by the lender, the licensee should refer the borrower to at least three lenders and encourage the borrower to meet with more than one.

Types of Loan Affects the Deal

The type of loan that a buyer seeks to secure for the property impacts a real estate deal in several ways. It affects the amount of money the borrower is required to include as a down payment. It affects the amount of existing debt the borrower may already have and the amount of housing debt the borrower may take on with the loan. It affects what type of property is acceptable. It affects what type of condition the property is required to be in to secure the loan. It may affect where the property is allowed to be located. It may also affect whether any repairs are allowed to be made as part of the loan. (If the buyer is looking to finance repairs, special loan types would be required.) Licensees should keep all of these things in mind when looking to close a deal where there is a loan involved.

Conventional Loans

A typical conventional loan requires that the borrower put between 5 to 20% down on the purchase of the house in order to qualify for the loan. Licensees often feel intrusive inquiring whether a buyer has the required funds to close, however, it is an important conversation to have. Licensees who are uncomfortable with this conversation can defer to the lender leading in this area.

Down Payment Calculation

To Calculate Required Down Payment

- Take the purchase price and multiply by the percentage required.

*Waldo wants to buy a home. He is required to put 10% down. How much down payment will he be required to make on a home he is purchasing for $275,000?

Answer: $275,000 x 10% = $27,500

With a conventional loan, the government is neither insuring or guaranteeing any repayment to the lender in the case of borrower default on the loans. Therefore, the lender may require private mortgage insurance to be paid by the borrower. The monthly cost of the private mortgage insurance must be included in debt calculations to determine whether the borrower qualifies for the loan. Borrowers securing a conforming conventional mortgage cannot exceed a maximum total monthly debt obligation ratio of 36%.

Buyers may use a conventional mortgage for various types of property including condominiums. However, conventional mortgages are generally not approved for manufactured homes. The condition requirements of the property may be somewhat flexible so long as the condition upholds a property appraisal. There are generally no limitations as to where a property may be located when the buyer is using a conventional loan.

Total Obligation Ratio

To Calculate Total Monthly Obligations

1. Total a buyer's Monthly INSTALLMENT debt already found on the Credit Report:

    - Credit card payments, auto payments, student loans, child support payments

2. Add the proposed House Payment:

    - PITI (House Principal Payment, Interest, Taxes, & Insurance) + PMI (Private Mortgage Insurance)

3. Divide Total Monthly Obligations by total of buyer's Monthly Gross

*Waldo wants to buy a home with a conventional mortgage. The total PITI for the home he wants is $1,000. He is already paying $800 in other long term debt obligations (car payment of $525 and total credit cards of $275). Waldo's gross monthly income is $3,200. Will he qualify for this home?

Answer:

$1,800 ($1,000 + $800) ÷ $3,200 = .5625 or 56%

Does NOT qualify!

★ **Students of the post-licensing 45-hour course are instructed to do the following exercise:**

> Buyer Cash Requirements
> You are working with a buyer that wants to purchase a home using a conventional loan. The lender has informed you that the buyer must put 5% down on the purchase. Plus, the buyer will need about 3.5% of the purchase price in order to pay required closing costs. Calculate how much cash the buyer would need to close on a property purchased at a price of $185,000.
>
> _____
> _____
> _____
>
> Answer: 5% + 3.5% = 8.5% x $185,000 = $15,725 cash required to complete purchase

FHA Loans

Borrowers that struggle to come up with the down payment requirement of a conventional mortgage may apply for a loan through the Federal Housing Administration – known as a FHA loan. The down payment requirement of a FHA loan is only 3.5%. FHA loans are insured by the government, however, to cover the insurance borrowers are charged an upfront and monthly insurance premium. As with a conventional mortgage, this adds to the monthly payment and affects how much home the buyer qualifies to purchase. Borrowers securing a FHA loan cannot exceed a maximum total monthly debt obligation ratio (TOR) of 43%. This means that a borrower may have more debt and still qualify for a FHA loan. However, with a FHA loan there is an added qualifying feature of having to be at or under 31% for a total Housing Expense Ratio (HER).

Housing Expense Ratio

To Calculate Housing Expense Ratio

1. Add the proposed House Expense:

   - PITI (House Principal Payment, Interest, Taxes, & Insurance) + MIP (Mortgage Insurance Premium)

3. Divide Total Housing Expense by total of buyer's Monthly Gross

Buyers may use a FHA mortgage for various types of property including condominiums and manufactured homes. However, in order for an FHA loan to be used with a condominium purchase, the condominium development must be on an approved list. To find out if a condominium development is on the approved list for a FHA loan look up the property here:
https://entp.hud.gov/idapp/html/condlook.cfm

The condition requirements of the property for FHA loans is more stringent than for conventional loans. However, there are generally no limitations as to where a property may be located when the buyer is using a conventional loan. Consult with a lender regarding other issues that may affect a home purchase with a FHA loan including maximum value loan limits.

Section 203(k)
Section 203(k) program is special type of FHA loan that is designed rehabilitation and repair of single family properties. It includes money for rehab and repair of the home right into the loan.

When a licensee works with a buyer that is looking at a "fixer upper," this may be a good loan product to allow the buyer to purchase the home. The borrower will have to qualify for the amount of the mortgage after the repairs have been done. Furthermore, the home will have to appraise for the total loan – taking into consideration what the value will be with the repairs completed.

VA Loans
Military service members, veterans, and eligible surviving spouses may obtain a loan through the Veteran's Administration – known as a VA loan. There is no down payment requirement with a VA loan. The VA loan has a partial guarantee by the government which partially protects the lender in case of default. There is a funding fee charged to the borrower. However, it is a one time fee only (which may be financed into the loan) so it does not increase the monthly payment. Borrowers securing a VA loan cannot exceed a maximum total monthly debt obligation ratio (TOR) of 41%. There is no Housing Expense Ratio requirement to be met.

Buyers may use a VA loan to purchase various types of property including condominiums and manufactured homes. However, check with the lender about guidelines regarding the age of a manufactured home as older ones tend to run into difficulty securing required homeowner insurance coverage required for VA loans. The condition requirements of the property for VA loans are the most stringent as compared to conventional loans or FHA loans. There are generally no limitations as to where a property may be located when the buyer is using a conventional loan. Consult with a lender regarding other issues that may affect a home purchase with a VA loan including the buyer obtaining the required Certificate of Reasonable Value for the property; Certificate of Eligibility which states the amount of entitlement available to the veteran or serviceman; loan guarantee limits and what fees can and cannot be paid by the seller on behalf of the buyer.

USDA Loans
For property located in qualifying rural areas, buyers may obtain 100% financing without monthly mortgage insurance premium using the USDA Guaranteed Rural Housing Loan – known as a USDA loan.

The 100% financing feature means that the buyer will not be required to put any money down. Furthermore, the monthly payment isn't increased by mortgage insurance. There is an upfront mortgage insurance premium, which can be financed into the loan. Consult with a lender regarding other issues that may affect a home purchase with a USDA loan.

Homebuyer Assistance Programs
In addition to understanding buyer loan options, licensees should also be familiar with existing home buyer assistance programs. These programs are offered county by county. Funds will often become available through these programs to help buyers cover down payment and closing costs. The terms of repayment, if required, varies from program to program. Qualifying terms also vary often including

participation in home buying education classes offered by the county. Licensees should check with lenders and local housing authority personnel to learn what programs may be available for local buyers.

Mortgage Fraud

Mortgage fraud is one of the fastest growing crimes in the United States. Mortgage fraud occurs when someone deliberately falsifies information to obtain mortgage financing that would not have been granted otherwise. Licensees must learn to recognize mortgage fraud.

One common type of mortgage fraud includes using "straw borrowers" to make the purchase. Straw borrowers are people who consent to the use of their names and personal details by someone else so that a mortgage can be obtained. Sometimes a straw borrower will be offered money for this "favor." Sometimes a straw buyer is used to illegally benefit a relative. "Inflated appraisals" are another type of mortgage fraud. Inflated appraisals involve an appraiser who acts in collusion with a borrower and provides a misleading appraisal report to the lender. The report inaccurately states an inflated property value. "Inflated contract prices" are a type of mortgage fraud often used when "flipping property." The goal is to artificially inflate the value of the property to obtain larger loans than what might otherwise be possible and to skim the equity off of the property.

Red Flags

Learning how to avoid and identify mortgage fraud can prevent licensees from becoming a victim as a party to a fraudulent deal.

Three types of red flags to watch involve:
1. An inflated appraisal that doesn't match the licensee's experience with the market and is not adequately supported by MLS sales data.
2. Someone requesting that a licensee alter the MLS list price to reflect appraised value.
3. Frequent ownership changes within a brief period of time, not having the property seller on the title, references to a double escrow or other closing disclosures, and large fluctuations of the sales price over a period of a few weeks or months.

Reporting Mortgage Fraud

Licensees that become suspicious or aware of mortgage fraud are obligated to report it. Not to do so could result in the licensee being charged as being culpable in the mortgage scheme.

- Mortgage fraud is a second-degree felony when the loan documents exceed $100,000.
- Fraud charges would also result in the loss of licensure as a licensee.

Students of the post-licensing 45-hour course are instructed to do the following exercise:

> Mortgage Fraud
>
> You have a buyer call you that you have never worked with before. You show the buyer a property that he requested to see and then write up an offer for the property. The buyer insists that the offer be made for $25,000 more than what similar properties have sold for in the area. You warn the buyer that it is unlikely that the property will appraise – a requirement since the buyer is obtaining a loan. To your surprise the property appraises. When you review the comparable properties used within the appraisal, you notice that the properties used were not very good matches for the property.
>
> Which is the best course of action to take?
> - A. You immediately contact your broker to point out the discrepancy.
> - B. Since the appraisal benefits your buyer, you say nothing.
>
> A is the better choice. The bad appraisal is a red flag that there may be mortgage fraud being committed. You should elicit the help of your broker as both you and the broker could be found guilty of being culpable in the mortgage scheme.
>
> *Mortgage fraud is a second-degree felony when the loan documents exceed $100,000.

7 CONDO/H.O.A/C.D.D
LEARNING TERMS AND PHRASES

- Condominium
- Creation of Condominiums
- Condominium Disclosures
- Articles of Incorporation
- Declaration of Condominium
- Bylaws of the Association
- Frequently Asked Questions
- Prospectus
- Financial Reports
- Governance Form
- Rules of the association
- Rules and Regulations
- Default of Fees
- Application for Ownership
- Homeowner Association
- Complaint Resolution
- HOA Disclosure
- Estoppel Certificates
- Community Development Districts
- CDD Disclosures
- Milestone Inspection
- Structural Integrity Reserve Study

Learning Objectives

- Licensees will understand how varying property types impact deal management.
- Licensees will be able to recognize a condominium from a legal description.
- Licensees will be able to manage required documents upon the sale of condominiums.
- Licensees will develop skill in comparing condominium features and fees.
- Licensees will develop skill in managing real estate deals involving homeowner associations.
- Licensees will be able to manage required documents upon the sale of an HOA property.
- Licensees will develop skill in comparing HOA related features and fees.
- Licensees will develop skill in comparing property located within community development districts and impact on cost of ownership.

The Property Type Can Affect the Deal

Beyond loan considerations, it is important for licensees to keep in mind the type of property that is being sold when structuring and handling the deal. For example, selling condominiums involves different legal issues than the sale of single family homes. Properties in Florida are often subject to homeowner associations which involves unique issues. Furthermore, being located within a community development district also involves different considerations.

Condominium Considerations

It is important that a buyer understand exactly what a condominium is, what the buyer is getting with the purchase, as well as what is expected of the buyer during the purchase and after ownership. The licensees involved with the sale as well as the seller each have disclosure requirements that must be made to the buyer regarding the purchase of a condominium.

What is a Condominium?

Condominium ownership is an alternative form of ownership as compared to single-family homes. Condominiums, also referred to as condos, involves ownership of individual units through fee simple ownership. When someone buys a condominium, ownership of the building unit is transferred by a deed. Use of the common elements are "legally attached" to the purchase and transferred as well. Property taxes are levied on the individual units and paid by each individual unit owner just the same as when someone purchases an unattached single-family home.

Recognizing a Condominium

Most people will think of a high-rise building when referring to a condominium. However, a condominium does not have to be a high-rise. In fact, what makes something a condominium is about how title is taken, not the "style" of the property. As already stated, with a condominium, ownership of the building unit is transferred to the property owner. However, even when a property condominium unit is situated directly on ground level, ownership of the land itself stays community property of the entire development.

On the other hand, when someone takes title to a single family residence, the person gets ownership of the land beneath the home as well as ownership of the land surrounding the home as defined by property lines detailed in the legal description. Townhouses and duplexes are both single family homes, not condominiums. Apartments are actually commercial property with the "owner" of the apartment receiving one deed for the entire apartment building, which includes ownership of the land.

Legal Property Description of Condominiums

Licensees must be able to recognize when working with a condominium. Keep in mind that property owners may not always understand what type of property he or she owns. This is often the case when property has been inherited! Licensees may look to tax records to determine whether a property is a condominium. Within the tax records, characteristics will be found of the property defining the county use description, the state use description, and the building type. The description for these fields will designate whether the property is a condominium. A trick a licensee may use to quickly determine whether a property is legally a condominium is to look at the legal description of the home. All legal descriptions of condominiums start with the word "unit."

Comparing Tax Records

The following property characteristics were pulled from tax records using realist.com

The description on the left is for a condominium.

The description on the right is for a single family residence.

Characteristics (Condominium)

County Use Description:	Condo-Hi-Rise 7+ Stories-0405
State Use Description:	Condominium-04
Land Use - CoreLogic:	Condominium
Building Type:	Condo Hi Rise
Year Built:	2004
Effective Year Built:	2004
Living Square Feet:	3,317
Total Building Sq Ft:	3,622
Heated Sq Ft:	3,317
Ground Level Sq Ft:	3,317
Stories:	1
Total Units:	18
Total Rooms:	6
Bedrooms:	2

Characteristics (Single Family)

County Use Description:	Single Family-0110
State Use Description:	Single Family-01
Land Use - CoreLogic:	SFR
Style:	Square Design
Building Type:	Single Family
Year Built:	1967
Effective Year Built:	1979
Living Square Feet:	1,781
Total Building Sq Ft:	2,421
Heated Sq Ft:	1,781
Ground Level Sq Ft:	1,781
Stories:	1
Total Units:	1
Bedrooms:	MLS: 2

★ **Students of the post-licensing 45-hour course are instructed to do the following exercise:**

Single Family or Condominium?
You are working with a buyer that only wants to look at single family homes.

Which of the following properties would you NOT want to show your buyer?
A. PEBBLE LAKE EST LOT 70
B. LOT 1, BLK C, FAIRFIELD ACRES UNIT TWO; LESS ROAD R/W PI#42580.0000/1
C. UNIT 9103 INN ON THE SEA PHASE 3

C is a condominium designated by starting with the word "Unit" in the legal description.

Popularity of Condominiums

There are several reasons why condominiums have become popular in Florida. One is rising land values. By building high-rise condominiums, developers are able to maximize space and increase the return on their investment by selling property units to more owners than would have been possible by selling detached single family homes. Another is the desire that so many people have to live near the Gulf of Mexico, the Atlantic, the many bays, or waterways in Florida. This has led to the sale of "air rights" and the creation of high-rise condominiums. By building up, condominium owners are able to enjoy spectacular views! Finally, by purchasing a condominium, owners are able to minimize the amount of maintenance and upkeep that is required on the property. This fits well with the lifestyle of many busy professionals and retiring individuals.

Creation of Condominiums

A condominium is created by recording a declaration in the public records of the county where the condominium is located. All condominium owners have rights and obligations which are detailed in the "Declaration of Condominium" and "Bylaws of the Association." Upon the creation of a condominium development, the developer must file these documents with the Division of Florida Condominiums, Timeshares, and Mobile Homes. Plus, if there are 20 or more residential units, the developer must prepare a "Prospectus" which is a summary of the major points contained in the condominium documents and file it with the division as well.

Condominium Complaint Resolution

The Division of Florida Condominiums, Timeshares, and Mobile Homes provides consumer protection for Florida residents living in the regulated communities through education, complaint resolution, mediation and arbitration and developer disclosure. This means that if anyone has a complaint about how an association is ran or the decisions of an association, then the person can contact this division for help. Licensees should explain this to potential buyers as one of the main concerns about purchasing condominiums is the fear of no control over a "runaway" board.

Condominium Disclosure Requirements

The disclosure requirements for the sale of condominiums are governed by the condominium act Florida statute 718. Per the statute, when a condominium is sold, specific documents must be provided from the seller to the buyer. Licensees involved in the sale of new condominiums are responsible for making sure that these documents are given to the buyer. Licensees could be found liable for not ensuring that disclosures are made. A purchase agreement addendum should note whether the buyer received the documents at the time of or prior to signing the purchase agreement. If the buyer received the forms after the purchase agreement was signed, then an addendum should later be added which clarifies the date that the buyer acknowledged being given the forms. Licensees must safeguard that all the required forms are given – as most buyers are uneducated about these forms. Should an unknowing buyer sign off of the addendum without adequate counsel from the licensee, the buyer could later sue the licensee and the licensee's broker for negligence. The forms that are required and the timeline to cancel the contract change with whether it is a new condominium sale or a resale.

Sale of New Condominiums

Upon the sale of a newly established condominium, the developer must provide the buyer with 6 different required documents. Once the buyer receives these documents, the buyer has 15 calendar days to cancel the purchase agreement. This provision is in place to give the buyer adequate time to evaluate the condominium development to make sure that the buyer is prepared to accept the organizational structure, financial health of the development and ongoing fees.

The documents required to be provided to the buyer include: Articles of Incorporation, Declaration of

Condominium, Bylaws of the Association, Frequently Asked Questions, Prospectus (if there are 20 or more units), and the Estimated Operating Budget.

Contracts for purchase of new condominiums must include in conspicuous type:

> This agreement is voidable by buyer by delivering written notice of the buyer's intention to cancel within 15 days after the date of execution of this agreement by the buyer, and receipt by buyer of all of the items required to be delivered to him or her by the developer under section 718.503, Florida statutes.

Until the developer has furnished the required documents, the buyer may void the contract and is entitled to a refund of deposits.

Resale of Condominiums

Upon the resale of previously owned condominium, the seller must provide the buyer with 7 different required documents. (Not including possible requirement of providing a Milestone Inspection and a Structural Integrity Reserve Study.*) Once the buyer receives these documents, the buyer has 3-business days to cancel the purchase agreement. This provision is in place to give the buyer adequate time to evaluate the condominium development to make sure that the buyer is prepared to accept the organizational structure, financial health of the development and ongoing fees.

The documents required to be provided to the buyer include: Articles of Incorporation, Declaration of Condominium, Bylaws of the Association, Frequently Asked Questions, Most Recent Year-End Financial Report, Governance Form, and Rules of the Association.

Contracts for purchase of resale condominiums must include the following:

> This agreement is voidable by buyer by delivering written notice of the buyer's intention to cancel within 3 days, excluding Saturdays, Sundays, and legal holidays, after the date of execution of this agreement by the buyer and receipt by buyer of a current copy of the declaration of condominium, articles of incorporation, bylaws and rules of the association, and a copy of the most recent year-end financial information and frequently asked questions and answers document if so requested in writing. Any purported waiver of these voidability rights shall be of no effect. Buyer may extend the time for closing for a period of not more than 3 days, excluding Saturdays, Sundays, and legal holidays, after the buyer receives the declaration, articles of incorporation, bylaws and rules of the association, and a copy of the most recent year-end financial information and frequently asked questions and answers document if requested in writing. Buyer's right to void this agreement shall terminate at closing.

Notice that the above statement clarifies that the buyer's right to void the agreement terminates at closing. This means that if a buyer purchases a property without having received any or all of the required disclosures, the sale is still valid. The buyer would no longer be able to hold the seller responsible for not having provided the disclosures. However, as it is the licensee's duty to safeguard the interest of his or her client. If the licensee fails to ensure that all of these forms are provided, the buyer could later take legal action against the licensee, claiming that the licensee failed to look out for the buyer's interests.

Condominium Disclosures

	DEVELOPER	RESALE
Articles of Incorporation	✓	✓
Declaration of Condominium	✓	✓
Bylaws of the Association	✓	✓
Frequently Asked Questions	✓	✓
Prospectus*	✓	
Estimated Operating Budget	✓	
Most Recent Year-End Financial Report		✓
Governance Form		✓
Rules of the Association		✓

*For condominium developments for 20+ units.

© Pamela Kemper

Condominium Documents

As licensees are responsible to oversee that disclosures are made to buyers of condominiums, it is important that licensees are familiar with the different documents that must be provided.

Articles of Incorporation

Articles of Incorporation is a document, filed with a U.S. state (Florida) by a corporation's founders, describing the purpose, place of business, and other details of a corporation.

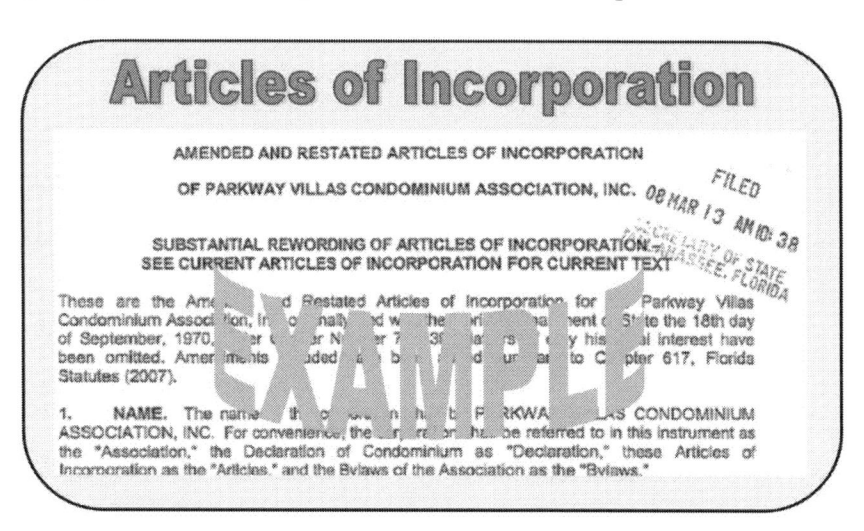

Declaration of Condominium

Declaration of Condominium is a legal document filed in the county in which the condominium will be located. Once filed, it establishes existence of the project and divides airspace into layers of ownership. It also describes property boundaries, the common elements, membership and voting rights in regard to the association, and the covenants and restrictions on the use of each individually owned unit plus the common areas.

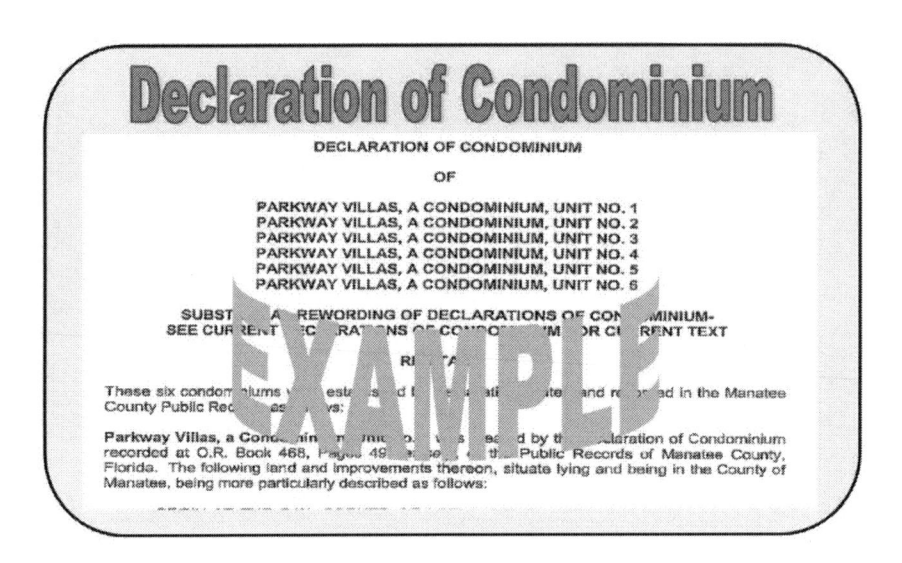

Bylaws of the Association

Bylaws of the association are the official rules and regulations which govern a corporation's management. Bylaws are drawn up at the time of incorporation, along with the charter.

Frequently Asked Questions

Frequently Asked Questions is a prepared document that informs prospective buyers about restrictions on things such as, leasing and pets and provides general information about assessments, etc. Also referred to as FAQ.

Prospectus

A prospectus is required if the condominium consists of more than 20 residential units. The prospectus acts as a summary of the major points that are detailed in other condominium documents.

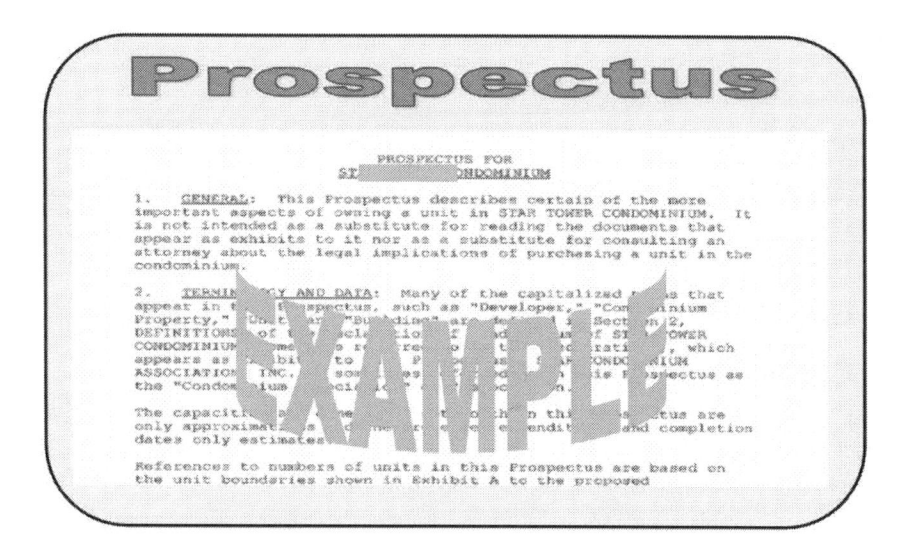

Estimated Operating Budget or Most Recent Year-End Financial Report

The estimated operating budget outlines expected expenses for the condominium development. Whereas the Most Recent Year-End Financial Report is a snapshot of the previous year's finances. This is an important document for buyers to review when considering the purchase of a condominium as it gives a picture of the financial health of the development.

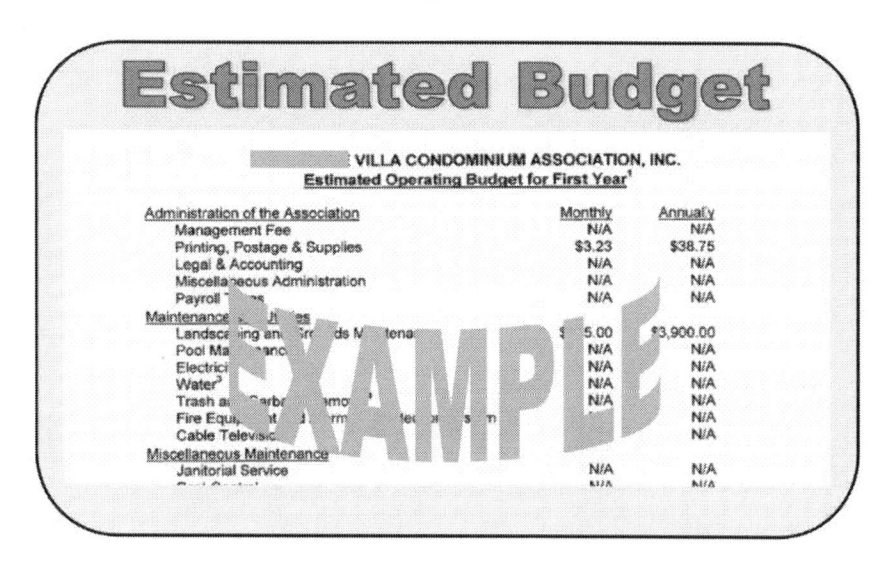

What is not included in the budget is also an important consideration. Some condominium developments put back reserves for replacements such as roofs and parking lots. When these reserves are not kept, it will be charged equally to the owners as an additional expense once the need for the expense comes due.

Governance Form

A Governance form must be provided by condo sellers (who are not the original developer) to prospective buyers. This is a disclosure from the Florida Department of Business and Professional Regulation (DBPR) which details the rights and responsibilities of condominium boards and unit owners, voting rights, meeting notices and other governance matters.

Rules of the Association

Rules of the association are the rules and regulations adopted by the board of directors of the association. The association elects a board of directors, which handles the maintenance and repair of common areas, disputes among unit owners, enforcement of rules and regulations, and condominium fees.

Locating Condominium Documents

Although it is the seller's responsibility to provide the required disclosure documents, licensees should be prepared to assist in obtaining the documents.

Declaration of Condominium documents may be accessed online records of county clerk. However, the easiest way to receive a copy of all the required documents is to contact the office of the management company for the condominium. There may be a cost to receive a copy of the documents.

Please note that it is the seller that is responsible for providing the actual forms. A licensee takes on legal liability of supplying outdated forms if the licensees gather the forms rather than having the seller do so. Always look to your broker for brokerage rules about procedures designed to limit liability.

Living with the Rules and Regulations

Buyers of condominiums should be advised to read rules and regulations carefully. These are conditions of ownership that buyers will have to live with upon the purchase. Licensees must be careful not to take on liability of these conditions if they aren't matched to what a buyer had expressed as "must haves" for ownership. For example, are pets allowed? Are trucks allowed? Is advertising for businesses on vehicles restricted? May the property be leased out a lessee?

Living with the Fees

Condominium fees may be charged annually, quarterly or monthly. Fees are generally paid ahead. What is included in the fees can be clarified by the management company. Understanding these fees aids a buyer in assessing the affordability of the condominium.

For example, a condominium that charges $300 a month may at first appear to be adding $300 in expense to the owner's monthly budget. However, if the condominium provides water, trash, cable, internet, and use of a community pool and exercise room – then the $300 fee may actually replace what the owner would be paying anyway even without the association. Only the buyer can decide whether taking on the expense of living in a condominium makes sense. It is the licensee's job, though, to make sure that the buyer has all the information to make a well-informed decision.

Failure to Pay Condominium Fees

When owners fail to pay condominium fees, the fees can become attached to the property as a lien. The condominium association may then initiate foreclosure on the property the same as a mortgage company may foreclose on property. Licensees should make sure that buyers understand that fees are not optional!

Maintenance

Many buyers of condominiums are attracted by the "maintenance free living." Generally, the condominium development oversees lawn and plant care. Whether things like trimming of shrubs is taken care of by the association should be investigated and clarified by the licensee.

Condominium Insurance and Owner Insurance

One of the advantages of condominium ownership is that the condominium acquires a combined insurance property for the condominium structure. This generally leaves the owner needing to only insure from the walls inward. This can actually be quite a savings in homeowner's insurance expense as compared to insuring a detached single-family home.

Application of Condominium Ownership

Licensees should also assist in ensuring that buyers have filled out any required applications for purchase. This process may require that the buyer pay a processing fee by the condominium association. It may also require a buyer interview. Conditions of ownership may be placed on buyers as written into the rules of the association including having background and credit checks.

Students of the post-licensing 45-hour course are instructed to do the following exercise:

> Condominium Analysis
> If a member of the Multiple Listing Service, do a search in the MLS for condominiums in the area that you plan to focus much of your real estate prospecting.
>
> - Note the types of condominium fees charged and what is included in the fees.
> - Note the rules and regulations including limitations on whether pets are allowed and whether there are age restrictions to live there.
> - Note the amenities and advantages of living within the condominium development.

Homeowner Association Considerations

Another property consideration that licensees need to be mindful of when managing a real estate deal is whether there is a homeowner association. Also known as HOAs, homeowner associations can be a factor whether dealing with a single-family residence or a condominium. When the property is a condominium, there may be both a condominium association fee and a homeowner's association fee charged to owners of the property.

What is a Homeowners Association?

An HOA is a legally formed organization for the intent to make, manage, and enforce rules for properties within its jurisdiction. Membership and abidance to the HOA is mandatory when a buyer purchases a property with an existing HOA. Many developments offer amenities similar to condominium developments in providing common areas for clubhouses, pools, parks, etc. These common areas require maintenance and oversight which falls to the task of the HOA.

HOA Complaint Resolution

Although the Division of Florida Condominiums, Timeshares, and Mobile Homes does not specifically refer to homeowner associations in the title, the division handles consumer complaints regarding associations just as it does for condominiums.

Fees, Restrictions, and Application

Just as condominiums must collect fees to cover expenses, homeowner associations also divide operating costs among the homeowners. If these fees are not paid, they become a lien on the owner's property just as unpaid condominium fees do. Just as condominiums may place restrictions on owners use of property,

HOAs may place similar restrictions. Just as condominiums may require an application process, so may the homeowner association.

HOA Required Disclosure

Licensees involved with the sale of a property where the property is subject to a homeowner's association must ensure that proper disclosure of the HOA has been made by the seller to the buyer. Per Florida Statute 720, a disclosure must be made to the buyer which specifically informs the buyer that the property is subject to the homeowners association. The disclosure must include the fact that the buyer may cancel the contract within 3-business days of having received the HOA disclosure form. Note that this is different from the condominium timeline which allows for the cancelling of the contract within 3-business days of having received the actual condominium documents. The 3 day right of rescission for HOA is based on receiving the HOA disclosure NOT the HOA documents! This is a point often confused by licensees in the practice of real estate. The right to cancel the contract cannot be waived by the buyer.

No Requirement for Seller to Provide HOA Documents

Although the seller is not required to provide homeowner association documents, a licensee could still be held liable if within the documents are terms and conditions contrary to what the buyer had told the licensee was acceptable. Therefore, it is always in the licensee's best interest to ensure that the buyer acknowledges receipt of the homeowner association documents.

Estoppel Certificates

A title company handling the transfer of property subject to a homeowner's association will order an estoppel certificate showing that all HOA fees are paid in full prior to closing. Fees paid by ahead by the seller will be prorated on the closing documents. See Chapter 10, "Closings."

HOA Disclosure Summary

DISCLOSURE SUMMARY
FOR
(NAME OF COMMUNITY)

1. AS A PURCHASER OF PROPERTY IN THIS COMMUNITY, YOU WILL BE OBLIGATED TO BE A MEMBER OF A HOMEOWNERS' ASSOCIATION.

2. THERE HAVE BEEN OR WILL BE RECORDED RESTRICTIVE COVENANTS GOVERNING THE USE AND OCCUPANCY OF PROPERTIES IN THIS COMMUNITY.

3. YOU WILL BE OBLIGATED TO PAY ASSESSMENTS TO THE ASSOCIATION. ASSESSMENTS MAY BE SUBJECT TO PERIODIC CHANGE. IF APPLICABLE, THE CURRENT AMOUNT IS $ PER . YOU WILL ALSO BE OBLIGATED TO PAY ANY SPECIAL ASSESSMENTS IMPOSED BY THE ASSOCIATION. SUCH SPECIAL ASSESSMENTS MAY BE SUBJECT TO CHANGE. IF APPLICABLE, THE CURRENT AMOUNT IS $ PER .

4. YOU MAY BE OBLIGATED TO PAY SPECIAL ASSESSMENTS TO THE RESPECTIVE MUNICIPALITY, COUNTY, OR SPECIAL DISTRICT. ALL ASSESSMENTS ARE SUBJECT TO PERIODIC CHANGE.

5. YOUR FAILURE TO PAY SPECIAL ASSESSMENTS OR ASSESSMENTS LEVIED BY A MANDATORY HOMEOWNERS' ASSOCIATION COULD RESULT IN A LIEN ON YOUR PROPERTY.

6. THERE MAY BE AN OBLIGATION TO PAY RENT OR LAND USE FEES FOR RECREATIONAL OR OTHER COMMONLY USED FACILITIES AS AN OBLIGATION OF MEMBERSHIP IN THE HOMEOWNERS' ASSOCIATION. IF APPLICABLE, THE CURRENT AMOUNT IS $ PER .

7. THE DEVELOPER MAY HAVE THE RIGHT TO AMEND THE RESTRICTIVE COVENANTS WITHOUT THE APPROVAL OF THE ASSOCIATION MEMBERSHIP OR THE APPROVAL OF THE PARCEL OWNERS.

8. THE STATEMENTS CONTAINED IN THIS DISCLOSURE FORM ARE ONLY SUMMARY IN NATURE, AND, AS A PROSPECTIVE PURCHASER, YOU SHOULD REFER TO THE COVENANTS AND THE ASSOCIATION GOVERNING DOCUMENTS BEFORE PURCHASING PROPERTY.

9. THESE DOCUMENTS ARE EITHER MATTERS OF PUBLIC RECORD AND CAN BE OBTAINED FROM THE RECORD OFFICE IN THE COUNTY WHERE THE PROPERTY IS LOCATED, OR ARE NOT RECORDED AND CAN BE OBTAINED FROM THE DEVELOPER.

Florida Statutes 720.401 (1) (a)

Restrictions Beyond Condominium and HOAs

Often buyers will choose to purchase property that does not involve either condominium or homeowner association restrictions to gain greater freedom in use of the property. Licensees are cautioned to keep in mind that homeowners may also experience restrictions on property usage by local city and county regulations. To avoid legal liability, buyers should be advised to refer to city and county ordinances to ensure that they are prepared to pursue the property.

★ **Students of the post-licensing 45-hour course are instructed to do the following exercise:**

> Home Ownership Restrictions
>
> You have been working with a buyer for months. The buyer has not liked any of the terms of the properties that you have shown the buyer due to restrictions placed by home owner associations.
>
> Finally, the buyer chooses to purchase a property that is not subject to a home owner or condominium association. However, the property is located within city limits. Right before closing, the buyer tells you that he is going to put up a 7 foot fence as soon as he closes on the property.
>
> Which of the following is the best action to take?
>
> A. Do nothing. You have worked too long and hard with this buyer to blow it now!
> B. Remind the buyer that the property may be subject to city and/or county restrictions. These restrictions may affect whether the buyer may install a fence or how tall the fence may be. Advise the buyer visit the zoning board prior to closing. Plus, have the buyer sign a form that you have advised the buyer to do so.
>
> B is the best choice. Failure to make this disclosure to the buyer could open you up to liability in a lawsuit later from the buyer.

Community Development Districts

Another property consideration licensees need to be aware of is whether a property is located within a community development district – known as a CDD. Community development districts are special tax districts created to take care of long-term needs of a community. These needs are usually tied to infrastructure issues such as the creation of neighborhood roads.

The infrastructure incurs costs which are passed onto homeowners. These costs are collected along with taxes. Licensees who are members of the multiple listing service should be careful presenting the CDD fees to buyers. The MLS system has a special place to note the CDD fee. However, the amount of taxes paid on the property already include the amount of the CDD as part of the tax payment. It is easy for listing agents and buyer agents to become confused with this information. As a buyer's agent, it is good practice to speak with the listing agent to clarify how the information was entered into the MLS so that it can be accurately passed onto the buyer.

CDD Disclosures

A CDD disclosure must be made prior to the purchaser signing a purchase agreement. The disclosure must be attached to the purchase agreement for it to be valid.

> THE (Name of District) COMMUNITY DEVELOPMENT DISTRICT MAY IMPOSE AND LEVY TAXES OR ASSESSMENTS, OR BOTH TAXES AND ASSESSMENTS, ON THIS PROPERTY. THESE TAXES AND ASSESSMENTS PAY THE CONSTRUCTION, OPERATION, AND MAINTENANCE COSTS OF CERTAIN PUBLIC FACILITIES AND SERVICES OF THE DISTRICT AND ARE SET ANNUALLY BY THE GOVERNING BOARD OF THE DISTRICT. THESE TAXES AND ASSESSMENTS ARE IN ADDITION TO COUNTY AND OTHER LOCAL GOVERNMENTAL TAXES AND ASSESSMENTS AND ALL OTHER TAXES AND ASSESSMENTS PROVIDED FOR BY LAW.

★ **Students of the post-licensing 45-hour course are instructed to do the following exercise:**

> Condominium Analysis
>
> If a member of the Multiple Listing Service, do a search in the MLS for properties located within community development districts.
>
> - Note the types of fees commonly associated with the CDD.
> - Practice determining how much of the taxes are for the CDD.
> - Practice determining how much of the taxes for the actual taxes not including the CDD.

*As of March 20, 2023, and Pursuant to changes to Chapter 718, F.S., a possible Milestone Inspection and Structural Integrity Reserve Study may have to be supplied with the resale of a condominium. This is in response to the Surfside condominium tragedy. This alters the language of the FAR BAR and CRSP Condominium Association Rider/Addendum. Be sure to use an updated version.

Not all sellers will be required to provide these additional documents as the law only applies to certain associations or may be within the grace period to provide. Look to your brokers for guidance.

Milestone Inspection: It's a structural inspection conducted for life safety purposes. Generally, the requirement for associations to obtain a milestone inspection applies to condominium and cooperative buildings three stories or higher which have been occupied 30 years or more or, if located within three miles of Florida's coastline, occupied 25 years or more.

Structural Integrity Reserve Study: It's a study of reserve funds required for future major repairs and replacement of the common areas which must be conducted for condo and cooperative association buildings that are three stories or higher.

8 CONTRACTS

LEARNING TERMS AND PHRASES

- Legal Guidelines
- Legal Liability
- Record Keeping
- Effective Date
- Contractual Capacity
- E-Signatures
- Written Listing Agreements
- Equitable Title of Spouse
- Co-brokerage Commission
- Excluded Fixtures
- Limited Brokerage Services Addendum
- Offer and Acceptance
- Consideration
- Misc. Addendums
- Wired Funds
- Personal Property
- Additional Terms
- As Is Agreements
- Required Disclosures
- Breach of Contract

Learning Objectives

- Licensees will develop skill in contract preparation and management.
- Licensees will be able to determine the effective date of the contract.
- Licensees will be able to calculate important timelines connected to contract terms.
- Licensees will be able to manage legal aspects and importance of signatures.
- Licensees will have an understanding of how to handle commissions with listing contacts.
- Licensees will have an understanding of how to handle fixtures versus personal property within listing contacts and purchase agreements.
- Licensees will understand the aspects of working with limited listing versus full service listings.
- Licensees will learn how to manage attached contract addendums.
- Licensees will understand how the accounting of funds is handled within contracts.
- Licensees will understand required information that must be included with purchase contracts.
- Licensees will be able to manage "as is" purchase agreements with required disclosures.

The Importance of Contract Expertise

All the hard work licensees pour into their real estate businesses culminates into the writing of contracts. Licensees work to secure listing contracts with sellers, buyer contracts with buyers, and to facilitate purchase contracts between buyers and sellers. Being able to master contracts is vital to licensees' skill set.

Following Legal Guidelines in Contract Preparation

First of all, it is important for a licensee to be careful not to fall into the unauthorized practice of law when working with contracts. Only lawyers can give "legal" advice to clients. This includes matters of real estate law such as advice on the title and transfer of property. A licensee must remember to always refer clients to other professionals including lawyers as appropriate.

Real estate licensees are granted authority by the Florida Department of Business and Professional Regulation to draw up four specific types of contracts: Listing Contracts, Buyer Broker Contracts, Sale and Purchase Contracts, and Option Contracts. A distinction is made between how you are legally allowed to handle lease agreements versus other types of real estate contracts. Licensees cannot draw up lease contracts from scratch. Instead, licensees may use fill-in-the-blank contracts that have been approved by the Florida Supreme Court.

Access to Contracts

Due to the legal liability taken on in drafting contracts from scratch, licensees are advised to use prepared fill-in-the-blank contracts for all real estate activities. For licensees that have joined the Florida Real Estate Association, contracts are available for use. These contracts can be accessed by registering an online account at www.floridarealtors.org. Licensees should look to their brokers for direction on what contracts are acceptable for use.

Legal Liability

When a licensee works with contracts, the licensee is actually working as a general agent of the broker. As a general agent, a licensee is empowered to create contracts on the broker's behalf. The acts of the licensee, then, obligates both the broker and the licensee to the terms. Both the broker and the licensee may be held liable for poorly written contracts.

Record Keeping

Brokers must follow strict guidelines for maintaining copies of contracts and brokerage disclosure forms. Florida Statutes 475.5015 requires that brokerages maintain business records for five years. These records must also be made available to the DBPR in the event of an audit. Records include books, accounts, and records that pertain to the real estate business such as earnest money deposits.

As such, licensees must provide brokers with copies of executed listing agreements, buyer broker agreements, offers to purchase (even if the deal failed to close), rental property management agreements, rental or lease agreements, or "any other written or verbal agreement which engages the services of the broker." Records of written disclosure documents must also be turned over to the broker. These copies may be in "electronic" format legally, but should match the practice of the employing broker.

Contract Dates

With any contract that a licensee handles, the licensee must be mindful of the pertinent dates involved. One of the most litigated actions taken against licensees and brokers involve the licensee failing to adequately monitor and meet important contract dates. Different contracts use different definitions of the term "days" which is then used to calculate contract deadlines. The contract terms define whether "days" are counted in the contract as calendar days or as business days.

Upon initiating a contract, the licensee should make immediate note of the effective date, the expiration date or end date, and dates for contingencies to be met such as inspections for purchase contracts. The effective date is generally defined as happening when the last person accepted or initialed a page turning an offer into a valid contract.

Effective Date

3. **TIME FOR ACCEPTANCE OF OFFER AND COUNTER-OFFERS; EFFECTIVE DATE:**
   (a) If not signed by Buyer and Seller, and an executed copy delivered to all parties on or before _____, this offer shall be deemed withdrawn and the deposit, if any, shall be returned to Buyer. Unless otherwise stated, time for acceptance of any counter-offers shall be within 2 days after the day the counter-offer is delivered.
   (b) The effective date of this Contract shall be the date when the last one of the Buyer and Seller has signed or initialed and delivered this offer or final counter-offer ("Effective Date").

★ **Students of the post-licensing 45-hour course are instructed to do the following exercise:**

> Calculating Effective Date
> You are representing a buyer who has entered into a purchase agreement with a seller. The buyer signed the offer on June 5th, 2017. The seller signed the offer on June 8th, 2017. The buyer agreed in the contract to have all inspections completed and responded to within 15 days after the effective date.
> When is the deadline?
> _____
>
> The end of day on June 23rd would be the date that all inspections must be completed and responded by per the contract. This would be 15 days "after the effective date of June 8th."

Contractual Capacity of the Parties

When handling contracts, it is imperative that the parties have "Contractual Capacity" otherwise the contract could be deemed void or invalid. Having contractual capacity means that the participating parties must have the legal and mental capacity to contract.

Someone preparing a listing contract for an elderly person, for example, should take note when the seller's decisions do not align with normal seller behavior and decisions. This could indicate declining mental capacity. Minors may enter a contract. However, any contract that the minor signs may be voided by the minor.

E-Signatures

When obtaining signatures on contracts, Florida law allows for the use of digital signatures. Florida Statute 668.001 is The Electronic Signature Act of 1996 (ESA). It declares that electronic signatures have the same legal effect as written signatures, unless "otherwise provided by law."

There are numerous services that facilitate electronic signatures. Licensees who are members of the Florida Association of Realtors may look to Form Simplicity to create electronic signing sessions for buyers and sellers. DocuSign and Dotloop are also popular options. These services send documents to recipients to "sign" by inserting a chosen image of their signature into designated signing areas.

There is a fee charged for this service, however, the ease and benefit provided to clients generally offsets the expense. Licensees should check with their brokers to see if signing services are already available or discounted for agents.

Listing Contracts

A listing contract is an agreement between a property seller and a listing broker for the broker to handle the details of marketing and handling the sale of the property.

The listing contract utilized determines the type of listing that was entered into between the broker and the seller. As explained in Chapter 3, "Listing Management," there are 3 overall types of listing agreements. There are open listing agreements, exclusive brokerage listing agreements, and exclusive right to sell listing agreements.

The net listing taught in the Florida 63-Hour Sales Course is not a type of listing contract. Rather, that is a different way to determine how much the listing broker will be paid to handle the sale.

The open listing and exclusive brokerage listing is not detailed in this chapter. The emphasis is on the exclusive right to sell listing agreement – the most popular contract that license must maneuver.

Written Versus Verbal Listing Agreements

Per the Florida Statute of Frauds, listing contracts may be verbal as long as it is for a period shorter than one year. That said, it is unlikely that a broker would authorize a licensee to operate under a verbal listing agreement. Terms of a verbal agreements are difficult to prove!

Information Included in Written Listing Agreements

According to Florida Statutes Chapter 475, written listing agreements must contain a definite expiration date, a description of the property, the listing price with acceptable sale terms, and the commission structure to be paid to the broker either at the time of listing or upon a sale. Plus, a written listing contract must be signed by all legal owners of the property in order to be valid. A copy of the signed listing agreement must be delivered to the owners either at the time of listing or within 24 hours. This copy may be delivered as a fax or email. Finally, the listing agreement must not contain a provision for automatic renewal. A provision for automatic renewal would be an automatic extension of the expiration date if the property doesn't sell.

Signature of All Owners

Licensees should be aware that per Florida law, homesteaded property becomes a legal homestead for both spouses even when one of the spouses is not listed on the deed. This gives a spouse who isn't listed on a deed "equitable title" to the property. So even if both spouses are not listed as owners of a property, when a property has been homestead - a signature from both spouses should be obtained on the listing agreement and all subsequent contracts.

★ **Students of the post-licensing 45-hour course are instructed to do the following exercise:**

> What would you do if...
> You have been working with a seller for months in the effort to sell her property. You have finally secured a purchase agreement from an eager buyer and you are preparing for a speedy closing.
>
> While communicating with the seller, the seller comments that she is glad that the sale is finally going to be completed. In passing, she also comments that her soon to be ex-husband objected to her moving out of state, but she was anxious to complete the move.
>
> This was the first you had heard that the seller was married. Only her name was noted in the tax records, so she was the only one who had signed the listing agreement. The property has been homesteaded.
>
> Which of the following is the best action to take?
>
> A. Explain to the seller that legally her spouse has equitable title to the property and needs to sign all documents related to the listing and sale of the property.
> B. Do nothing. So long as the title company doesn't make a big deal about it, it will be fine.
>
> A is the correct choice. Failure to get the sellers signature could create a "cloud" on the title if that person ever tried to make a claim on the property.

Co-brokerage Commission

Sellers pay brokers to sell their home. This is often through a percentage of the purchase price and is referred to as a commission on the sale. Brokers are legally able to pay other brokers a part of the commission to assist in the sale of the home by bringing and representing the buyer.

Listing contracts generally define how much of the commission will be paid to a co-broker who brings the buyer. Brokers and licensees, as members of the multiple listing service, will then advertise this amount in the MLS in an attempt to draw buyers who are represented by agents other than the listing agent to consider the property for purchase.

> **Commission**
>
> **Compensation:** **Seller** will compensate **Broker** as specified below for procuring a buyer who is ready, willing, and able to purchase the Property or any interest in the Property on the terms of this Agreement or on any other terms acceptable to **Seller**. **Seller** will pay **Broker** as follows (plus applicable sales tax):
> (a) _____ % of the total purchase price plus $_____ OR $_____, no later than the date of closing specified in the sales contract. However, closing is not a prerequisite for **Broker's** fee being earned.
> (b) _____ ($ or %) of the consideration paid for an option, at the time an option is created. If the option is exercised, **Seller** will pay **Broker** the paragraph 8(a) fee, less the amount **Broker** received under this subparagraph.
>
> **Cooperation with and Compensation to Other Brokers: Notice to Seller:** The buyer's broker, even if compensated by **Seller** or **Broker**, may represent the interests of the buyer. **Broker's** office policy is to cooperate with all other brokers except when not in **Seller's** best interest and to offer compensation in the amount of
> ☐ _____ % of the purchase price or $_____ to a single agent for the buyer; ☐ _____ % of the purchase price or $_____ to a transaction broker for the buyer; and ☐ _____ % of the purchase price or $_____ to a broker who has no brokerage relationship with the buyer.
> ☐ None of the above. (If this is checked, the Property cannot be placed in the MLS.)

Fixtures Excluded from Listing

Occasionally sellers will sight attachments to the property and request that the item not be sold with the property. Licensees should be very careful about this for two reasons. First of all, if an item is left on the property but detailed in a listing that it is "not included in the sale" - - this draws attention to the item as being something of "value." Often this results in the buyer demanding that the item remain as part of the contract negotiations.

Second, if an item is detailed in a listing agreement that it is being excluded from the listing – but then the licensee fails to ensure that it is also excluded on a purchase agreement, the licensee will be held liable to the seller for the loss of the item. It is recommended, instead, that the item be "removed" from the property rather than from the listing. For example, if the seller has a favorite chandelier that the seller doesn't want to be included in a sale, licensees might advise the seller to remove the chandelier before buyers start visiting the property for showings.

Limited Listings

As noted in Chapter 3, "Listing Management," a limited listing allows for a broker to offer limited representation to sellers. This provision allows a broker to be paid for specific listing tasks rather than the agent being required to offer services that the client does not wish to pay the agent for providing. Despite the picking and choosing of tasks contracted, this is an exclusive right of sale listing agreement. Licensees who access contracts through Florida Realtor Association will find a prepared Limited Listing agreement available for use.

Also available is prepared "Addendum to Listing Contract – Limited Brokerage Services." This breaks apart the many services that a licensee may offer to sellers. The addendum clarifies that unless a service is checked then it is not provided! Assistance with price, advertising, providing signage, inclusion in MLS, inclusion on websites, holding open houses, showing of the property, use of a lockbox, presenting and managing offers, contract negotiations, and transaction closing assistance are all tasks that can be specifically contracted as a limited listing service.

Changes to Listings

Terms of listings, including pricing, should be kept current by making addendums to the listings.

Buyer Broker Contracts

As noted in Chapter 4, "Buyer Management," Buyer Broker Agreements are formal contracts that secure a commitment from a buyer not to purchase a home through some other agent. Buyer broker contracts are not necessary in order to represent a buyer in a real estate purchase. However, use of a buyer broker agreement increases the likelihood that an agent will be adequately compensated for all of his or her hard work.

As a contract, a Buyer Broker Agreement must identify the parties in the agreement – the buyers and the broker; the length of the agreement, the type of property desired, the broker and buyer obligations and compensation.

Sale and Purchase Contracts

A sale and purchase contract is a contract for the purchase of property between a buyer and a seller. Licensees representing buyers, sellers, or both in the purchase of real estate will prepare the terms of the contract in an offer. Upon acceptance or acceptance of a counter, the offer becomes a contract. Real estate contract purchase agreements must be in writing.

Offer and Acceptance

To have a valid contract, there must have been an offer made that was accepted. This offer and acceptance should be of a natural meeting of minds. This means they came to a decision under mutual assent. Mutual assent is the offer made by an offeror and accepted by the offeree.

Licensees must be careful to make sure that an offer is still valid based on the set expiration date of an offer when the contract is accepted. Many times, a contract may involve a lot of back and forth causing that original expiration date to expire. It is important to write new valid contracts if this happens.

Consideration

Consideration is the promise to perform and fulfill the contract. Valuable consideration can be measured in terms of money. Good consideration cannot be measured in terms of money such as love and affection. This is a concept that is often confused by licensees.

Earnest money, also called a good faith deposit or binder deposit and is NOT required to have a legal contract. However, most sellers will not take a property off the market and enter into a purchase agreement without the buyer showing "good faith" by providing earnest money along with the offer.

★ **Students of the post-licensing 45-hour course are instructed to do the following exercise:**

> What would you do if…
> You have listed a seller's home for $340,000 and you receive two competing offers on the seller's home.
>
> Which of the following offers would you advise the seller to accept?
>
> A. A cash offer for $335,000 with $20,000 in earnest money deposit.
> B. A cash offer for $338,000 with $2,000 in earnest money deposit.
>
> A is the more common choice. Even though offer B is for a bit higher of a purchase price, the higher earnest money deposit with offer A will normally win out as it puts more money at risk from the buyer showing that buyer as more likely to close the deal.

Holding of Earnest Money

As earnest money often involves a large amount of funds, it is a requirement by state law that purchase contracts specify where earnest money is being held. Many times, when an offer is made, the contract is written for the seller to choose the title company. If the title company is also to hold the earnest money, then the contract is written without knowing who to designate as holding earnest money.

To accommodate the unknown holder of earnest money, "TBD" is often written on the contract in place of the name. Then once the name of the title company is decided upon, it can be added to the contract. A common infraction found when the state audits brokerages and contracts is that once the title company has been decided upon, the name is written on the contract by the licensee. This is not allowed. Once a contract has been made official by the last person signing the contract – an addendum should be added which specifies where the earnest money is being held. The addendum must be signed by all parties to the contract and attached to the contract.

Addendums

All changes to contracts should be made through the use of addendums, signed by all parties, and attached to the contracts. As a deal progresses, it is common for contingencies to result in changes to the contract. These changes should be detailed on the addendum. The addition of the addendum does not change the effective date of the contract.

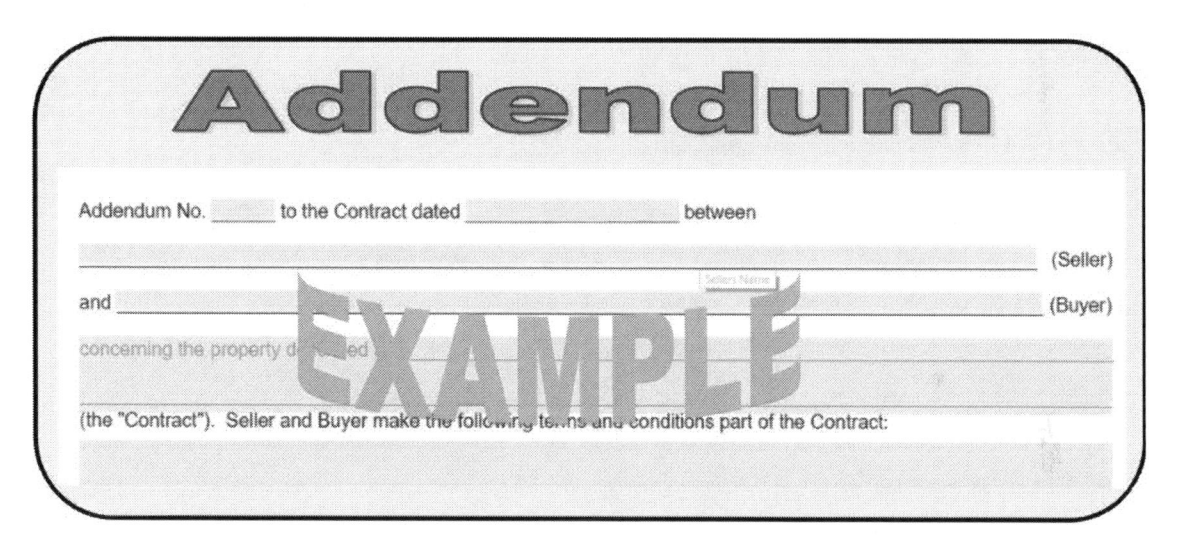

Accounting of Funds

When licensees accept earnest money deposits as cash (which would NEVER be recommended) or as "checks," the licensees must turn the deposits into their broker by the "end of the next business day." Brokers must deposit the funds into an earnest money account by the end of the third business day AFTER the business day that the licensees receive the funds.

When a title company handles the earnest money, rather than a broker – the process is different. In that case, if the buyer has chosen the title company, then within 10 business days after the deposit is due, the buyer's broker (usually left to the licensee) must make a written request to the title company (attorney) for verification of receipt of deposit. Then, within 10 business days after the broker had made the written request, the buyer's broker must provide to the seller's broker a copy of the written verification of deposit.

Wired Funds

With today's financial environment, it is prudent to avoid having buyers make deposits with checks. This includes cashiers/bank checks. When deposits are made using checks, it can slow down a closing by several weeks while the check waits to clear through the banking system. Instead, buyers should be directed to wire the funds. Contact the title company to get wire instructions. The buyer will then take the instructions to the bank to make the deposit. The buyer should follow the same wire instructions to wire the funds needed for the day of closing.

★ **Students of the post-licensing 45-hour course are instructed to do the following exercise:**

> What would you do if…
> You are working with a buyer and recently wrote an offer on a house that was accepted. Your buyer chose the title company and you received an email from the title company telling you that the wire had been received.
>
> Which is the correct course of action to take?
>
> A. Keep a copy of the email for the brokerage records and forward the email to the seller's broker.
> B. Because the law states that the buyer's broker must make a written request for confirmation of the deposit – send off a request of confirmation to the title company.
>
> A is the correct choice. In this situation, the title company saved you a step. You received confirmation of earnest money deposit without having to request it.

Information Included in the Purchase Contracts

In addition to stating where earnest money funds are being held, real estate purchase agreements must also contain the following specific information to be a valid, legal contact:
- Date, time and Place of closing
- Price and Financing Terms of Purchase
- Quality of Title to Be Conveyed
- Type of Deed
- Items of Personal Property Included
- Type of Title
- Prorated Items

Appliances and Personal Property

Sales Contracts should clearly specify which items are being included in the contract in regard to items such as appliances. Many licensees rely on the language of an MLS listing rather than specifying in the contract what is included in the sale. This is risky practice for a licensee. When a buyer discovers that expected appliances are not still in the house upon the purchase, the buyer may look to the licensee to replace the appliances. Clear and concise language is the key guideline when writing contracts.

> ★ **Students of the post-licensing 45-hour course are instructed to do the following exercise:**
>
> What would you do if...
> You are working with a buyer and have sat down to write an offer. The home is listed for $225,000. The MLS lacked details about appliances and there were no pictures included of the interior. During the showing, though, you noticed that the home had a stove, refrigerator, dish washer, washer, and dryer. The buyer is counting on the home having these appliances to save on expenses upon moving into the home.
>
> Which is the correct course of action to take?
>
> A. Specify on the contract all of the appliances.
> B. Rely on standard language of the contract that appliances stay that are on the property at the time of contract acceptance.
>
> A is the better choice. With the absence of the details on the MLS, there is no evidence to support the fact that appliances were in the property at the time the contract was accepted. Even with details and pictures, it is ALWAYS best practice to list the appliances on the purchase agreement.

Additional Terms

Even with prepared contracts, licensees have the option of writing in additional terms. Take care with any verbiage that is added to this area to make sure that it accurately reflects the needs of the buyer or seller being represented. A very slight word choice can make for a big difference in meaning and consequences to the parties involved. For example, a removal of a contingency "within three days" has a different meaning than "three days after."

As Is Agreements

Traditional real estate purchase contracts set aside a specific amount that a seller would be willing to spend on needed repairs that were sighted in property inspections. An advantage of this traditional contract for the seller is that unless there is a significant issue with the property that takes repairs beyond that agreed upon amount, the buyer cannot be released from the contract to purchase. The advantage to the buyer is that the seller agrees to this allowance for repairs during the original negotiations for the property.

A disadvantage of this type of contract is that whatever the amount is that was set aside for repairs equally causes the seller to demand more for the property in order to offset the allowance. With property that is in good repair, often the allowance is overestimated – unnecessarily driving the cost of the property up making the deal more difficult to come together.

With as is contracts, no amount for repairs is set aside in advance. Instead, buyers are given an opportunity to conduct inspections. During the inspection period, the buyer may choose to walk away from the contract – for ANY reason. The language of the contract doesn't require that the buyer provide a reason to cancel the contract. It simply allows it if within the inspection period. This type of contract is seen as more of an advantage for the buyer than the seller as it is only the buyer that has the right to cancel the contract during the inspection period.

As Is Agreements

> **PROPERTY INSPECTION; RIGHT TO CANCEL:**
> (a) **PROPERTY INSPECTIONS AND RIGHT TO CANCEL:** Buyer shall have _____ (if left blank, then 15) days after Effective Date ("Inspection Period") within which to have such inspections of the Property performed as Buyer shall desire during the Inspection Period. If Buyer determines, in Buyer's sole discretion, that the Property is not acceptable to the Buyer, Buyer may terminate this Contract by delivering written notice of such to Seller prior to expiration of Inspection Period. If Buyer timely terminates this Contract, the Deposit paid shall be returned to Buyer, thereupon, Buyer and Seller shall be released of all further obligations under this Contract; however, Buyer shall be

EXAMPLE

Disclosure of Material Defects

Any fact that may have a significant and reasonable impact on the market value of the property is material fact or a material defect and must be disclosed. The issue of whether a disclosure was made is a major source of litigation. These court cases involve suits against sellers and real estate agents.

Johnson vs. Davis is the landmark case that set the legal precedence that material defects must be disclosed by the seller. Rayner vs. Wise Realty of Tallahassee set the precedence of the licensee's duties to disclose. In fact, failure to disclose can open a licensee up to misrepresentation or fraud charges.

As Is contracts do not alleviate the duty to disclose. Licensees should encourage sellers to use prepared written seller disclosure questionnaires. This written disclosure is not required by law. However, it is a great tool to facilitate disclosure about property conditions. This form can later be used by proof by a seller that disclosure was made.

Additional Sales Contract Required Disclosures

Other disclosures that must be made include Radon Gas Disclosure, Energy Efficiency Disclosure, Lead-based Paint Disclosure, HOA Disclosure, Flood Insurance Disclosure, Condo, Co-Op Disclosures, Property Tax Disclosure, and Building Code Violation Disclosure.

Agency disclosure rules must also be followed as presented in Chapter 15 "Agency in Practice."

Radon Disclosure

Buyers and renters who enter into a purchase or rental agreement must receive a written disclosure regarding radon gas before or at the time of executing the purchase or lease agreement. This disclosure must be contained in at least one document. The disclosure describes what radon gas is.

Energy Efficiency Brochure

Another disclosure that must be made prior to signing a purchase and sale agreement, is the fact that a buyer may choose to get an energy-efficiency rating of the structure prior to closing. This disclosure is made through an information brochure.

Lead-Based Paint Disclosure

A lead based paint disclosure must be made to buyers and renters for homes built prior to 1978. The purpose is to disclose whether knowledge of or records exist of lead based paint in the home.

HOA Disclosure Requirement

A disclosure summary must be included with a purchase and sale agreement for property that is subject to mandatory Homeowner Association membership, fees and assessments, and restrictions.

Property Tax Disclosure

A Property Tax Disclosure must be given to a buyer before or at the time of signing purchase agreement. The Property tax disclosure is designed to warn the buyer that the amount of ad valorem taxes for the existing owner may be different for the buyer. These differences can result from reassessment and the loss of prior Homestead exemption.

Building Code Violation Disclosure

The building code violation disclosure is given prior to closing. Sellers are not required to rectify the situation, but must make available to the buyer notices and nature of the violation. Also, the new owner's name and address must be forwarded to code enforcement within 5 days. Failure of the seller to disclose Building Code Violations may constitute fraud and lead to civil charges.

Breach of Contract

Should a buyer or seller fail to deliver based on the terms of the contract, that party would be in breach of contract. The most common cause of breach of contract is running out of time to perform, such as trying to get a loan funded in time to close. The party that is in breach of contract risks being sued for specific performance or compensatory damages (sum of the loss plus lawyer and court fees).

If the party that is in breach is the buyer, the buyer may end up legally forfeiting the earnest money deposit. This is referred to as liquidated damages. If the buyer and seller are in dispute about the earnest money being returned, the licensee's broker would need to institute a settlement procedure if the broker is in possession of the earnest money. When the title company is holding the earnest money, the buyer or seller would have to initiate a lawsuit to determine who would be awarded the earnest money.

Handling contracts is a great responsibility for licensees. With care and diligence, licensees can ensure that the task is completed successfully.

9 INSPECTIONS

<u>LEARNING TERMS AND PHRASES</u>

- Caveat Emptor
- Inspection Contingency
- Strength of Offer
- Election of No Inspections
- Inspection Timelines
- Legal Liability of Inspections
- Pre-Deal Inspections
- Whole House Inspection
- Wood-Destroying Organisms Inspection
- Mold Inspection
- Radon Inspection
- Electrical Inspection
- Plumbing Inspection
- Roof Inspection
- 4-Point Inspection
- Wind Mitigation
- Methamphetamine Inspection
- Conflict of Interest
- Inspection Report
- Negotiated Repairs

Learning Objectives

- Licensees will gain an understanding about how to work with inspection contingencies.
- Licensees will gain knowledge about how inspection contingencies affect the strength of deals.
- Licensees will understand the risk to brokerages and licensees when deals are closed without inspections.
- Licensees will be able to manage inspection deadlines.
- Licensees will gain knowledge about muting risk to brokerages and licensees by having buyers pick and order their own inspections.
- Licensees will gain knowledge about the different types of inspections.
- Licensees will gain an understanding of how to handle renegotiations and repairs based on inspections.

The Importance of Inspections

The majority of real estate deals close after the buyer has conducted one or more inspections. Inspections are an important way that buyers protect themselves on the purchase of a property. If there are problems with the home found through inspections, the seller and buyer may negotiate repairs or the buyer may be able to cancel the deal. Other times, the buyer may choose to move forward with the deal accepting the property with the results of the inspection. How the inspection results affect the deal depends upon how the contract was written. Licensees need to be knowledgeable in assisting sellers and buyers throughout the inspection process.

Caveat Emptor

"Let the buyer beware" is a phrase that dominated real estate before licensing laws were put in place to protect consumers. Today, sellers and licensees have the legal duty to disclose any fact that may have a significant and reasonable impact on the market value of the property. As noted in Chapter 8, "Contracts," Johnson vs. Davis is the landmark case that set legal precedent that material defects must be disclosed by the seller.

Rayner vs. Wise Realty of Tallahassee set precedence of the licensee's duties to disclose. As is contracts do not alleviate this legal obligation. However, from the buyer's perspective, buying a property with problems and having to pursue a legal remedy is generally something that buyers want to avoid. Most prudent buyers conduct inspections to gain knowledge about the property rather than relying on reports from the seller or the agent.

Inspection Contingency

The majority of contracts are written subject to an inspection period. Licensees must explain the verbiage of a contract inspection contingency and explain how it affects the deal. The specifics of the contingencies vary with the contract used. Furthermore, licensees may write additional inspection terms under the "Additional Terms" or "Further Conditions."

When an inspection contingency is in place, it generally defines a specific period of time for the buyer to conduct inspections. Licensees should be aware that this inspection period generally includes the time that the buyer reviews the inspection results and provides a written response to the seller.

Strength of Real Estate Offer

Although most real estate contracts are written subject to inspections, buyers should also be made aware that by adding the inspection contingency, this can be seen as a negative by the seller. Where this particularly becomes an issue is in a seller's market where the same property quickly receives multiple offers.

Because the inspection contingency can result in the seller having to accommodate request repairs or having the deal fail – contracts written without an inspection contingency may be accepted over offers written subject to inspections. Offers written subject to inspections in these competitive seller markets often find it is easier to get the seller to accept when accompanying the contingency with an aggressive purchase price.

Consequence of Advising Against Inspections

Licensees working in a seller's market may be tempted to advise buyers to forgo the inspection contingency. This is especially tempting when a property appears to be in "good condition." Licensees should be aware that this opens up the licensee and the licensee's broker to future liability. Even homes that appear to be in top condition may have hidden defects.

It is good practice to advise inspections with every deal. In a seller's market, the risks to including versus not including the inspection contingency should be neutrally presented. Ultimately, it is the buyer's decision as to whether to include it as part of the offer to purchase. Should a buyer choose to skip inspections, it is good practice to get the buyer to sign a statement stating that the licensee advised the buyer that inspections may be conducted to investigate the condition of the property.

Students of the post-licensing 45-hour course are instructed to do the following exercise:

> What would you do if…
> You are working with a buyer in a very competitive seller's market. You have written several offers for the buyer and each time the buyer lost out on the home to another buyer. Each of the offers had been written subject to inspections. Finally, the buyer decides to write an offer without including an inspection contingency.
>
> Which is the best course of action to take?
>
> A. Warn the buyer about the risks and then write the contract exactly as the buyer has directed.
> B. Warn the buyer about the risks and then write the contract exactly as the buyer has directed. In addition, have the buyer sign a statement that the buyer was advised by the licensee to conduct inspections.
>
> B is the better choice. Although choice A is legally correct, by having a standard policy of always recommending inspections and having the buyer sign a statement stating it was advised, it will help licensees avoid litigation.

Adhering to Inspection Timelines

Most real estate contracts are written with tight timelines that must be adhered to in order to have a successful closing. Inspections must be ordered, completed, and responded to all within the timeline agreed to within the real estate purchase contract.

If the timeline runs over, the buyer may be locked into a contract to purchase the home despite any issues. Should the buyer choose to walk away from a home after the inspection timeline has ended, the seller normally has the right to claim the earnest money deposit as liquidated damages – this, of course, depends upon the wording of the contact. Or the seller could sue the buyer for "specific performance" to try to force the buyer to purchase the home as contracted.

Ordering Inspections

Some real estate licensees handle the ordering of inspections as a service to their clients. This is a practice that is waning, though, as brokerage offices adhere to policies that avoid potential financial liability for the inspections. When a licensee orders an inspection, if the client fails to pay for the inspection, the inspection company will hold the licensee liable for the cost of the inspection. This said, most inspection companies expect payment for the inspection before or at the time of the inspection. It used to be common for inspection costs to be paid at the time of closing. This practice became less common following the down turn of the real estate market of 2008. As inspection companies found themselves with more and more unpaid bills, it became commonplace for payment to be made upfront.

Licensees working with buyers who have purchased other homes may find that the buyers aren't prepared for this current practice. Licensees should prepare buyers for the cost of inspections and keep this in mind when drafting an offer. It is possible to negotiate for the seller to order and pay for inspections.

Legal Liability of Inspections

The licensee may also take on legal liability of the inspection by referring the buyer or seller to a specific inspector/inspection company to use.

For this reason, most licensees refrain from even referring an inspection company to the client. For licensees that do make referrals, it is important to make sure that the inspection companies do good work and are properly licensed. To further insulate the licensee from the inspector, most licensees always refer the individual to multiple inspectors and never less than three.

Agent Sued For Ordering Inspection

Schoembs v. Schena (Massachusetts Superior Court, Jan. 23, 2015)

In this case, the real estate licensee offered to contact a inspection company to check on a foundation. It had been disclosed by the sellers that some years before there had been significant settling of the foundation. The licensee attended the inspection.

Not all of the foundation was accessible to the inspector, so the licensee suggested that hiring a structural engineer was prudent. However, the buyers declined doing so and instead purchased the home.

6 years later, the buyer sued the licensee, his broker, the sellers, the seller's salesperson and broker, and the inspector and his employer.

Because the licensee had failed to check the qualifications of the inspection company, this was considered negligent behavior by the licensee.

Property Condition Disclosure Highlights: 1Q 2015. February 2017. https://www.nar.realtor/publications/legal-pulse/property-condition-disclosure-highlights-1q-2015

⭐ **Students of the post-licensing 45-hour course are instructed to do the following exercise:**

> Inspection Companies
> You should take the following steps to be prepared to work with buyers and sellers in regard to inspection companies.
>
> 1. Consult with your broker to determine company practice and policy for ordering and referring inspection companies.
> 2. Research area inspection companies.
>   a. Determine what type of inspection services are offered
>   b. Cost for inspections
>   c. Turn around average timeline for inspection reports
>   d. Verify that company complies with mandatory licensing
>   e. Compile a list of the gathered information to have available as needed.

Advantages of Sellers Ordering Pre-Deal Inspections

Licensees may advise sellers to order inspections to have on hand for home showings. This is a common practice particularly in a buyers' market. By ordering inspections in advance and taking care of any issues that were pointed out from the inspections, the home may stand out to a buyer as being a safer home to purchase.

It may also speed up the closing process if buyers, in turn, choose not to order additional inspections. Keep in mind, though, that many buyers will still choose to do their own inspections. Sellers should be advised about this possibility. In this case, the advanced inspection may have still been helpful in assisting the seller to find issues to be repaired prior to the buyer's inspection.

Types of Inspections

The most common types of inspections are whole house inspections and inspections for wood-destroying organisms such as termites. Specific inspections may also be ordered to check for mold, radon, issues with electrical, plumbing, the roof or the structure. Insurance companies may require 4-Point Insurance Inspections and wind mitigation reports. Another inspection that has become more common with the rise of "meth labs" in homes is a meth inspection.

Whole House

A whole house inspector inspects the total home structure, major appliances, plumbing, electrical, roof and property near structures. The condition of the home is presented in detail including: foundation, walls, roof, insulation, windows, doors, kitchen, bathroom, laundry, water heater, furnace, ventilation, air conditioning, electrical systems, plumbing and outdoor areas. The ASHI and the National Association of Home Inspectors (NAHI) offer home inspector accreditations. To qualify for accreditation, home inspectors must pass training classes, pass the National Home Inspection Exam, complete 250 or more fee-paid home inspections, plus promise to adhere to industry practice and ethical standards.

In order to work in Florida as a home inspector, the person must be licensed by the Department of Business and Professional Regulations. The Department's Bureau of Central Intake and Licensure processes applications for licensure and refers complex applications to the home inspectors licensing office for final review. The Division of Regulation is responsible for complaint analysis and investigations, and the Office of the General Counsel provides prosecutorial services for disciplinary cases. The Department engages in rulemaking to implement the provisions set forth in its statutes and conducts other general business, as necessary.

Licensees may double check that an inspector's license is current at www.myfloridalicense.com. Because whole house inspections cover so many areas – the entire home – it is not unusual for the report to come back with many things cited as being imperfect. Lengthy reports often overwhelm buyers. Licensees will need to guide those buyers through the report to find items that pose a risk to the property or to the value of the property. Yet, in doing this, licensees must be careful not to take on liability of "sugar coating" the importance of issues.

Wood-Destroying Organisms

Termite prevention and structural damage costs approximately $1 billion annually according to the Department of Agriculture and Consumer Service.

Because wood-destroying organisms, such as termites, can cause structural damage, many buyers choose to obtain inspections to look for active termites or evidence of damage. It is also common for lenders to require termite inspections. The practice of pest control in Florida is regulated under the Structural Pest Control Act, Chapter 482, Florida Statutes (F.S.). This law is administered and enforced by the Department of Agriculture and Consumer Services.

The inspector must evaluate accessible areas of the property where infestation could occur, including the attic and crawlspace, for signs of live insects, dead insects or insect parts, and signs of infestation such as shelter tubes running through wood or other material, exit holes and insect staining. In addition, the inspector checks for visible damage to wood and other structural materials.

Licensees should be wary of termite inspectors that offer to provide an inspection for free. Free termite inspectors are part of many pest company "sales departments." Companies often "waive" termite inspection fees in hopes to gain a contract to treat for wood-destroying organisms. These treatments can be costly.

Mold

The Department of Business and Professional Regulation is responsible for licensing and regulating mold inspectors and mold remediators. Molds can grow on cloth, carpets, leather, wood, sheetrock, and insulation when moist conditions exist. People can become exposed to molds by direct contact on surfaces or through the air. Indoor spaces that are wet, and have organic materials that mold can use as a food source, can and do support mold growth.

Mold spores or fragments that become airborne can expose people indoors through inhalation or skin contact causing illness. Because of the serious threat that mold creates, many buyers choose to order mold inspections. Whole house inspectors may take note of obvious conditions in the home that are often associated with mold. Mold inspectors take this a step further by testing for mold in the air.

Radon

Radon is a natural occurring odorless gas from decaying uranium in the soil. It causes lung cancer. Newer, efficient, "tightly sealed homes" increases the likelihood of radon becoming trapped inside the home exposing residents to harm.

Because of this, Florida Statute 404 mandates that a Radon disclosure warning officially be provided prior to a buyer signing a purchase agreement. There is no requirement for the buyer to test for radon. However, many buyers choose to do so.

According to floridahealth.gov, about 1 in 5 radon tests made in Florida are found to have elevated levels of radon. Anyone offering professional radon services must have a Florida Department of Health Radon Certification. Mitigation solutions for radon involve different options ranging from inserting pipes as ventilation into floor slabs to using fans to create counter pressure to prevent radon from entering a home.

Frequently Asked Questions. March 2017. http://www.floridahealth.gov/environmental-health/radon/radon-faq.html

Electrical and Plumbing

Electrical and plumbing systems are checked as part of the whole house inspection. Generally, "electricians" or "plumbers" are called in to give a more extensive check of the systems. Similar to wood-destroying organism inspectors, the individuals doing the inspection are often hoping to "fix found problems."

Licensees should be guarded when working with un-vetted individuals as the "inspectors" may be tempted by an inherent conflict of interest to find problems. However, licensees who try to avert these types of inspections could find themselves later liable for electrical and plumbing problems.

Roof

The Florida Department of Business and Professional Regulation certifies commercial and residential roofing inspectors. To become certified, the inspector must have four years of roofing experience and pass standardized state testing. Some insurance companies will require that the condition of the roof be certified before a homeowner's policy can be bound on the property.

Structural

Beyond the structural inspection conducted by a whole house inspector, structural engineers may be hired to perform a more detailed inspection. These services often offer repair solutions for issues uncovered.

4-Point Insurance Inspection

Buyers should be encouraged to contact insurance agents during the inspection period. In order to secure insurance on the property, the buyer may need a 4-point insurance inspection or a wind mitigation report. Whole house inspectors are often able to perform these needed reports. Or they can be ordered separately.

The four points of inspection include:
1. Heating and air systems
2. Electrical wiring and panels
3. Plumbing and plumbing fixtures
4. Roof

Condition along with age of the units are included in the reports.

Wind Mitigation

Home buyers often order wind mitigation reports to provide to their homeowner's insurance company. State law requires that insurance companies give discounts on the cost of insurance if certain steps have been taken to mitigate potential wind damage during storms. The wind mitigation report rates the home based on features such as exterior construction type, roof shape and construction methods, age of roof covering, door and window opening protection as well as the actual year the home was built.

Meth

Meth labs operated in homes leaves residue within the home that can cause ongoing health problems to individuals living in the home. Crystal meth is short for crystal methamphetamine. Methamphetamine is a white crystalline drug ingested by inhaling through the nose, smoking, injecting, or taking orally. A meth lab is an illegal operation where crystal meth is produced.

Licensees and buyers should take extra note of experiencing headaches, nausea, shortness of breath, dizziness, chest pain, or a dry mouth after visiting a property as these may be signs that a meth lab operated in the home. To test for meth, kits are used test swabs taken from within the house. Professionals can be hired to gather these swabs

What is Crystal Meth. March 2017. http://www.drugfreeworld.org/drugfacts/crystalmeth.html

Conflict of Interest

Regardless of the type of inspection being conducted, licensees should watch out for "inspectors" that will also benefit from repair issues by then being paid to make repairs or conduct treatment. A good rule of thumb is to never tie the repair and the inspection together with the same company. When items are flagged as being an issue, it may also be prudent to get a second opinion.

★ **Students of the post-licensing 45-hour course are instructed to do the following exercise:**

> What would you do if . . .
> You are representing a seller in a purchase agreement between the seller and a buyer. As part of the contract, the buyer has conducted wood-destroying organism inspection. Before the end of the inspection period, the buyer provided a copy of the report which reported that the house had termite damage in part of the house trim. The buyer is asking for a $2000 credit for the cost of termite tenting that was offered with the inspection.
>
> The seller tells you that the house is under contract with another termite company for biannual inspections and that company had been out to the home just the month before. That company offered a report that the house did not have evidence of termites.
>
> Which is the correct choice:
>
> A. Because the buyers have a report showing active termites, you tell the seller that they should do what the buyers want because if the deal fails, the seller will be legally obligated to share the new termite inspection report with other potential buyers.
> B. You get a copy of the report from the termite company that the seller has been using to share with the buyer's agent. You negotiate for a third termite company to check on the property – a company approved by both the buyer and the seller – to provide a neutral report. That company is told, beforehand, that no treatment service work will be given to the company. Both the buyers and the sellers attend the third inspection.
>
> B is the correct choice. Although it is true that sellers and licensees must disclose the existence of material defects, if the seller truly believed that the 2nd report was invalid, it would warrant pulling in another company to validate or invalidate the findings.

Renegotiating the Deal Based on Inspection Reports

If the items cited on an inspection report seem significant, the buyer may want either a reduction in the sales price or to have the seller make repairs to the property. The buyer's agent must write up a requested price reduction on an addendum to the purchase contract. This request must be submitted to the other party prior to the inspection period ending to keep the buyer out of risk in the deal.

If a buyer wants repairs to be made based on inspections, the licensee would also write up an addendum requesting that the repairs be made. Inspection reports conducted by buyers are owned by the buyer and should go directly to the buyer and/or the buyer's agent. With requested repairs, though, these inspections are normally shared with the seller to show evidence of the needed repairs. Negotiating for repairs is often a contentious time. Items that a buyer may deem as needing repaired may not seem as important to the seller.

It is not uncommon for the negotiating process to require going "back and forth" between the parties several times before they come to some sort of agreement. The licensee's goal is to avoid the contract being canceled!

Managing Repairs

If repairs are agreed to in the deal, the licensee may face having to oversee the repair process. Again, because of risk of liability it is most prudent as a licensee to remain as removed from the repair process as much as possible. The buyer and the seller should be in charge of choosing the person who makes the repairs – not the licensee.

All paid receipts should be shared between parties to ensure that there is no risk of unpaid work becoming attached to the property as a mechanic's lien. Licensees should encourage buyers to either personally inspect the property after repairs have been made or to rehire an inspector to do so. The licensee should never take on the liability of vouching for repairs.

Licensees who are able to successfully navigate the inspection period will find that they have served the best interest of their clients.

10 CLOSINGS

<u>LEARNING TERMS AND PHRASES</u>

- Real Estate Closings
- Use of Title Company vs. Title Attorney
- Chain of Title vs. Abstract of Title
- Title Opinion
- Title Insurance
- Clear to Close
- Surveys
- Insurance
- Associations
- 72 Hours
- Closing Disclosure Check
- Proration Check
- Single Entry Check
- Commission Check
- Misc. Fee Check
- Repair Escrow
- Closing Funds
- Mail Away Closings
- Final Walk Throughs
- Failed Deals

Learning Objectives

- Licensees will gain an understanding of how to limit risk to the seller, the buyer, the brokerage, and the licensees by having either title companies or title attorneys handle closing.
- Licensees will understand how to manage lenders "clear to close" with closing agents.
- Licensees will understand how to communicate with buyers, sellers, lenders and closing agents to keep the deal moving forward.
- Licensees will understand how to manage surveys, insurance, and associations to prepare for closing.
- Licensees will be able to analyze figures contained on closing disclosures.
- Licensees will understand how to manage "mail away" closings.
- Licensees will understand the importance of "walk throughs" prior to closings.
- Licensees will understand aspects of managing deals that fail to close.

The Importance of Closings

Finally, all the hard work of a licensee has come together and it is time to "close" the deal! This may also be referred to as a real estate settlement. A real estate closing is when the seller formally signs over property to the buyer.

Licensees must manage the "clear to close from a lender", ensure that any required buyer insurance is in place, ensure that all debits and credits are accounted for on the closing disclosure, manage closing procedures for out of town buyers or sellers, manage a final property walk through, and manage any last-minute issues which could halt the closing and jeopardize the deal. Plus, licensees must be able to unwind a deal if it does fail.

Importance of Working with a Title Company or Title Attorney

Once a buyer and seller enter into a purchase agreement for real estate, the licensee must go to work to ensure that the transfer of title takes place. Although this can legally happen without the aid of a title company or lawyer, a licensee would be open to massive legal liability for being involved with a closing that didn't utilize the services of either a title company or a title attorney.

The title company or attorney researches the history of the property, issues title insurance to protect the parties involved and draws up the paperwork required at closing including the deed. Licensees may not provide legal advice in the manner of how the parties should take title, may not provide an opinion on the marketability of title, and may not draw up deeds!

Title Insurance

In Florida, either a title company or a title attorney may issue title insurance. The property's title must be free of defects in order to qualify for the title insurance policies. Previous ownership records of a property are reviewed to establish a Chain of Title. This information is gathered in an Abstract of Title which is then used to execute a Title Opinion in regard to the marketability of the title – the ability of the owner to transfer the property to the buyer.

Chain of Title Vs. Abstract of Title

A Chain of Title is the "linking" of one owner to another as the property has been conveyed from one person to the next. Each person is connected through the ownership history and is said to form a "chain" of ownership.

An Abstract of Title is the search through recorded documents to find evidence of title transfer history and mortgages or other liens against the property including judgments and unpaid taxes. The abstract briefly summarizes the various activities affecting ownership of a parcel of land.

Title Opinion

Once the chain of title has been established and an abstract of title has been reviewed by an attorney, the attorney provides an opinion of title. A title opinion is the written opinion of an attorney, based on the attorney's title search into a property, describing the current ownership rights in the property, as well as the actions that must be taken, if any to make the stated ownership rights marketable. The title opinion is, as the name implies, an "opinion" and does not guarantee that it is correct and without errors.

Purpose of Title Insurance

To protect the parties against title problems, title insurance companies offer title insurance. With title insurance, if any claims are brought regarding the property as a result of a pre-existing problem with the title, the title insurance will likely cover the expense. Title insurance is not required by law, however, because of the risk involved with an unmarketable title. Title insurance may be required as part of the closing when a mortgage is involved. There are two types of title insurance: owner's title insurance, which protects the property owner from title issues and lender's title insurance, which protects the mortgage company.

Owner's Policy Vs. Lender's Policy

Licensees must understand the differences between an owner's policy and a lender's policy. An owner's policy is to protect the new owners whereas the lender's policy is put into place only to protect the lender. An owner's policy is issued for the price of the house where the lender's policy is issued for the price of the mortgage the policy is protecting. How much the lender's policy will cover goes down as the mortgage is paid – as it actually protects the unpaid balance!

With the owner's policy if the owner dies and the property is passed on to an heir, the title protection remains in place. However, the owner's policy does not pass to a new owner upon the sale of the property. The lender's policy is always transferable to a new lender if the mortgage is sold in the secondary market after the closing. Both the owner's policy and the lender's policy are paid as a one-time fee at closing.

Comparing Types of Title Insurance

Owner's Policy
- Issued for price of house (sale price)
- Protects the new owner (buyer) and his heirs
- Not transferable to another party upon a sale
- One-time premium is charged (at closing)

Lender's Policy
- Issued for mortgage amount
- Protects the lender against title defects (not the owner)
- Transferable (assignable to someone else buying the loan)
- One-time premium paid at closing

Choosing Title Company

As explained in Chapter 8, "Contracts," the contract will specify whether the buyer is choosing title or if the seller is choosing title. In the standard contracts prepared by the Florida Bar for the Florida Realtor Association, whomever chooses the title company also pays for the cost of the closing including the owner's title policy, search fee and closing fee. Licensees should refer to the details of the contract to know whether an owner's policy is to be provided and which party is paying for it.

Just as with mortgage professionals and inspectors, buyers and sellers will most often look to the licensee for direction as to which title company or attorney to use. Licensees are best served by offering the buyer several options so as not be deemed as liable for the actions of the closing agent. Once the title company has been chosen, the licensee should make sure that the contract and relevant information is quickly sent to the title company. The title company will need to know the contact information for the buyers, sellers, and any lenders. Delay in providing this information to a title company could result in a delay in closing!

Clear to Close

When a lender is involved, the goal is to receive a "clear to close." Clear to close means that the deal has been approved and the final lender paperwork is being drawn up to send to the title company to be signed at closing along with the deed. To facilitate a quick clear to close, as soon as a contract has been entered into between a buyer and a seller, the licensee working with the buyer should forward a copy of the contract to the lender. Even with pre-approved buyers there will be a series of contingencies that will have to be met before the loan will approve the lender and issue the clear to close.

- Completion of property appraisals to verify condition and value
- Providing additional documents needed to verify income, assets or debts
- Providing updated copies of bank statements
- Providing proof that the earnest money deposit check has cleared (another reason to use "wires")
- Verification of buyer employment – usually conducted near the very end of the process
- Providing proof of homeowner's insurance and/or title insurance
- Providing proof of flood insurance – if in a flood zone

Keeping the Deal Moving Forward

The items on the lender's contingency checklist may seem to be out of a licensee's control. The licensee, though, should be checking in with the buyer and lender to ensure that everything is moving forward with a "sense of urgency." Updates should also be shared with the seller's licensee or seller. Contracts include a timeline for loans to be approved. Delays in finance contingency is one of the most common reasons deals fail to close on time or fail completely.

For this reason, buyers and sellers often find that the time from contract to closing to be extremely stressful. Licensees can help to alleviate anxiety by staying involved in the process offering information, guidance, and reassurance.

Refer to Chapter 6, "Financing Considerations."

Surveys and Insurance

Licensees should coordinate with the buyer, the title company and the lender to determine whether a survey of the property is required or requested. A property survey establishes and describes the legal description as a written word statement and also as a sketch or map of a piece of land showing the property boundaries and physical features. The licensee should also coordinate with the buyer, the buyer's lender, and the buyer's chosen property insurance company as to whether an elevation certificate will be required. An elevation certificate compares the building's elevation to the estimated floodwaters in the area. This is used to determine risk of flooding which affects the cost of flood insurance.

If the property is located in a flood zone and a loan is being secured on the property, the lender will require the property insurance and flood insurance be in place before the lender will approve the loan. It can be a cost savings to order the survey and the elevation certificate together as generally the same surveyor can provide both. It is also prudent to check with the seller to see if both have already been done and if available whether copies of the seller's documents will satisfy the insurance company and lender.

Associations

If the property is governed by a condominium association or a homeowner association, the licensee must ensure that contact information for the association is quickly provided to the title company to facilitate the issuance of an estoppel certificate to verify that fees have been paid current to date. The contact information should also be given to the buyer as most associations require some type buyer of application process. Evidence of the application being approved must be provided to the title company for the closing to move forward.

72 Hours

Once the lender has issued a clear to close, the title company will pull together the closing documents including the closing disclosure. The closing disclosure details all the costs associated with the closing including lender fees, real estate agent commissions, title closing fees, and costs to be prorated between the buyer and the seller.

The closing disclosure form must be provided to the borrower within 3-business days before the loan closing. This mandatory timeline was established in 2010, when congress passed the Dodd-Frank Act. Dodd-Frank established the CFPB to regulate rules under the Truth-in-Savings Act, Funds Availability Act, Equal Credit Opportunity Act and Truth-in-Lending Act.

Checking the Closing Disclosure

Licensees must be able to read closing disclosures to ensure that the figures reflect the terms of the contract between the buyer and the seller. Items are credited (+) or debited (-) to each party according to who is liable or owed money from the other party. These calculations are based on the day of closing (as defined in the contract). A credit means that the person who gets the credit is receiving money. A debit means that the person who gets the debit is being charged money.

See a sample Closing Disclosure form at the end of this chapter.

Prorated Items

Expenses or income connected to owning the property which are paid in advance or in arrears are prorated between buyers and sellers according to date of closing. This includes city and/or county property taxes, homeowner association fees, mortgage interest on an assumed loan, and prepaid rent collected on a rental property.

Proration methods

Unless otherwise indicated on the contract, the buyer will "own" the day of closing. This means that expenses or income is calculated with the buyer taking over the expense as of the day of closing or receiving the income benefit as of the day of closing. The actual number of days for the time period being calculated is used as a basis for the calculations.

City and/or County Property Taxes

City and county property taxes are paid in arrears. This means that the tax bill becomes due at the end of the tax year. With this payment timeline, the seller normally has not paid his or her portion of the tax bill before closing. So, the seller owes the buyer money at closing to account for the unpaid taxes as the buyer will legally be liable to pay all the taxes when the bill is issued.

To make this equitable, the seller's portion of the tax bill is calculated and entered as a credit to the buyer and debit to the seller on the closing disclosure.

★ **Students of the post-licensing 45-hour course are instructed to do the following exercise:**

> Property Taxes Prorated
> You are checking closing figures on a closing disclosure.
> $580.05 has been entered on the seller's side as a debit for property taxes. $580.05 has been entered as a credit for the buyer.
> Is this correct based on the following information?
> - The property taxes are $1,580 for the year and are unpaid.
> - The day of closing is May 15th and is charged to the buyer.
>
> _____
> _____
> _____
> _____
>
> Solution:
> - First you have to calculate how many days the seller owes the buyer at closing:
>   - January 1 to May 14 = 134 days
>   - 31 (Jan) + 28 (Feb) + 31 (Mar) + 30 (Apr) + 14 (May) = 134 days
> - Then you have to calculate how much is owed for each day and multiply the # of seller days owed
>   - $1580 ÷ 365 = $4.3287671 per day × 134 days = $580.05
>   - Debit seller $580.05, Credit buyer $580.05
> - Yes, the closing disclosure is correct!

Homeowner Association Fees

Homeowner association fees are paid ahead. Meaning that the seller has paid a billing period that the buyer will now owe the seller for at closing. Homeowner association fees may be billed as an annual bill, a quarterly bill, or as a monthly bill. This billing period has to be known in order to calculate the prorated entries. The title company will verify that the fees have been paid in full to date through an Estoppel Certificate from the management of the association. This will be entered as a credit to the seller and a debit to the buyer.

See Chapter 7, "Condo/HOA/CDD" for more details.

★ **Students of the post-licensing 45-hour course are instructed to do the following exercise:**

> Homeowner Association Fees Prorated
> You are checking closing figures on a closing disclosure.
> $90 has been entered on the seller's side as a credit for home owner association fee. $90 has been entered as a debit for the buyer.
> Is this correct based on the following information?
> - The association fees are paid monthly at $225.
> - The day of closing is July 10th and is charged to the buyer.
> - The July association bill has been paid by the seller.
>
> _____
> _____
> _____
> _____
>
> Solution:
> - First you have to calculate how many days the buyer owes the seller at closing:
>   - July 1 to July 9th belongs to the seller
>   - 31 (Days in July) – 9 = 22 days that the buyer owes the seller
> - Then you have to calculate how much is owed for each day and multiply the # of seller days owed
>   - $225 ÷ 31 = $7.25806452 per day × 22 days = $159.68 (rounded up)
>   - Debit buyer $159.68, Credit seller $159.68
> - NO the closing disclosure is NOT correct!

Mortgage Interest on an Assumed Loan

Mortgage interest is paid in arrears. When a buyer assumes a mortgage from the seller, interest that the seller owes for the number of days he owned the property that month will be given as a credit to the buyer and charged as a debit to the seller.

★ **Students of the post-licensing 45-hour course are instructed to do the following exercise:**

> Mortgage Interest on an Assumed Loan Prorated
> You are checking closing figures on a closing disclosure.
> $184.93 has been entered on the seller's side as a debit to account for mortgage interest on an assumed loan. $184.93 has been entered as a credit for the buyer.
> Is this correct based on the following information?
> - The assumable mortgage loan balance is $150,000 at 5% interest rate.
> - The day of closing is June 10th and is charged to the buyer.
>
> _____
> _____
> _____
> _____
>
> Solution:
> - $150,000 x 5% = $7,500 ÷ 365 days = $20.547945 per day
> - $20.547945 x 9 days = $184.93
> - Debit the seller $184.93, Credit the Buyer $184.93
> - Yes, the closing disclosure is correct!

Prepaid Rent Collected on a Rental Property

Rent is generally paid in advance. For investment property that has a tenant, the rent that the seller collected at the first of the month will need to be prorated on the closing disclosure. Credit will be given to the buyer and a debit to the seller for the amount of the rent owed to the buyer who will be taking over the rental property.

⭐ **Students of the post-licensing 45-hour course are instructed to do the following exercise:**

> **Prepaid Rent Collected on a Rental Property Prorated**
> You are checking closing figures on a closing disclosure.
> $800 has been entered on the seller's side as a debit to account for rent collected that is due to the buyer. $800 has been entered as a credit for the buyer.
> Is this correct based on the following information?
> - The monthly rent is $1,500.
> - The day of closing is April 15th and is given to the buyer.
> - April rent has been collected by the seller.
>
> _____
> _____
> _____
> _____
>
> Solution:
> - The Buyer is due rents from closing date to end of month.
> - From the 15th of April to the 30th is 16 days of rent due buyer
> - $1,500 ÷ 30 = $50 per day × 16 days = $800.
> - Debit seller $800, Credit buyer $800.

Single Entry Items

Not everything gets entered on the closing disclosure to both the buyer and the seller (known as double entry). Several items are only entered on either the buyer side or the seller side, but not both (known as single entry). Buyer's earnest money deposits along with credit for the mortgage balance gets entered as a credit to the buyer. (Not entered on the seller's side.)

If the seller was holding a mortgage on the home which is paid off as part of the closing, this is entered as a debit to the seller. (Not entered on the buyer's side.) Other expenses may be entered on only one side or the other as agreed upon in the contract. This includes expenses such as document preparation fees, recording fees, broker's commission and title insurance.

Debits & Credits

The allocation as show below may be changed per the terms of the contract.

Items Debited to the Seller

Broker's commission
Mortgage(s) paid off or held by seller
Deed preparation
Seller's attorney fees
State documentary stamps on the deed
Owner's title insurance
Prorated taxes, interest, advance rent
Rental security deposit

Items Debited to the Buyer

Purchase Price
State documentary stamps all notes
Mortgage note prep
Title insurance (lender's policy)
Recording Deed
Recording Mortgage
Attorney's fees (buyer)
Home Owner Association Fees Prorated

Items Credited to the Seller

Purchase Price
Prepaid items
Homeowner Association Fees Prorated

Items Credited to the Buyer

Mortgages, new or assumed
Earnest money deposit
Prorated property taxes, unpaid interest and paid rents
Rental security deposits

Commission and Fees

Licensees will want to notify the title company or attorney about agreed upon commission and ensure that it has been added to the closing disclosure. If the brokerage company charges a processing administrative fee to the buyer or seller, the licensee would need to request that this also be added.

In Florida, licensees may be paid at closing with the title company issuing a check to the licensee for the licensee's portion. This is legal despite the fact that by law only a broker may be paid a direct commission with the broker paying the licensee. A special provision in license law allows the licensee to be paid at closing as long as the broker provides written permission (may be by email).

Other Fees

Finally, the licensee must keep in mind the terms of the contract and anything that transpired as a result of inspections. For example, if repairs were made to the property, it is legally correct to turn paid receipts in to the title company. These charges will be added to the closing disclosure as "paid outside of closing."

Repair Escrow

Occasionally, money will be set aside in the deal and paid by the title company after closing for repairs that could not be completed prior to closing. This would be per the terms as agreed by both the buyer and seller. Licensees would watch for this accounting on the disclosure as well and confirm with the title company that the company is willing to issue the check post proof that the work has been completed.

Transfer of Earnest Money

If earnest money is being held by the broker (rather than the title company), the licensee will need to ensure that the earnest money is transferred to the title company immediately before closing. The broker would follow the agreement of the purchase contract should the money have been kept in an interest-bearing account.

Closing Funds

Once the closing disclosure has been approved by all parties and the lender, the buyer should be advised to "wire" any amount needed for closing the title company. Keep in mind that in the case of a "short sale," the seller would also need to wire funds to the title company to reconcile the shortage of the seller's mortgage and fees. The majority of title companies will no longer accept either a personal check, bank check or cashier's check due to potential fraud.

Mail Away Closings

Not all buyers and sellers are able to attend closings. Title companies or attorneys should be notified about out of town buyers and sellers in order to make provisions to "mail away" the closing documents. With today's technology, the closing documents are often provided by email. The parties may have to visit a notary for some of the document signatures. Once signed, the party will generally overnight the documents back to the title company or attorney.

Company Disclosure Forms

Most brokerage companies have custom disclosures that must be signed by the buyers and sellers for every deal. These documents often disclose affiliated relationships, potential environmental hazards, and contain "hold harmless" clauses designed to lessen potential legal liability.

Final Walk Through

Immediately prior to a closing, licensees should be prepared to take the buyer through the property for one last look. The goal is to ensure that the property condition matches the condition when the buyer entered into the purchase agreement. This is when things such as appliances that are supposed to transfer with the property are verified as still being on the property. Buyers are satisfied with the property should sign a "Walk Through" form verifying that the walk through was conducted and that the buyer accepts the property. Buyers that waive the walk through should sign a form stating such. Buyers that are unhappy with the condition of the walk through should be advised not to close until the condition is brought to a satisfactory standard.

★ **Students of the post-licensing 45-hour course are instructed to do the following exercise:**

> Compare the two possible outcomes:
> You are working with a buyer who is purchasing a home. The home has been vacant with the power and water turned off. As a result of negotiations, the seller removed the existing washer and dryer from the property. Because the water was turned off, the mover didn't think to turn off the water at the back of the washer before disconnecting and removing the unit. Preparing for ownership, the buyer contacted the water company and had the water turned on the day before closing.
>
> Outcome A: The morning of the closing, the buyer walked through the house and found it flooded.
>
> Outcome B: The buyer waived the final walk through. Instead, the buyer closed on the house and arrived at the property later that day to find it flooded.
>
> With Outcome A, the buyer would halt the closing – and the seller would be responsible for any necessary repairs.
>
> With Outcome B, the buyer would have now own a flooded house and have to carry any repair costs!

When the Deal Fails to Close

Despite all the licensee's hard work, occasionally deals fail to close. This often happens as the result of financing problems, appraisal problems, or inspection problems. Occasionally, deals close due to the buyer or seller changing their mind about the purchase. When this happens, licensees should first work to ensure that every effort has been made to keep the deal together – assuming that this is in the best interest of the licensee's client. Sometimes it is not!

Licensees should draft a "Cancellation and Release of Funds" form to obtain a signed agreement from both parties noting that the deal is canceled and as to how the earnest money funds will be distributed. When the buyers and sellers disagree about the disbursement of earnest money, licensees should involve their broker. If the broker is holding the funds, there are specific procedures the broker must follow to determine how the funds will be released. If the title company is holding the funds, the buyer and seller would need to come to an agreement or sue each other in court to resolve the issue. Licensees should focus on the best interest of the client in this situation and move the client toward another deal as quickly as possible.

Closing Gifts

Although not necessary, upon the successful closing many licensees gift their clients with a closing gift. The gift should be thoughtful and aid the client in thinking of the licensee first for future real estate needs!

Closing Disclosure

Closing Disclosure

This form is a statement of final loan terms and closing costs. Compare this document with your Loan Estimate.

Closing Information
- Date Issued: 4/15/2013
- Closing Date: 4/15/2013
- Disbursement Date: 4/15/2013
- Settlement Agent: Epsilon Title Co.
- File #: 12-3456
- Property: 456 Somewhere Ave, Anytown, ST 12345
- Sale Price: $180,000

Transaction Information
- Borrower: Michael Jones and Mary Stone, 123 Anywhere Street, Anytown, ST 12345
- Seller: Steve Cole and Amy Doe, 321 Somewhere Drive, Anytown, ST 12345
- Lender: Ficus Bank

Loan Information
- Loan Term: 30 years
- Purpose: Purchase
- Product: Fixed Rate
- Loan Type: ☒ Conventional ☐ FHA ☐ VA ☐
- Loan ID #: 123456789
- MIC #: 000654321

Loan Terms

		Can this amount increase after closing?
Loan Amount	$162,000	NO
Interest Rate	3.875%	NO
Monthly Principal & Interest See Projected Payments below for your Estimated Total Monthly Payment	$761.78	NO

		Does the loan have these features?
Prepayment Penalty	YES	• As high as $3,240 if you pay off the loan during the first 2 years
Balloon Payment	NO	

Projected Payments

Payment Calculation	Years 1-7	Years 8-30
Principal & Interest	$761.78	$761.78
Mortgage Insurance	+ 82.35	+ —
Estimated Escrow Amount can increase over time	+ 206.13	+ 206.13
Estimated Total Monthly Payment	**$1,050.26**	**$967.91**

| Estimated Taxes, Insurance & Assessments
Amount can increase over time
See page 4 for details | $356.13
a month | This estimate includes
☒ Property Taxes
☒ Homeowner's Insurance
☒ Other: Homeowner's Association Dues
See Escrow Account on page 4 for details. You must pay for other property costs separately. | In escrow?
YES
YES
NO |

Costs at Closing

Closing Costs	$9,712.10	Includes $4,694.05 in Loan Costs + $5,018.05 in Other Costs – $0 in Lender Credits. See page 2 for details.
Cash to Close	$14,147.26	Includes Closing Costs. See Calculating Cash to Close on page 3 for details.

CLOSING DISCLOSURE PAGE 1 OF 5 • LOAN ID # 123456789

This Disclosure Summary can be located through The Consumer Financial Protection Bureau

http://www.consumerfinance.gov/owning-a-home/closing-disclosure/

Closing Disclosure

Closing Cost Details

Loan Costs		Borrower-Paid At Closing	Borrower-Paid Before Closing	Seller-Paid At Closing	Seller-Paid Before Closing	Paid by Others
A. Origination Charges		**$1,802.00**				
01 0.25 % of Loan Amount (Points)		$405.00				
02 Application Fee		$300.00				
03 Underwriting Fee		$1,097.00				
04						
05						
06						
07						
08						
B. Services Borrower Did Not Shop For		**$236.55**				
01 Appraisal Fee	to John Smith Appraisers Inc.					$405.00
02 Credit Report Fee	to Information Inc.		$29.80			
03 Flood Determination Fee	to Info Co.	$20.00				
04 Flood Monitoring Fee	to Info Co.	$31.75				
05 Tax Monitoring Fee	to Info Co.	$75.00				
06 Tax Status Research Fee	to Info Co.	$80.00				
07						
08						
09						
10						
C. Services Borrower Did Shop For		**$2,655.50**				
01 Pest Inspection Fee	to Pests Co.	$120.50				
02 Survey Fee	to Surveys Co.	$85.00				
03 Title – Insurance Binder	to Epsilon Title Co.	$650.00				
04 Title – Lender's Title Insurance	to Epsilon Title Co.	$500.00				
05 Title – Settlement Agent Fee	to Epsilon Title Co.	$500.00				
06 Title – Title Search	to Epsilon Title Co.	$800.00				
07						
08						
D. TOTAL LOAN COSTS (Borrower-Paid)		**$4,694.05**				
Loan Costs Subtotals (A + B + C)		$4,664.25	$29.80			

Other Costs						
E. Taxes and Other Government Fees		**$85.00**				
01 Recording Fees	Deed: $40.00 Mortgage: $45.00	$85.00				
02 Transfer Tax	to Any State			$950.00		
F. Prepaids		**$2,120.80**				
01 Homeowner's Insurance Premium (12 mo.) to Insurance Co.		$1,209.96				
02 Mortgage Insurance Premium (mo.)						
03 Prepaid Interest ($17.44 per day from 4/15/13 to 5/1/13)		$279.04				
04 Property Taxes (6 mo.) to Any County USA		$631.80				
05						
G. Initial Escrow Payment at Closing		**$412.25**				
01 Homeowner's Insurance $100.83 per month for 2 mo.		$201.66				
02 Mortgage Insurance per month for mo.						
03 Property Taxes $105.30 per month for 2 mo.		$210.60				
04						
05						
06						
07						
08 Aggregate Adjustment		– 0.01				
H. Other		**$2,400.00**				
01 HOA Capital Contribution	to HOA Acre Inc.	$500.00				
02 HOA Processing Fee	to HOA Acre Inc.	$150.00				
03 Home Inspection Fee	to Engineers Inc.	$750.00			$750.00	
04 Home Warranty Fee	to XYZ Warranty Inc.			$450.00		
05 Real Estate Commission	to Alpha Real Estate Broker			$5,700.00		
06 Real Estate Commission	to Omega Real Estate Broker			$5,700.00		
07 Title – Owner's Title Insurance (optional) to Epsilon Title Co.		$1,000.00				
08						
I. TOTAL OTHER COSTS (Borrower-Paid)		**$5,018.05**				
Other Costs Subtotals (E + F + G + H)		$5,018.05				
J. TOTAL CLOSING COSTS (Borrower-Paid)		**$9,712.10**				
Closing Costs Subtotals (D + I)		$9,682.30	$29.80	$12,800.00	$750.00	$405.00
Lender Credits						

CLOSING DISCLOSURE   PAGE 2 OF 5 • LOAN ID # 123456789

EXAMPLE

This Disclosure Summary can be located through The Consumer Financial Protection Bureau

http://www.consumerfinance.gov/owning-a-home/closing-disclosure/

Closing Disclosure

Calculating Cash to Close

Use this table to see what has changed from your Loan Estimate.

	Loan Estimate	Final	Did this change?
Total Closing Costs (J)	$8,054.00	$9,712.10	YES • See **Total Loan Costs (D)** and **Total Other Costs (I)**
Closing Costs Paid Before Closing	$0	−$29.80	YES • You paid these Closing Costs **before closing**
Closing Costs Financed (Paid from your Loan Amount)	$0	$0	NO
Down Payment/Funds from Borrower	$18,000.00	$18,000.00	NO
Deposit	−$10,000.00	−$10,000.00	NO
Funds for Borrower	$0	$0	NO
Seller Credits	$0	−$2,500.00	YES • See Seller Credits in **Section L**
Adjustments and Other Credits	$0	−$1,035.04	YES • See details in **Sections K and L**
Cash to Close	$16,054.00	$14,147.26	

Summaries of Transactions

Use this table to see a summary of your transaction.

BORROWER'S TRANSACTION

K. Due from Borrower at Closing		**$189,762.30**
01 Sale Price of Property		$180,000.00
02 Sale Price of Any Personal Property Included in Sale		
03 Closing Costs Paid at Closing (J)		$9,682.30
04		
Adjustments		
05		
06		
07		
Adjustments for Items Paid by Seller in Advance		
08 City/Town Taxes to		
09 County Taxes to		
10 Assessments to		
11 HOA Dues 4/15/13 to 4/30/13		$80.00
12		
13		
14		
15		

L. Paid Already by or on Behalf of Borrower at Closing		**$175,615.04**
01 Deposit		$10,000.00
02 Loan Amount		$162,000.00
03 Existing Loan(s) Assumed or Taken Subject to		
04		
05 Seller Credit		$2,500.00
Other Credits		
06 Rebate from Epsilon Title Co.		$750.00
07		
Adjustments		
08		
09		
10		
11		
Adjustments for Items Unpaid by Seller		
12 City/Town Taxes 1/1/13 to 4/14/13		$365.04
13 County Taxes to		
14 Assessments to		
15		
16		
17		

CALCULATION

Total Due from Borrower at Closing (K)	$189,762.30
Total Paid Already by or on Behalf of Borrower at Closing (L)	−$175,615.04
Cash to Close ☒ From ☐ To Borrower	**$14,147.26**

SELLER'S TRANSACTION

M. Due to Seller at Closing		**$180,080.00**
01 Sale Price of Property		$180,000.00
02 Sale Price of Any Personal Property Included in Sale		
03		
04		
05		
06		
07		
Adjustments for Items Paid by Seller in Advance		
09 City/Town Taxes to		
10 County Taxes to		
11 Assessments to		
12 HOA Dues 4/15/13 to 4/30/13		$80.00
13		
14		
15		
16		

N. Due from Seller at Closing		**$115,665.04**
01 Excess Deposit		
02 Closing Costs Paid at Closing (J)		$12,800.00
03 Existing Loan(s) Assumed or Taken Subject to		
04 Payoff of First Mortgage Loan		$100,000.00
05 Payoff of Second Mortgage Loan		
06		
07		
08 Seller Credit		$2,500.00
09		
10		
11		
12		
13		
Adjustments for Items Unpaid by Seller		
14 City/Town Taxes 1/1/13 to 4/14/13		$365.04
15 County Taxes to		
16 Assessments to		
17		
18		
19		

CALCULATION

Total Due to Seller at Closing (M)	$180,080.00
Total Due from Seller at Closing (N)	−$115,665.04
Cash ☐ From ☒ To Seller	**$64,414.96**

This Disclosure Summary can be located through The Consumer Financial Protection Bureau
http://www.consumerfinance.gov/owning-a-home/closing-disclosure/

SECTION 3 LEGAL ISSUES

SECTION 3 LEGAL ISSUES, of this course, focuses on legal issues that pertain to real estate licensing.

Chapters include:

11. Licensing Law – Maintaining Compliance
12. Ethics and Business Practices
13. Fair Housing Applied
14. ECOA / TILA / RESPA – In Practice
15. Agency in Practice

Upon completion of this section, licensees should be re-familiarized with the license law learned in the 63 hours pre-licensing course – with particular emphasis on remaining compliant. The licensee should have a good grasp of the importance of following ethical standards within the practice of real estate, the licensee should understand how to apply fair housing to real estate dealings, and the licensee should understand the application of the Equal Credit Opportunity Act, the Truth in Lending Act and the Real Estate Standards of Practice Act affecting all real estate transactions.

11 LICENSING LAW – MAINTAINING COMPLIANCE

Learning Terms and Phrases
- DBPR as a Resource
- FREC as a Resource
- Conduct of Practice
- Broker Advancement
- Prima Facie Compliant
- Maintaining Current Active Status
- Choosing Voluntary Inactive Status
- Consequences: Involuntary Inactive Status
- Employing Broker
- License Ceases to Be Enforce
- Null and Void License
- Renewal
- Reactivation Education
- Florida Realtors® Association
- Florida Realtors® Legislative Center
- Legislative Tracker
- Florida Realtors® Political Action Committee
- Ask an Attorney
- Florida Senate Bills
- Legislative Summary

Learning Objectives

> - Licensees should have a good grasp of how different levels of licensing can be used to maintain and advance a career in real estate.
> - Licensees should be able to identify the rules regarding the reporting of legal infractions following obtaining a license.
> - Licensees should understand the application of the rule of Prima Facie in regard to keeping a wallet license in their possession while practicing real estate.
> - Licensees should be able to identify legal requirement of keeping registration records with the DBPR updated regarding change of address and employing broker.
> - Licensees should understand the importance of staying aware of an employing broker's license status as it affects the licensees ability to practice real estate legally.
> - Licensees should understand how to maintain an active or inactive license beyond initial licensing.
> - Licensees should be familiar with online resources to stay updated with changes to licensing laws.

License Law in Review

It is important, especially beyond initial licensing, in the real estate industry to remain knowledgeable of licensing law. Following is a quick review of Florida real estate licensing law with an emphasis on staying compliant, recruiting others, and advancing licensees' credentials. Resources for remaining updated on changes within license law are also presented.

Applicable Statutes

Prior to licensing laws, all risk and responsibility was on the buyer known as **caveat emptor** meaning "Let the buyer beware!" Today, licensees should be aware that license laws must be strictly adhered to in the practice of real estate. This includes remaining knowledgeable about changes in license law.

- **Florida Statute 20** created the organizational structure of the Executive Branch of the Florida government. The purpose of the **Executive Branch** is to carry out the executive duties of the government that was established in the state constitution.
  - **Under Statute Chapter 20, The Department of Business and Professional Regulation (DBPR)** was established to implement policies and oversee professions to be regulated - when the unregulated practice can harm the public, the public is not adequately protected by other laws, and less restrictive means of regulation are not available.
- **Florida Statute 455** was then passed as **The Regulation of Professions and Occupations** to define the general legal practice and procedures for the DBPR. Statute 455 set a standard from profession to profession.
- **Florida Statute 120** was passed as the **Procedural Process** and established **Discipline Procedures** for licensees for ALL governmental professions authorized under the Florida Constitution.
- **Chapter 475** of the Florida Statutes was passed specifically to regulate Real Estate. The intent of real estate regulation is to protect the health, safety, and welfare of the public. It follows the standards of professional regulation set forth under Chapter 455 and is called the **Real Estate Professions Act**.

Beyond initial licensing, the DBPR will continue to be an important resource for licensees. It is through the DBPR, aided by the Division of Real Estate, that the licensee will maintain their professional license through renewals and apply for advanced licenses – if choosing to do so.

FREC

The Florida Real Estate Commission, also known as FREC or "the Commission," was put in place as a body of people to implement, interpret, and enforce the provisions of Chapter 475.

FREC was **granted the authority** to keep records, conduct investigations, and the power to grant, deny, suspend, and revoke licenses.

- To hold FREC and licensees to specific standards, the Florida Real Estate Commission Rules were established in the **Florida Administrative Code 61J2**.

Duties and Powers of the Commission

The primary purpose of FREC is to enforce duties and obligations as they apply to the real estate business. While decisions and policies are carried out by the (DRE) Division of Real Estate, the FREC may regulate and enforce license law, foster education, adopt a seal, establish fees, create and pass rules and regulations, regulate professional practices, grant or deny applications, suspend or revoke licenses, issue administrative fines, and make determinations of license violations. This means that if a licensee faces discipline related to the practice of real estate, FREC members will decide the licensee's fate.

Services Requiring a Real Estate License

According to Florida Statutes 475, performing the services of real estate on behalf of another person, for compensation, requires a real estate license. The term "real estate" is defined in statute to include both interest in land and/or real property and business opportunities. The term "compensation" includes monetary compensation as well as valuable consideration, which includes benefits other than cash or tangible goods. This means that if someone receives anything of value in exchange for "helping" someone sell or lease property, the person may be breaking license law, which is a third-degree felony.

Real Estate Activities

Real Estate activities cover a broad range of activities. Anyone engaged in the following activities for compensation for others is required to have a real estate license. It is important that the licensee maintain their real estate license in order to be compensated by anything of value for the following activities. It is also important that licensees not pay a fee to an unlicensed person for assisting in the following:

- Assisting in ADVERTISING a property for sale if the person is paid upon a successful sale or lease.
- Assisting a buyer to BUY.
- Assisting a seller to SELL.
- Assisting in AUCTIONING real estate.
- Assisting in the EXCHANGE of property.
- Assisting a tenant to RENT.
- Assisting a seller to LEASE.
- Assisting in APPRAISING property.

Exemption from Licensure

Among the exemptions from licensing are the following which tend to cause confusion within the general public and real estate community. Licensees must understand the nuances of these exceptions as the licensee works for others and in hiring assistants.

- **Owners** may buy, sell, exchange or lease their own property without a license. Therefore, **owner developers** can employ salaried employees to sell property as long as there is NOT compensation based on the actual sales.

- Any **salaried** employee of an owner, or of a registered broker for an owner, of an **apartment community** who works in an onsite rental office.

- **Any salaried manager of a condominium or cooperative apartment complex** for the renting of individual units within such condominium or cooperative apartment complex if rentals arranged by the person are for periods no greater than 1 year.

- Any property management firm or any owner of an apartment complex for the act of paying a **finder's fee** or referral fee to an unlicensed person who is a tenant in such apartment complex provided the value of the fee does not exceed $50 per transaction.

- An **owner of one or part of one or more timeshare** periods for the owner's own use and occupancy who later offers one or more of such periods for resale.

License Categories

There are three types of real estate license categories available in Florida that allow licensees to help other people buy and sell or lease real property and be paid a commission for that work. As licensees advance in their career, it may make sense to also advance to a higher licensing category:

- **Broker** - A real estate broker acts as an intermediary between buyers and sellers and tenants and landlords. They oversee the activities of sales agents in a brokerage or real estate office. They are licensed by the DBPR to carry out real estate services and may receive compensation for the services. The most notable distinction with the license level of a broker is that the broker can work on his or her own and receive compensation for real estate activities.

- **Sales Associate** - Real estate sales associates are licensed and registered by the DBPR to work under the direction of a broker. They are employed by the broker and receive compensation from the broker. All real estate licensees start at this level.

- **Broker Associate** - A broker associate qualifies for licensure as a broker, however, chooses to work under the direction of a broker.

⭐ **Students of the post-licensing 45-hour course are instructed to do the following exercise:**

> What would you do if...
> You have been working for two years as a real estate sales associate in a very competitive real estate market. You have successfully handled sales representing buyers and sellers and on two occasions both! Despite this success, you still find that you are losing too many listing appointments to other agents. Which of the following steps would make sense to take?
>
> A. Do nothing. Real estate is competitive. Sometimes you win some, sometimes you lose some.
> B. Consider taking the steps to advance your license level to Broker-Associate.
>
> B is clearly the best choice. Although real estate is a competitive business, there are many ways to stand out from the competition. Becoming a Broker-Associate is one of those ways. Many clients appreciate the knowledge and dedication that the license level requires. It also prepares you to run your own brokerage – should circumstances create that opportunity!

Licensees should remain aware of these qualifications as licensees recruit others to work in the real estate business. It also remains relevant if the infractions occur after a license was obtained.

- **Qualifications to Become Licensed**
    - In order to become a real estate licensee in Florida, there are certain provisions that must be met. These include being 18 years of age or older, having a high school diploma or equivalent, possessing a social security number, being of honest and of good character, and being competent and qualified.
- **Disclosure of Crimes**
    - Applicants and licensees are expected to disclose when under investigation, convicted of a crime or ever having entered a plea of nolo contendere/no contest, adjudication withheld, or a guilty plea.

- *Nolo Contendere* **(no contest)** also called a plea of no contest, is a Latin term meaning "I will not contest" the charges as a defendant in a criminal charge. The result is the same as having plead guilty.

- **Adjudication Withheld** means that instead of having been found guilty by a judge, a person is put on probation.

- **Disclose if Ever Denied**

    Applicants must disclose if the applicant has ever been denied a license, or had a license disciplined or pending discipline in another jurisdiction.

- **U.S. citizenship is not required (Chapter 455.10)**
    - It is not a requirement for any professional license in Florida for the applicant to be a United States Citizen. Per Chapter 455.10, realize that it is possible for a "non" U.S. Citizen to obtain a social security number. The qualification requirement is not for the applicant to be a U.S. Citizen – only that the applicant have a social security number.

- **The length of time a licensure application is valid**
    - Once an application has been received by the applicant, it is valid for two years. This means that if the application is approved to take the license exam, the applicant has up to two years to complete licensing requirements and become a licensee.

Florida Statutes 475.181

Conduct of Practice

Once an applicant has obtained a license, the licensee must disclose if the licensee is ever found guilty of any conduct or practice that would have been grounds for suspension or revocation under Chapter 475, F.S.

With the exception of minor traffic violations that do not need to be reported, if a licensee gets in trouble after having obtained a license – even if in another state besides Florida– the licensee must report the infraction to the DBPR. Failure to do so is a violation of licensure. This disclosure must be made within 30 days.

★ **Students of the post-licensing 45-hour course are instructed to do the following exercise:**

> What would you do if…
> You are going through a difficult divorce. One day your soon to be ex-spouse confronts you about an issue you have had an ongoing argument about. You get so mad that you drive away in such a hurry that you end up running over his motorcycle (on accident!). He tells the police that you did it on purpose. It goes to trial and you end up being found guilty of vandalism!
>
> A. Notify FREC within 30 days of being found guilty.
> B. Do nothing; you already have your license so it isn't any of the FREC's business!
>
> A is the correct choice. Chapter 475 requires you to report the guilty charge within 30 days. It would also be a good idea to include in the report a description of the circumstances so that FREC has all the information. Plus, include letters of recommendations from your Broker and other individuals. It would not necessarily impact your licensing status. That would be up to the discretion of FREC.

Broker Education

For licensees who wish to qualify as a broker, the following provision applies:

An individual licensed as a sales associate, may take a qualifying 72 Broker Pre-Licensing Sales Course (Course II). The end-of-course-exam must be passed at 70% or higher. Then, once the individual has completed two years as an active real estate sales associate licensee, either within or outside of Florida, the licensee may submit an application to the DBPR to become eligible to take the state broker exam. The Broker exam must be passed at 75% or higher.

Within the first renewal period following having qualified as a broker, the licensee must complete 60 hours of required broker post-licensing education. If a licensee fails to complete the requirement, the broker license would become null and void. However, the individual could request to have the license as a sales associate reinstated.

Broker Education Exemptions

As with the Sales Associate licensing, persons with a 4-year college degree (or higher) in real estate are exempt from the 72-hour Broker course (Course II). However, they must take the broker exam. They are also exempt from the post license broker course. They will be required to do the continuing education component to maintain their license.

Persons that are attorneys in good standing with the Florida bar ARE required to take the 72-hour broker pre-license course or Course II. They must take the state exam and must take the post license brokers course. However, they will not be required to do any other continuing education to maintain their license.

Mutual Recognition

Florida currently has mutual recognition agreements with:
- Alabama, Arkansas, Connecticut, Georgia, Illinois, Kentucky*, Mississippi, Nebraska, Rhode Island, and West Virginia**.

If someone is already a licensed real estate agent in a state that Florida has "Mutual Recognition" agreement, that individual may be exempt from some of the education and testing requirements to become a Florida licensee.

*effective as of 6/17/2021.
**effective as of 12/14/2021.

This also means that as a Florida real estate licensee, the licensee may obtain a license in the other 7 states by following their mutual recognition provisions!

- The purpose of mutual recognition is that the state of Florida recognizes the education and experience of these individuals and, therefore, provides special licensing provisions.
    - The definition of a Florida Resident is applied to see if someone can get their license through Mutual Recognition! Even if the individual is licensed by one of the states recognized for mutual recognition, if the individual is a "resident" of Florida, the rules of mutual recognition do NOT apply.
    - Anyone applying for a Florida license, either at the sales associate level or at the broker level, under mutual recognition will not have to take the pre-license courses. If applying as a sales associate – exempt from Course I. If applying as a broker – exempt from Course II.
    - And instead of a regular 100 question exam, the applicant will instead be required to take the Florida law portion of the Florida Real Estate exam. This is a 40-question exam pertaining to Florida specific real estate practice and laws. This verifies that the person's knowledge transfers to specific Florida licensing provisions. This exam must be passed at 75% or higher.

Florida Residents

Anyone who has resided in Florida continuously for a period of four calendar months or more within the preceding year is considered to be a Florida Resident. Remember to follow this rule for reporting to the DBPR when no longer a Florida resident.

Distinguish Between Mutual Recognition and Reciprocity

Mutual Recognition is not the same thing as **Reciprocity** – which is NOT allowed in Florida! Reciprocity is the exchange of licensing privileges between states, nations, businesses or individuals. In regard to real estate, reciprocity refers to recognizing the license of a real estate agent from another state without the necessity of taking the local state's examination. Whereas mutual recognition credits the experience and education, yet still requires proof of competency through passing the Florida law exam. Florida does NOT have reciprocity with any state.

Prima Facie Evidence

Prima Facie is Latin meaning at first sight; on the first appearance; on the face of it; so far as can be judged from the first disclosure; presumably.

Licensees are required to have their wallet license in their possession anytime they are conducting real estate activities with the public. A real estate license is considered prima facie evidence that the individual holding the license has a valid license and may conduct real estate services. The license contains all identifying license information including name, license number, type of license and expiration date. The code at the start of the license number indicates the type of license granted.

★ Students of the post-licensing 45-hour course are instructed to do the following exercise:

> What would you do if...
> You have a vacant home listed. While you are at a nearby beach, a buyer calls you wanting you to show her a house right away. There's a coded lock box on the house so entry is no problem, but you have left your normal business items at home including your wallet real estate license.
>
> A. Go and immediately show the home (apologizing for your beach attire).
> B. Schedule the showing long enough out that you can go home and collect your wallet license.
>
> B is the correct choice. Florida license law requires that you have your license with you as prima facie evidence whenever you are conducting real estate business.

Continuing Education

Regardless of whether a sales associate, broker associate, or broker, licensees must take 14 hours of continuing education before every renewal period ends after the initial renewal period. It doesn't apply during the first renewal period as post license courses are taken instead. Three of the 14 hours must be in the area of core law. The other 11 hours can be a specialty course offered by approved schools.

A licensee may take a second three hours of core law during the second year if the first three hours were taken during the first year for a total of six hours of core law. A licensee may substitute the three-hour core law requirement by attending a legal agenda session of the Florida Real Estate Commission – FREC. This can be done one time during a renewal cycle. If a licensee is REQUIRED to attend a legal session due to a disciplinary action against the licensee. This would not be allowed to count to replace the core law continuing education requirement! Also, to get credit for attendance toward the core law, the licensee must notify the Division of Real Estate (DRE) at least seven days in advance of the session.

Beginning October 1, 2017, licensees must also take the 3-hour Ethics and Business Practices course once during each licensure renewal period. This will change the 11 hours of specialty courses to being only 8 hours.

- Note that licensees who also have a four-year degree in real estate are NOT exempt from continuing education. However, licensed Florida lawyers in good standing are exempt.

Continuing Education Change
Effective October 1, 2017
Licensees must take:
- 3-hours Core Law
- 3-hours Ethics and Business Practices
- 8-hours Electives

Due every renewal cycle past the first.

License Statuses
Once a licensee has obtained a license, there is more than one type of status that the license can be attributed as.
- **Active** status indicates that the licensee has fulfilled all requirements (including if a sales or broker associate having an employer on record with the DBPR) and may practice real estate.
- **Inactive** means that there is a license in place, but the licensee may not practice real estate. An inactive status can be voluntary specifically by choice and request of the licensee. This would be appropriate for a licensee who would like to retain the license but is not currently working in real estate. When a licensee's license is inactive, the licensee is still required to pay all renewal fees and complete post license education and/or continuing education and renewal requirements.
- **Involuntary inactive** is when the licensee fails to fulfill the renewal requirements. However, the state allows a licensee to reactivate a license if the licensee fulfills the renewal requirements within two years of expiration. Reactivation is not possible if the licensee fails to meet requirements of the first renewal period.
- After 2 years, the license becomes **null and void** and the licensee would have to repeat the entire application process and retake the pre-license course to obtain a new license.
- **Current** status indicates that all requirements have been completed and the license has not expired.

Canceled Status
A license is considered canceled when the commission mistakenly approved a license. Falsifying an application is a third-degree Felony.

Employing Broker License Becomes Suspended or Revoked
When an employing broker has his or her license suspended or revoked for discipline reasons (or retires, quits or is fired from the brokerage), the licenses of all sales associates and broker associates employed by the broker are automatically placed in involuntary inactive status. A licensee may activate the license by having the license registered under a new employing broker.

License Ceases to be in Force

A license shall cease to be in force whenever a broker changes her or his business address and fails to notify the department of the change. Per Florida Statutes 475.23, the licensee must notify the department of address changes within 10 days after the change. The distinction here is that upon verifying a license within the DBPR system, it would appear to be active and valid as the Department would be yet unaware of the infraction. Yet technically, the license would fail to be in force until notification was made and the licensee could not practice real estate.

★ **Students of the post-licensing 45-hour course are instructed to do the following exercise:**

> What would you do if...
> You hold a Florida real estate license and you move from one home address to another.
>
> A. Notify FREC within 10 days of the change of address.
> B. Do nothing as it is your broker's responsibility to keep your records with the state current.
>
> A is the correct choice. Licensees must notify the DBPR within 10 days of change to current mailing address. A failure to notify the DBPR could result in a citation and a fine of $1,000.

Null and Void License
A license is null and void when it no longer exists.
- License has been involuntarily inactive for more than two years
- Revoked following disciplinary proceedings
- Voluntarily relinquish (does not involve disciplinary action)

Renewal
It is important for a licensee to track his or her license renewal dates to avoid having a license lapse. Remember that failure to renew within the first renewal period would result in an immediate loss of license. The license would be null and void. Licenses are only renewed during one of two dates in a year- either March 31st or September 30th. Once a license is approved, the license is in effect (not the same as active) and the first renewal date will be between 18 to 24 months from the license date. To calculate the first renewal period date, add 2 years to the calendar year of the new license. Because a license must be renewed within 24 months, go backwards to the either March 31st or September 30.th This will be the renewal date.
Florida Statute 475.183

Reactivation Education
Occasionally a licensee fails to renew his or her license before the end of a license renewal period. To renew a license, the licensee must have completed the continuing education or post education requirements AND have paid the renewal fee. If the licensee fails to renew the license by the first renewal term, the license is lost with no chance to recover it. The license is null and void.

After the first renewal period, if the licensee fails to take the required 14 hours of continuing education the license will be considered involuntary inactive and the licensee cannot practice real estate until the license is once again active. If the license has expired for no more than 12 months, the licensee simply needs to make up the 14 hours of continuing education in order to activate the license. If more than 12 months has passed but less than 24 months, then the licensee is required to take a special Reactivation Course which equals 28 hours of education. If the licensee fails to renew the license and allows 24 months to pass, then the license cannot be renewed.

Florida Statute 475.183

⭐ **Students of the post-licensing 45-hour course are instructed to do the following exercise:**

> What would you do if...
> You really liked being a real estate agent, but due to personal reasons you need to move out of the area to help your mother. You plan to come back eventually, but it could be a couple of years. Your broker charges a monthly fee to have your license hung under her brokerage and you really can't afford to keep up with that while you are away. Your license is due to expire in two months. What should you do?
>
> A. Notify the state to remove your broker as being your employer and instead place your license in Current Inactive Status. You also inform the state of your change in address. Plus, you take the required 14 hours of continuing education courses and pay the licensing fees to the DBPR to maintain the current status.
> B. Quit your brokerage and let your license lapse.
>
> A is the best choice. You've worked hard to earn your license and if there is a chance you will be using it in the future, it makes sense to keep it current. By going inactive, you can avoid paying any required brokerage or multiple listing services fees.

Members of the Armed Forces (F.S. 455.02)

Military members and their spouses are exempt from initial license fees.

Spouses of military personnel who hold a real estate license in another state or jurisdiction when the military duty is stationed in Florida, he or she may be awarded a Florida Real Estate license. The spouse must submit an application, proof of existing professional license, and fingerprints for a background check. A real estate class nor a state test is required.

A licensee in good standing who is a member of the U.S. Armed Forces is exempt from renewal requirements during active duty and for 2 years after discharge from active duty. If military duty is out of state, the exemption also applies to a licensed spouse (Assuming that the person is not active in real estate).

Multiple Licenses

Multiple licenses are issued to a broker who qualifies as the broker for more than one business entity or brokerage. For each business/brokerage that a person is a broker, a separate broker license must be obtained.

Here is a scenario in which multiple licenses could become useful:
- "The broker of Walden Realty suddenly dies. The broker of Helpful Realty agrees to also become the broker of Walden Realty so that the agents working under Walden Realty can continue to legally conduct real estate business."

Group License

According to the Florida DBPR, a group license is for an owner/developer who owns properties through various entities, but all such entities are connected so that such ownership or control is by the same individual or individuals. A sales associate or broker associate may have a "group license" in order to sell for all the entities owned by the owner/developer.

Owner-developer sends the DBPR a list of legal company names and the sales associate or broker associate receives ONE license under ONE employer. Licensees who choose to work in new construction may find this situation relevant.

License Law Updates

It is extremely important that licensees remain current with license law as it is subject to change. Licensees are encouraged to periodically log into the Department of Professional Regulation Website to remain updated on any such changes.

Links to real estate licensing law can be found at:
http://www.myfloridalicense.com/dbpr/re/statutes.html
By going to that link, licensees will find:

FLORIDA STATUTES AND FLORIDA ADMINISTRATIVE CODE

Florida Real Estate Commission (FREC)

- Florida Statutes Chapter 475 - Part I
- Florida Administrative Code Chapter 61J2

Florida Real Estate Appraisal Board (FREAB)

C. Florida Statutes Chapter 475 - Part II
D. Florida Administrative Code Chapter 61J1
E. Uniform Standards of Professional Appraisal Practice

Department of Business & Professional Regulation (DBPR) General

Business and Professional Regulation - General Provisions Chapter 455
Financial Matters; General Provisions Chapter 215
Administrative Procedures Act Chapter 120
Organizational Structure Chapter 20

★ **Students of the post-licensing 45-hour course are asked to follow the above link to read the Florida Statutes and Administrative Code - as this is the best way to absorb the information – directly from the source!**

Florida Realtors® Association
Another great resource to remain current on license law changes is to log into the Florida Realtors website and go to the Legislative Center: http://www.floridarealtors.org/LegislativeCenter/index.cfm

Topics covered within the Legislative Center include:
    Legislative News Updates - News and videos.
    Top Initiatives - Yearly End of Session Reports of continuing initiatives of the Florida Realtors Political Action Committee PAC.
    Legislative Tracker - Real estate bills as being considered in the House and Senate.
    Realtor Action Center - An online "Call to Action system" encouraging agents to contact legislators regarding crucial real estate issues.
    Great American Realtor Days – An annual event held in Tallahassee where Realtors and legislators come together.
    Florida Realtors PAC – Political Action Committee.
    Ordinance Watch – City and County Government News feeds.
    Flood Insurance Toolkit – Videos and resources to learn about flood insurance issues.

Ask an Attorney
Found on the Florida Realtors Org website, are "Ask an Attorney" legal questions and answers:
http://www.floridarealtors.org/LegalCenter/AskanAttorney/Legal-FAQs-Categories.cfm

Topics are divided into: Advertising, Appraisals, Broker Business, Brokerage Disclosure, Code of Ethics, Commercial Lien, Commissions, Community Associations, Complaints, Condominiums, Contracts, Disclosure, Escrow, Fair Housing, Federal Law, Foreclosure, Homeowners' Associations, Landlord/Tenant, and License Law.

There is a Florida Realtors Legal Hotline which is free to members of the Florida Realtor Association. The hotline number is: **407-438-1409**. Hours for calls are between 9 a.m. - 4:45 p.m., Monday - Friday.

★ **Students of the post-licensing 45-hour course are asked to follow the above links to become familiar with resources available through the site.**

Summary of Recent License Law Changes
Following are significant, applicable changes passed by the Florida Senate/House, Florida Statute, and Florida Administrative Code since 2017. Please review to ensure that you have the most current understanding of the laws:

- **Chapters 196.202, F.S. – Property of widows, widowers, blind persons, and persons totally and permanently disabled, Effective 2023 Ad Valorem Tax Role**
"Increased the additional exemption from $500 to $5,000 of every widow, widower, blind person, or totally and permanently disabled person…"

                                                    https://flsenate.gov/Laws/Statutes/2022/196.202

- **Chapters 553.899, 718.301, and 719, F.S. – Mandatory structural inspections for condominium and cooperative buildings and Seller's Disclosure of Milestone Inspection Report and Structural Integrity Reserve Study, Effective March 20, 2023**

"Some condominiums and cooperatives are subject to providing Milestone Inspection Reports and Structural Integrity Reserve Study. This is in response to the Surfside condominium tragedy and desire for increased structural safety. Also updated Riders/Disclosures include wording to add these documents."

https://flsenate.gov/Laws/Statutes/2022/553.899

- **Chapter 83.53, F.S. – Landlord's access to dwelling unit Effective 01/01/2023, 2021**

"Changed reasonable notice for nonemergency entry into a tenancy from 12 hours to 24 hours. Also related bill increased security measures by requiring apartments to background check employees."

http://www.leg.state.fl.us/statutes/index.cfm?App_mode=Display_Statute&URL=0000-0099/0083/Sections/0083.53.html

- **Executive Order by President Biden –Preventing and Combating Discrimination on the Basis of Gender Identity or Sexual Orientation, Effective January, 2021**

"Based on 2020 Supreme Court Ruling in Bostock v. Clayton County, the order extends Fair Housing prohibition of sex discrimination to include gender identity and sexual orientation."

https://www.whitehouse.gov/briefing-room/presidential-actions/2021/01/20/executive-order-preventing-and-combating-discrimination-on-basis-of-gender-identity-or-sexual-orientation/

- **Florida Bill 615 Professional Regulation --The Occupational Opportunity Act**
  Chapter 2017-135, Laws of Florida Effective July 1, 2017

"Revised the length of time active duty servicemember may remain in good standing with administrative board; requires that spouse or surviving spouse be kept in good standing and be exempt from licensure renewal provisions; requires DBPR to issue professional license to spouse or surviving spouse of active duty member; provides requirements to application, fees, and renewal; provides for a fee waiver for specified persons." See 455.02 F.S. for implementation.

https://www.flsenate.gov/Session/Bill/2017/615

- **455.02 Licensure of members of the Armed Forces in good standing and their spouses or surviving spouses with administrative boards or programs.**

Changed the time of being exempt from continuing education and renewal fees from 6 months after discharge to 2 years after discharge. Plus, spouses of military members serving in Florida who have a real estate license in another state will now be issued a regular license rather than a temporary license:

(1) Any member of the United States Armed Forces now or hereafter on active duty who, at the time of becoming such a member, was in good standing with any of the boards or programs listed in s. 20.165 and was entitled to practice or engage in his or her profession or occupation in the state shall be kept in good standing by the applicable board or program, without registering, paying dues or fees, or performing any other act on his or her part to be performed, as long as he or she is a member of the United States Armed Forces on active duty and for a period of 2 years after discharge from active duty. A member, during active duty and for a period of 2 years after discharge from active duty, engaged in his or her licensed profession or occupation in the private sector for profit in this state must complete all license renewal provisions except remitting the license renewal fee, which shall be waived by the department.

(2) A spouse of a member of the United States Armed Forces who is married to a member during a period of active duty, or a surviving spouse of a member who at the time of death was serving on active duty, who is in good standing with any of the boards or programs listed in s. 20.165 shall be kept in good standing by the applicable board or program as described in subsection (1) and shall be exempt from licensure renewal provisions, but only in cases of his or her absence from the state because of his or her spouse's duties with the United States Armed Forces. The department or the appropriate board or program shall waive any license renewal fee for such spouse when he or she is present in this state because of such member's active duty and for a surviving spouse of a member who at the time of death was serving on active duty and died within the 2 years preceding the date of renewal.

(3)(a) The department shall issue a professional license to an applicant who is or was an active duty member of the Armed Forces of the United States, or who is a spouse or surviving spouse of such member, upon application to the department in a format prescribed by the department. An application must include proof that:

1. The applicant is or was an active duty member of the Armed Forces of the United States or is married to a member of the Armed Forces of the United States and was married to the member during any period of active duty or was married to such a member who at the time of the member's death was serving on active duty. An applicant who was an active duty member of the Armed Forces of the United States must have received an honorable discharge upon separation or discharge from the Armed Forces of the United States.

2. The applicant holds a valid license for the profession issued by another state, the District of Columbia, any possession or territory of the United States, or any foreign jurisdiction.

3. The applicant, where required by the specific practice act, has complied with insurance or bonding requirements.

4.a. A complete set of the applicant's fingerprints is submitted to the Department of Law Enforcement for a statewide criminal history check.

b. The Department of Law Enforcement shall forward the fingerprints submitted pursuant to sub-subparagraph a. to the Federal Bureau of Investigation for a national criminal history check. The department shall, and the board may, review the results of the criminal history checks according to the level 2 screening standards in s. 435.04 and determine whether the applicant meets the licensure requirements. The costs of fingerprint processing shall be borne by the applicant. If the applicant's fingerprints are submitted through an authorized agency or vendor, the agency or vendor shall collect the required processing fees and remit the fees to the Department of Law Enforcement.

(b) The department shall waive the applicant's initial licensure application fee.

(c) An applicant who is issued a license under this section may renew such license upon completion of the conditions for renewal required of licenseholders under the applicable practice act, including, without limitation, continuing education requirements. This paragraph does not limit waiver of initial licensure requirements under this subsection.

History.—s. 2, ch. 21885, 1943; s. 5, ch. 79-36; s. 95, ch. 83-329; s. 1, ch. 84-15; s. 71, ch. 85-81; s, 6, ch. 93-220; s. 186, ch. 97-103; s. 5, ch. 2010-106; s. 4, ch. 2010-182; s. 2, ch. 2017-135; s. 7, ch. 2018-7.

http://www.leg.state.fl.us/Statutes/index.cfm?App_mode=Display_Statute&Search_String=&URL=0400-0499/0455/Sections/0455.02.html

- **61J2-1.011 License Fees and Examinations**

License fees are updated frequently and must be reviewed for current fees by licensees.

https://www.flrules.org/gateway/RuleNo.asp?title=REGISTRATION DETAILS AND FEE STRUCTURE&ID=61J2-1.011

- **61J2-3.008 Pre-licensing Education for Broker and Sales Associate Applicants**

1/17/2019 Changes to this rule has happened several times over the past few years. Recent workshopped changes include clarification about live streaming versus regular online delivery of continuing education courses; clarification that a classroom hour is 50 minutes not 60 minutes and clarification that distance education may involve the internet. There have also been changes about course submission requirements.

https://www.flrules.org/gateway/RuleNo.asp?title=MINIMUM EDUCATIONAL REQUIREMENTS&ID=61J2-3.008

- **61J2-3.009 Continuing Education for Active and Inactive Broker and Sales Associate Licensees**

12/27/2018, clarified changes to continuing education requirements adding a requirement for an ethics component. "Licensees must take the 3-hour Core Law course once during each renewal period. A licensee who takes the 3-hour Core Law course in each year of the renewal period shall be allowed a total of 3 hours of Core Law education and 3 hours of specialty education toward the 14 hour requirement. Real estate licensees who hold a license that expires on September 30, 2018, or thereafter, must also take the 3-hour Business Ethics course once during each licensure renewal period. A licensee who takes the 3-hour Business Ethics course in each year of the renewal period shall be allowed a total of 3 hours of Business Ethics and 3 hours of specialty education toward the 14 hour requirement. Licensees who complete the Core Law course and Business Ethics course will receive 6 hours credit toward the 14 hour requirement. The "specialty" course hours must total at least 8 hours."

https://www.flrules.org/gateway/RuleNo.asp?title=MINIMUM EDUCATIONAL REQUIREMENTS&ID=61J2-3.009

- **61J2-3.011: Continuing Education for School Instructors**

12/11/2019, along with other changes from 2012, provided for distance continuing education for real estate instructors and added a required provision for instruction on teaching methods altering the requirement hours of continuing education for instructors.

https://www.flrules.org/gateway/RuleNo.asp?title=MINIMUM EDUCATIONAL REQUIREMENTS&ID=61J2-3.011

- **61J2-3.012 Equivalency for Pre-licensing Education**

12/24/2017, clarified that someone with a "higher" education than a bachelor's degree in real estate also qualifies as being exempt from pre-licensing courses.

https://www.flrules.org/gateway/RuleNo.asp?title=MINIMUM%20EDUCATIONAL%20REQUIREMENTS&ID=61J2-3.012

- **61J2-3.020 Post-licensing Education for Active and Inactive Broker and Sales Associate Licensees**

03/25/2018, this rules provided language clarifying between providers and schools for course submissions. It clarified provided clarification of the 50 minute class hour (Also see 475.17 F.S.) It clarified the requirement to provide material and delivery mechanism for approval requests for live streaming courses. It removed the requirement for having to wait 30 days when failed a 45 hour post-licensing course. It added clarification that if the first exam is failed, retest must be taken "within one year of the original examination."

https://www.flrules.org/gateway/RuleNo.asp?title=MINIMUM%20EDUCATIONAL%20REQUIREMENTS&ID=61J2-3.020

- **61J2-10.026 Team or Group Advertising**

07/01/2019, this added rule puts requirements in place for team or group advertising to ensure that the public understands the broker that is legally responsible. It was implemented to stop confusion by the public that teams were the broker. The rule is as follows:

(1) "Team or group advertising" shall mean a name or logo used by one or more real estate licensees who represent themselves to the public as a team or group. The team or group must perform licensed activities under the supervision of the same broker or brokerage.

(2) Each team or group shall file with the broker a designated licensee to be responsible for ensuring that the advertising is in compliance with chapter 475, Florida Statutes, and division 61J2, Florida Administrative Code.

(3) At least once monthly, the registered broker must maintain a current written record of each team's or group's members.

(4) Team or group names. Real estate team or group names may include the word "team" or "group" as part of the name. Real estate team or group names shall not include the following words:

(a) Agency	(h) Inc.
(b) Associates	(i) LLC
(c) Brokerage	(j) LP, LLP or Partnership
(d) Brokers	(k) Properties
(e) Company	(l) Property
(f) Corporation	(m) Real Estate
(g) Corp.	(n) Realty

(o) Or similar words suggesting the team or group is a separate real estate brokerage or company

(5) This rule applies to all advertising.

(6) In advertisements containing the team or group name, the team or group name shall not be in larger print than the name of the registered brokerage. All advertising must be in a manner in which reasonable persons would know they are dealing with a team or group.

(7) All advertisements must comply with these requirements no later than July 1, 2019.

Nothing in this rule shall relieve the broker of their legal obligations under chapter 475, Florida Statutes, and division 61J2, Florida Administrative Code.

https://www.flrules.org/gateway/RuleNo.asp?title=OPERATION,%20BUSINESS%20AND%20OFFICES&ID=61J2-10.026

- **61J2-24.002 Citation Authority**

02/11/2019 and 2/11/2019, updated text including that this rule added wording for violation of newly added rule regarding teams and group advertising 61J2-10.026. "Rule 61J2-10.026, F.A.C. – failed to follow the requirements for team or group advertising; a citation shall only be issued for a second violation of the rule committed after July 1, 2019. --$500.

https://www.flrules.org/gateway/RuleNo.asp?title=DISCIPLINARY%20MATTERS&ID=61J2-24.002

- **61J2-24.003 Notice of Noncompliance**

02/11/2019 and 2/11/2019, corrected wording and this rule added wording for violation of newly added rule regarding teams and group advertising 61J2-10.026. "(o) Rule 61J2-10.026, F.A.C. – for a first violation, failure to adhere to team advertising requirements after July 1, 2019. (2) The DBPR shall issue a notice of noncompliance to the licensee, registrant or permitholder subject to the statute and rule that the statute and rule have been violated."

https://www.flrules.org/gateway/RuleNo.asp?title=DISCIPLINARY%20MATTERS&ID=61J2-24.003

- **61J2-24.003 Disciplinary Matters**

11/02/2021, this rule clarified handling of ending of probation.

https://www.flrules.org/gateway/RuleNo.asp?title=DISCIPLINARY%20MATTERS&ID=61J2-24.006

- **61J2-10.025 Advertising**

08/16/2021, add wording to emphasize that the Internet is included for rules of advertising.

https://www.flrules.org/gateway/RuleNo.asp?title=OPERATION,%20BUSINESS%20AND%20OFFICES&ID=61J2-10.025

- **61J2-24 Disciplinary Matters**

03/02/2023, increased fees and fines and updated notice changes.

https://www.flrules.org/gateway/ChapterHome.asp?Chapter=61J2-24

12 ETHICS AND BUSINESS PRACTICES

- Administrative Penalties of Unethical Behavior
- Business Ethics
- Civil Penalties of Unethical Behavior
- Company Policies
- Customer Feedback
- Discipline within NAR
- Duties to Clients
- Duties to Customers
- Duties to Public
- Duties to Real Estate Licensees
- Ethical Standards

Learning Terms and Phrase

- Legal Penalties of Unethical Behavior
- NAR Code of Ethics
- National Association of Realtors®
- Procuring Cause
- Real Estate Recovery Fund
- REALTOR®
- Reputation Management
- Social Entrepreneurship
- Unethical Behavior

Learning Objectives

- Licensees should be able to identify the importance of business ethics and the impact of managing online reputations.
- Licensees should be able to identify how unethical behavior puts the public at risk within the real estate industry.
- Licensees should be able to identify when subjected to the tenants of the National Association of REALTORS® versus basic business ethics.
- Licensees should be able to apply the concept of cooperation among REALTORS® versus professional behavior among all agents.
- Licensees should be able to apply the concept of honesty in dealing with others based on REALTORS® Code.
- Licensees should be able to apply the concept of competence in providing real estate services verses just being legally able to do so.
- Licensees should understand the legal consequences of unethical behavior.

Application of Business Ethics

Business ethics and the application of ethics within business practices is a form of professional conduct based on principles and morals. It applies to the entire scope of business dealings and involves the conduct of all individuals within an organization ranging from ownership and top management to entry level held positions. Following is a presentation of ethics and the application of ethical practices – specifically within the real estate field.

Rules and Standards of Behavior

Every day, an individual's behavior is governed by rules and standards that have been adopted. Following ethical behavior is considered to be a conscious choice. Individuals are confronted continually with the possibility of committing an act that would be considered either the right thing to do or the wrong thing to do based on standards of conduct.

Some believe that the actual choice to follow ethical conduct is ruled by an instinctive act to do so. And that even without external forces, the majority of individuals would choose to do well. Others believe that the decision to follow ethical behavior is driven instead by the knowledge of consequences which have been ingrained into each person by external forces.

Influence from the family and friends are considered to be the first and primary external force. Religious and educational influences are formed next. With community standards and laws following. Business company conduct along with professional organizations forms the last influences for many individuals.

Business Ethics. October 2016. https://en.wikipedia.org/wiki/Business_ethics

Law versus Ethics

Law and Ethics do not always converge. Just because something is legal does not mean that it is ethical. And just because something is unethical does not mean that it is illegal. In theory, law and ethics would line up and reflect the other. When laws are passed, it is based on the ethical foundation of acceptable behavior. Yet, across a small group of people – what is considered "acceptable behavior" can vary widely.

One only needs to look at the abortion debate to understand this possible dichotomy. Those who stand for the Right to Life movement lobby for different laws than those who stand for the Right to Choice movement. Each group believes that their views are backed by ethics.

Ethical Standards Change Over Time

What is considered to be ethical behavior is not static. Instead, a person's behavior should be judged within the dated society that the person existed. For example, there is currently a trend within the United States to discredit certain forefathers based on the fact that they owned slaves. Indeed, compared to modern day ethics, the owning of slaves is considered abhorrent. Yet, within the time period of the birth of United States, it was considered ethical behavior. Or was it? As even within that time period there were those that viewed the practice as wrong and fought against it! It was the very fight against the practice which led to the change of ethical standard within society and ultimately affected the law.

Business Ethics. October 2016. https://en.wikipedia.org/wiki/Business_ethics

Ethical Practices with Individual Businesses

It is important for individual businesses to incorporate ethical practices into the business. This can set the business apart in being viewed as a good company among consumers and employees. Being known as a good company helps to maintain relationships allowing the company to grow and to meet business goals. Customer loyalty developed from ethical business practices means repeat business from the same customers and new business when loyal customers refer a business to someone else.

The Value of Strong Ethical Business Practices and Social Responsibility. By Audra Bianca. October 2016. http://smallbusiness.chron.com/value-strong-ethical-business-practices-social-responsibility-24231.html

Company Policies of Practice

Standards of practice do not happen haphazardly and require consistent follow through in monitoring the behavior of all employees within the company. This may include clearly communicating expectations for standards of practice within company manuals, companywide mandatory training which encompasses expectations of ethical conduct, and creating an environment where employees feel that they can report unethical behavior of other employees without fear of repercussions.

The Value of Strong Ethical Business Practices and Social Responsibility. By Audra Bianca. October 2016. http://smallbusiness.chron.com/value-strong-ethical-business-practices-social-responsibility-24231.html

Reputation Management

Customer loyalty and trust can be enhanced when a company makes policies and practices public by including standards within marketing literature and also by publishing standards of practice on company websites. The result of consistently following ethics in business is seen in a strong business reputation which becomes part of the brand associated with the company. Brand loyalty is the goal. Regardless of the type of business being conducted, standing out from the competition becomes easier with a solid reputation.

Even one incident can affect a brand when that incident becomes part of public awareness. If anyone representing the company makes the appearance of unethical behavior in a transaction, the damage can be far reaching. Today's business environment involves a degree of reputation management through social media. Someone is twice more likely to share about a bad experience through online networks than if the experience had been positive.

Customer Feedback

Businesses must be careful to monitor comments that mention their company to try to manage them. Often, by reaching out to individuals who have had a bad experience, the negative comments will be removed or altered.

Businesses must be proactive with presenting a positive company image by encouraging customers with positives interactions to share about it online. And whenever the company participates in outreach activities with the community, these activities should be shared to demonstrate an ongoing commitment to society.

Bad Customer Service Interactions More Likely to be Shared Than Good Ones. By Marketing Charts Staff. October 2016. http://www.marketingcharts.com/online/bad-customer-service-interactions-more-likely-to-be-shared-than-good-ones-28628/

Students of the post-licensing 45-hour course are encouraged to examine their own online business profiles to check for negative comments and to reach out to individuals to request reviews.

Social Entrepreneurship

Some businesses take the concept of ethical business practices to the level of social entrepreneurship. The idea of being a social entrepreneur involves developing a business that specifically works to meeting or solving a social problem. Even *for-profit* companies can take on the goal of social entrepreneurship. However, while traditional for-profit companies generally use metrics of revenues and stocks to measure success; social entrepreneurs broaden the definition of success to include improvement in community issues.

Social Entrepreneurship. October 2016. https://en.wikipedia.org/wiki/Social_entrepreneurship

Ethical Practices within Business Industry

The opposite of developing a good reputation is developing a bad reputation. Bad reputations developed by one company can spill over to other companies causing a bad reputation within the business industry as a whole. Take, for example, the reputation of "used car salesmen." For years, the industry of selling used cars has been plagued by the unethical practices of a few. The remaining companies who practice good standards of behavior are often left scrambling to stand out from the bad.

Ethical Practices within Associations

In an effort to elevate the reputation of an industry as a whole, industry associations are often formed that adopt strict standards of behavior which members must follow. One of the goals of associations is that by banding together and advertising the standards that the public will trust businesses that belong to reputable associations.

Bad Behavior within the Real Estate Industry

The real estate industry is another type of business that once suffered from an overall bad reputation. This stemmed from the fact that before licensing laws, the practice of real estate was basically a free for all in behavior. Most people selling real estate were not licensed or simply licensed as "peddlers."

★ Students of the post-licensing 45-hour course are encouraged to view the following video which demonstrates how unscrupulous sales behavior in real estate can take advantage of buyers: https://youtu.be/EIvjz2X-Kok

National Association of REALTORS

The National Association of Realtors®, NAR, was established in 1908. In 1913, a full decade before the Florida Senate passed real estate licensing laws, the National Association of Realtors® made moves to bring standards to the real estate industry through the adoption of a Code of Ethics. Real Estate agents that join the National Association of Realtors and become REALTORS® are held to a standard of conduct established by the Code of Ethics. The Code of Ethics establishes obligations that may be higher than those mandated by state laws, "and in any instance where the Code of Ethics and the law conflict, the obligations of the law must take precedence" - per the Code.

National Association of REALTORS. October 2016.
https://en.wikipedia.org/wiki/National_Association_of_Realtors

Required NAR Ethics Training

REALTORS® are required to complete ethics training of not less than 2 hours, 30 minutes of instructional time within four-year cycles. The training must meet specific learning objectives and criteria established by the National Association of REALTORS®. The National Association of Realtors, referred to as NAR, has a voluntary membership of brokers who can then refer to themselves as "Realtors®" and sales associates and broker associates who can then refer to themselves as "Realtor-Associates®." Nar is the largest trade association in North America.

There is a difference in being a real estate licensee and a Realtor®. The only people that are allowed to use the designation as Realtor® with their names are licensees that belong to the National Association of Realtors®. Real estate licensee who choose to become members of NAR can find the required Code of Ethics training at: http://www.realtor.org/code-of-ethics/training

★ Students of the post-licensing 45-hour course are instructed to read the NAR Code of Ethics which can be found: http://www.realtor.org/sites/default/files/policies/2016/2016-NAR-Code-of-Ethics.pdf

Use of the Term REALTOR®

As stated, only members of NAR are allowed to refer to themselves as REALTORS®. The term is reserved for real estate brokers who are members of NAR. The concept of REALTOR® was first brought forth by Charles N. Chadbourn in 1916. He proposed that the word REALTORS® be adopted as a means to differentiate members of NAR from licensees who had opted not to join the association. The term REALTORS® was made an official legal trademark protected by U.S. registry office in 1949. The term REALTOR® was registered in 1950. Other variations have also been trademarked.

Three attempts have been made to try to get term REALTOR® unprotected. The most recent attempt was March 2015, when Jeffrey Schermerhorn petitioned to have the trademark cancelled based on the fact that it had become a generic term. He lost his bid based on the fact that he, himself, was a member of the National Association of REALTORS®.

FLORIDA REAL ESTATE 45-HOUR COURSE COMPANION

National Association of REALTORS. October 2016.
https://en.wikipedia.org/wiki/National_Association_of_Realtors

REALTOR® Code of Ethics

The basis of the Code of Ethics is to protect the public. With the Code preceding Florida state real estate law, many of the premises of the Code were incorporated into law. Yet, whenever there is a conflict between the Code and Florida law, law prevails. There are four sections in the REALTORS® Code of Ethics: Preamble, Duties to Clients and Customer, Duties to the Public, and Duties to REALTORS®.

Preamble – Training Among REALTORS®

The preamble begins by stressing the importance to our society of encouraging property ownership. "Under all is the land. Upon its wise utilization and widely allocated ownership depend the survival and growth of free institutions and of our civilization."

And because the promotion of property ownership is of such high importance, REALTORS® must be diligent in training and in following standards. The industry is constantly changing and REALTORS® must participate in ongoing educational efforts to remain abreast of the best ways to represent the public. REALTORS® must hold other individuals accountable who appear to be engage in unethical behavior.

Preamble – Cooperation Among REALTORS®

The preamble sets the tone for cooperation among licensees: "Realizing that cooperation with other real estate professionals promotes the best interests of those who utilize their services, Realtors® urge exclusive representation of clients; do not attempt to gain any unfair advantage over their competitors; and they refrain from making unsolicited comments about other practitioners."

★ **Students of the post-licensing 45-hour course are instructed to do the following exercise:**

> What would you do if…
> You go to a listing appointment and you find out that the sellers are also talking with another real estate agent in town that you have had conflict with in the past. The sellers are trying to decide whether to list with that agent or to list with you. Which of the following statements would be in accordance with the preamble "do not attempt to gain any unfair advantage over their competitors; and they refrain from making unsolicited comments about other practitioners?"
>
> A. I know that agent. He is a horrible person! Listing with him would be a huge mistake because he has a terrible reputation!
>
> B. I appreciate the fact that you are looking for the agent that will do the best job for you. I can assure you that I have the track record to take good care of you. If you like, we can pull my sales statistics and compare them with the other agent.
>
> B is clearly the correct choice. It is against the Code of Ethics to make disparaging remarks about another agent. However, providing factual information is appropriate.

Preamble - The Golden Rule

The preamble concludes with the Golden Rule: "Whatsoever ye would that others should do to you, do ye even so to them."

Duties to Clients and Customers – Article 1

Article 1 – 9 address REALTORS® Duties to Clients and Customers. With Article 1 setting the tone for putting the public first: "When representing a buyer, seller, landlord, tenant, or other client as an agent, Realtors® pledge themselves to protect and promote the interests of their client. This obligation to the client is primary, but it does not relieve Realtors® of their obligation to treat all parties honestly. When serving a buyer, seller, landlord, tenant or other party in a non-agency capacity, Realtors® remain obligated to treat all parties honestly."

Client or Customer

The difference between a Client and a Customer is a significant issue for real estate licensees to understand. Not all work done for buyers and sellers constitute the creation of an agency relationship. The distinction between the two roles can blur together legally. A client in common language often refers to a principal who is in a binding contractual relationship with a broker obligating the broker to act in an agency capacity. This relationship is often created through a formal Buyer Representation Agreement or a Listing Agreement.

Be aware, however, that even without a formal agency agreement; a broker (and the licensee) can be held accountable for an agency relationship that was created through the implication of the actions taken by the licensee or broker. A customer, in common language, is when the broker provides a limited task for the buyer or seller. Customers must be treated honestly and fairly.

Duties to Clients and Customers – Article 2

Article 2 continues to set the tone for honesty in transactions: "Realtors® shall avoid exaggeration, misrepresentation, or concealment of pertinent facts relating to the property or the transaction. Realtors® shall not, however, be obligated to discover latent defects in the property, to advise on matters outside the scope of their real estate license, or to disclose facts which are confidential under the scope of agency or non-agency relationships as defined by state law."

★ **Students of the post-licensing 45-hour course are instructed to do the following exercise:**

> What would you do if...
> You go to a listing appointment and the seller tells you that he is replacing wall board in the bathroom the hide the fact that there is a slow leak?
>
> A. You inform the seller that he must either repair the leak properly or disclose to any potential buyers that the leak exists. Otherwise, you will not be able to list his home.
> B. You aggressively price the home hoping to get it sold quickly before the water stains can resurface. Plus, you avoid representing buyers yourself so that you can avoid having to tell the buyer anything about the leak.
>
> A is the correct choice. "Realtors® shall avoid ... concealment of pertinent facts relating to the property..." regardless of whether you are representing the party.

Duties to Clients and Customers – Article 3

Article 3 addresses the need for REALTORS® to cooperate with other brokers unless to do so is contrary to the best interest of the client. Note, however, that cooperation is not a guarantee of commission sharing.

Generally, the more exposure a property gets, the more likely that the seller will get a good offer of purchase for the property. Article 3, follows this premise. As such, Standard of Practice 3-8- under Article 3, for example; details that REALTORS® should not misrepresent the availability of property for showing. And Standard of Practice 3-10 details the obligation to share details about property information.

★ **Students of the post-licensing 45-hour course are instructed to do the following exercise:**

> What would you do if...
> You have a buyer coming into town in two days that you think will love a property that you have listed. You are excited because you are hoping to be able to keep all of the commission by representing both the seller and the buyer in a sale. In the meantime, another real estate agent has called and requested to show the property the next day.
>
> A. You inform the other agent that the house is not available to show for three days.
> B. You set up the showing as the agent requested.
>
> B is the correct choice. To not set up the showing, the listing agent could find him or herself in breach of contract. As it is the agent's duty to represent the seller to the best of his ability. And postponing the showing could actually harm the seller...also making it unethical.

Duties to Clients and Customers – Article 4

Article 4 addresses the issue of licensees who wish to purchase property for themselves or who are assisting family members. Whenever this is the case, it is imperative that the licensee disclose the fact of the relationship or that he or she is a licensed agent. The idea behind this is that the holding of a real estate license gives the licensee knowledge that can create an unfair negotiating advantage over the other party. So, the license and/or the relationship must be disclosed.

Duties to Clients and Customers – Articles 5 - 9

Article 5 requires that a licensee disclose if the licensee has or has had interest in the property. Article 6 addresses the need to fully disclose when receiving fees for referring other types of services to your real estate client. Article 7 requires disclosure to all parties when being compensated by either or both. Article 8 requires that client's monies be held in escrow accounts. Article 9 involves the need to make sure that all contracts are clear and concise representing the client's actual intention in the creation of the contracts.

Duties to the Public – Articles 10 – 14

Article 10 makes it clear that a REALTOR® should not engage in discriminatory practices. Article 11 addresses the issue of needing to be competent in the services being offered to a buyer or seller. Article 12 requires licensees to include their license status whenever they advertise property or real estate services. Article 13 is a reminder to take care not to cross the line into the unlicensed practice of law. And Article 14 mandates that if an ethics charge is brought against a REALTOR®, that he or she will aid in facilitating the investigation rather than blocking it.

⭐ **Students of the post-licensing 45-hour course are instructed to do the following exercise:**

> What would you do if...
> You are a fairly new licensee and have been focused on training to sell residential property. While out for dinner at a restaurant you have been frequenting for years, you overhear the restaurant owner state that she wants to sell the restaurant. You have no idea how to sell a business, but when you tell her you have your real estate license; the owner announces that as her best customer - that of course you can list the business for sale.
>
> A. You agree to list the property and then immediately go to your broker for help who matches you up to co-list the business with an agent that specializes in selling restaurants.
> B. You pretend that you know what you are doing and forge ahead alone with the listing.
>
> A is the correct choice. Although licensed to sell businesses, as a real estate licensee not having the knowledge or skills to do so would make taking the listing unaided unethical.

Duties to REALTORS® – Article 4

Article 15 warns against making false statements or bringing false ethics charges against another REALTOR®. Article 16 addresses the need to honor exclusive listing or buyer representation agreements held by other REALTORS®. And Article 17 dictates that REALTORS® will not sue each other in court but rather use mediation or arbitration channels available through their local or state associations.

⭐ **Students of the post-licensing 45-hour course are instructed to do the following exercise:**

> What would you do if...
> You are a fairly new licensee who has joined the National Association of Realtors®. You realize that your neighbor's house has just been listed by a competing Realtor®. You are sure that your neighbor would have listed with you had they known that you had just gotten your license.
>
> A. When you see your neighbor, you mention your real estate license and tell them that you hope to bring them a buyer and wish them luck with the sale of the home.
> B. You knock on your neighbor's door and tell him that if he cancels the listing with the other broker that you will only charge half as much commission.
>
> A is the correct choice. As both licensees are REALTORS®, it is against the Code of Ethics to solicit a listing already being represented by another REALTOR®. This does not prevent you from going after the listing if it fails to sell.

Commission Disputes

Recall that agreement to cooperate between licensees is not an agreement to be compensated. When a property is listed within the Multiple Listing Service, the listing agent includes the amount of commission that will be paid to an agent who closes the sale representing the buyer.

If a licensee is not a member of the MLS, the licensee should obtain a separate agreement from the broker that a commission or fee will be paid. Otherwise, the listing real estate broker would be under no obligation to compensate the licensee's broker even if that licensee had brought the buyer to the deal and represented the buyer through closing!

Procuring Cause

Cases brought to local or state REALTOR® associations requiring mediation or arbitration involve either conduct charges from another REALTOR® or monetary disputes involving the payment of commission between REALTORS®. Cases among REALTORS® involving commission disputes are resolved by following the REALTOR® rules of Procuring Cause. The concept of procuring cause is rooted in the courts based on resolving contract issues. To earn a commission a broker (or sales associate or broker associate working on behalf of the broker) must prove that they initiated an unbroken chain of events that led to the sale. The ambiguity of the definition of procuring cause results in many cases seeming muddled as to who actually has earned the commission. In those cases, it is up to the hearing panel to make a decision as to which agent has earned the commission.

Discipline within NAR

Consequences of an ethics charge within the National Association of REALTORS® may result in one or a combination of the following: letter of warning, letter of reprimand, education, fines of up to $15,000, probation for up to one year, suspension from membership between 30 days and a year, expulsion from membership for between one to three years, and suspension or termination of MLS Privileges.

Ethics Beyond NAR

It is common in Florida for real estate licensees to hold active real estate licenses without also being a member of the National Association of Realtors. According to the Association of Florida Realtors, they have approximately 155,000 members. (Licensees sign up for the Florida Association of Realtors at the same time as the National Association of Realtors.) With more than 350,000 real estate licensees in Florida, that means that approximately 56% are NOT members of NAR.

This means that 56% of licensees are not required to participate in the Ethics training courses mandated for members of NAR. Because of this absence of ethics training for 56% of licensees, beginning October 1, 2017; all licensees must take 3-hours of Ethics and Business Practices training as part of the 14-hour continuing education requirement.

Ethics and the Law

Real estate licensees that are NOT members of NAR should not consider themselves relieved of the duty of ethical behavior. In fact, the opposite is true. Real estate law was shaped by the Code of Ethics. The code existed first. So, when lawmakers decided to regulate the real estate industry, they looked to the Code of Ethics. This is particularly true with issues that directly affect the public, customers and clients, and actual real estate transactions. (Not particularly true regarding the Code that address competition among agents.)

Let's revisit the scenario where the seller was planning to hide a plumbing leak. Should the listing agent have gone along with the plan, not only would the agent have been breaking the code of ethics, the agent would have been breaking license law. According to Florida Statute 475, licensees must ALWAYS disclose material defects about a property and deal all parties fairly and honestly!

Violating the Code of Ethics Can Get You Sued. By Larry Lowenthal. October 2016.
http://www.hg.org/article.asp?id=26904

Legal Consequences of Unethical Behavior

If a real estate licensee acts in an unethical manner that directly affects the public regarding a real estate transaction, the licensee is likely to be found guilty of breaking license law. There are three types of penalties that can be imposed for violation of license law.

Administrative penalties include FREC suspending a license, imposing fines, and revoking licenses. Civil penalties which are handled in civil court and include the public suing the licensee and/or broker for monetary damages. Criminal penalties which are handled in criminal court, often with a referral from FREC, and include possible prison sentences for license law violations. *Note: FREC does not have to power to imprison individuals!*

Administrative Penalties

Per Florida Statutes 475, The Florida Real Estate Commission is authorized to:

- deny an application for licensure, registration, or permit, or renewal thereof;
- place a licensee, registrant, or permittee on probation;
- suspend a license, registration, or permit for a period not exceeding 10 years;
- revoke a license, registration, or permit;
- impose an administrative fine not to exceed $5,000 for each count or separate offense;
- issue a reprimand,
- and any or all of the foregoing.

Denial of License:

If a license is denied, the DBPR mails a copy of the order to the applicant by registered or certified mail. The applicant has 21 days from date of receipt to request a hearing with FREC to dispute the denial.

Revoke without Prejudice

Per Florida Statutes 475.25, "a license may be revoked or canceled if it was issued through the mistake or inadvertence of the commission." The individual may reapply for a license.

Issuance of Citations

The DBPR/DRE has the authority to issue citations for minor violations. The licensee has 30 days to accept or reject the penalty. The penalty involved with a citation are fines from $100 to $500 per infraction. Additional education could also be placed on the licensee. See Administrative Code 61J2-24.02 for a complete list under Citation Authority.

Issuance of Fines

Per Florida Statutes 475.25, FREC may impose an administrative fine not to exceed $5,000 for each count or separate offense.

Impose Probation

Per Administrative Code 61J2-24.006, FREC may place the licensee on probation. Generally, probation will last 90 days with the probation period to begin 30 days after the filing of the final order.

Civil Penalties

If someone feels that they have been harmed by a licensee, they may sue the licensee in court and seek a civil remedy such as compensatory and punitive damages. This action may be taken in addition to or in place of reporting the licensee for administrative action.

Criminal Penalties for Certain License Law Violations

A licensee may also face criminal penalties depending upon the nature of infraction. Criminal penalties range as follows:

    Third-degree felony   = $5,000 fine and up to 5 years in prison
    First-degree misdemeanor   = $1,000 fine and up to 1 year in prison
    Second-degree misdemeanor = $500 fine and up to 60 days in jail

Criminal Violations Compared

The unlicensed practice of real estate (practicing real estate with a license resulting from a falsified application)
- Third-degree Felony

Selling a rental list that is inaccurate
- First-Degree Misdemeanor

Just about every other violation you may be asked about
- Second-Degree Misdemeanor

Legal Consequences

FREC may only refer suspicion of criminal activity to the judicial system.

FREC MAY NOT impose prison sentences!

Florida Real Estate Recovery Fund

If civil penalties are pursued by a member of the public and the licensee loses the case, the licensee would have to pay the plaintiff money as required by the judge in the case. Should the licensee fail to do so, the plaintiff could make a claim against The Florida Real Estate Recovery Fund. The plaintiff can collect up to $50,000.00 for a single case of misconduct. Court costs and attorney fees can be reimbursed as well as actual money lost. Punitive damages, treble damages, and interest cannot be paid from the fund. The payout from the fund results in immediate suspension of the license until the licensee has paid back the amount paid by the fund, plus interest.

F.S. 475.482

⭐ **Students of the post-licensing 45-hour course are instructed to do the following exercise:**

> What would you do if...
> You were working as a buyer's agent and ended up being sued in court by the buyer and lost. The judge awarded the buyer a total of $25,000 plus $5,000 in court and attorney fees. Unfortunately, you didn't have the money to pay the buyer.
> A. Nothing. If you don't have the money, you don't have it!
> B. If the buyer seeks the settlement from the Real Estate Recovery Fund, your license would be suspended until you were able to pay back the $30,000 plus interest.
>
> B is the correct choice. The buyer could receive up to $50,000 in settlement from the fund.

13 FAIR HOUSING APPLIED

<u>Learning Terms and Phrases</u>

- Civil Rights Act Application
- Jones Vs. Mayer
- Fair Housing Act Application
- Familial Status
- Handicap Status
- Discriminatory Advertising
- Steering
- Blockbusting
- Redlining
- Housing for Older Persons Act Application
- Florida Fair Housing Act Application
- Reasonable Accommodations
- Reasonable Modifications
- Multi-Family Housing
- Florida Residential Landlord and Tenant
- Landlord Access to Property
- Notice to Cancel Lease
- Eviction
- Broker Property Management
- Advance Rent

Learning Objectives

- Licensees should be able to identify the groups protected under Fair Housing Laws and apply it to common situations.
- Licensees should be able to identify when exemptions to Fair Housing Laws do and do not apply.
- Licensees should be able to apply the housing provisions allowed for religious groups and private clubs.
- Licensees should be able to recognize the illegal act of steering and understand how to avoid it in the practice of real estate.
- Licensees should be able to correctly apply the Americans with Disabilities Act to real estate situations.
- Licensees should be able to correctly apply landlord and tenant protections provided under the law.

The Importance of Fair Housing

Being mindful of fair housing laws through the course of practicing real estate is not only the right thing to do, it can actually keep a licensee's career intact and keep the licensee out of jail! Rights under fair housing is protected by Federal and State Laws. It is important for a licensee to not just know the law, but to understand how to apply it in actual practice.

Civil Rights Act of 1866

Civil rights laws that affect real estate date back to 1866 when the Civil Rights Act of 1866 was passed. The act makes it illegal to discriminate in the sale or leasing of real estate (housing) based on race – without exception.

- **Jones v. Alfred H. Mayer Co:** The Supreme Court upheld in the case *Jones v. Mayer* that the Civil Rights Act of 1866 made discrimination based on race unlawful. This is true whether within the public or private housing domain.

Students of the post-licensing 45-hour course are instructed to do the following exercise:

> What would you do if…
> You are a real estate licensee who has agreed to sell a property. The home is owned by an older Caucasian woman who has heard in the news that homeownership for non-Caucasian people is down in her area. This concerns her greatly, so she tells you that she will only consider an offer from someone who isn't white – so that she can make a contribution to create a more equitable society.
>
> A. You tell her that you are very impressed with her awareness of social issues and that you will do your best to help!
>
> B. You explain that although you appreciate that she is well intentioned, due to the Civil Rights Act of 1866, it is illegal to discriminate in the sale of a home to *anyone based on race*.
>
> B is the correct choice. Although the Civil Rights Act of 1866 resulted from discrimination against non-Caucasian people, the language of the law protects everyone. Also, the exemptions in place under the Fair Housing Act of 1968 never applies to race due to the Civil Rights Act of 1866.

Civil Rights Act of 1968 – Fair Housing Act

Title VIII of the Civil Rights Act of 1968 is referred to as the Fair Housing Act as it expanded the 1964 Civil Rights Act to prohibit discrimination in the **sale, rental, and financing of housing** based on race, religion, national origin, and since the 1974 Amendment- gender; and since the 1988 Amendments - the act protects people with disabilities and families with children. Based on Title VIII, discrimination is illegal in sales, leasing, advertising sales or rentals, financing, or brokerage services if based on:

- Race
- Color
- Religion
- National origin
- Sex (as amended in 1974)*
- Familial Status (as amended in 1988)
- Handicap Status (as amended in 1988)

Civil Rights Act of 1968 – Fair Housing Act
- Race
- Color
- Religion
- National origin
- Sex (as amended in 1974)
- Familial Status (as amended in 1988)
- Handicap Status (as amended in 1988)

*See final note in chapter regarding Executive Order by President Biden affecting definition of Sex

Definition of Familial Status Protection

Protection from discrimination based on familial status means that under United States law **24 CFR 100.20**, one or more individuals (who have not attained the age of 18 years) living together cannot be discriminated against. This protection extends to someone who is pregnant or in the process of getting custody.

Definition of Handicap Status Protection

Protection from discrimination based on handicap status means that under the United States law 24 CFR 100.201, anyone with a physical or mental impairment which substantially limits one or more major life activities cannot be discriminated against, including persons recovering from alcoholism and drug addiction.

There are two categories of housing covered by the 1968 Fair Housing Act:
  (1) Single-family
  (2) Multifamily

If it is a **Single-family house** and
- Government owned housing or
- Privately owned if real estate agent is employed to sell or rent it or
- Property owned by person who owns four or more residential properties total or
- If someone has sold two or more houses (not owner-occupied) in the past 2 years

… then requires compliance with the act.

If it is **multi-family/unit housing** and
- Has five (5) or more units or
- Has four (4) or fewer units (when the owner doesn't live in one of the units)

… then requires compliance with the act.

Real estate transactions exempt under the Fair Housing Act:
- If the seller owns three or fewer single-family dwellings or
- If the seller was not living in the house and was not the most recent resident when the property was sold or rented, still allowed one exempt sale within a 24-month period or
- For rentals in multi-family dwellings with four or fewer family units when the owner lives in one of the units or

… then exempt from Fair Housing ACT **if ALSO a real estate agent was not involved in the sale or lease and there was no discriminatory advertising involved.**

★ **Students of the post-licensing 45-hour course are instructed to do the following exercise:**

> What would you do if...
> You are a real estate licensee who has agreed to do property management for a female duplex property owner. The owner lives in the second unit and tells you that she is very nervous around men. Therefore, she wants you to rent it to a woman. It doesn't matter whether the female tenant has children.
>
> A. You tell the owner that she is in luck! Because she lives in the other side of the duplex, the owner is legally allowed to limit who lives in the other unit.
> B. You explain to the owner that using the services of a real estate agent to rent the property means that she may NOT discriminate based on sex per the Fair Housing Act.
>
> B is the correct choice. Although the owner lives in the other unit, using the services of a real estate agent means that the exemptions under Fair Housing Act DO NOT APPLY. Although the owner might be tempted to just rent out the property without using an agent; the owner should also be advised that advertising the property to just women would also be a Fair Housing violation.

Housing Operated by Religious Organizations and Private Clubs

Sometimes clubs and churches will offer housing exclusively to their members. This is legal under limited circumstances. Religious organizations may restrict units to members of their religion **provided** they do not discriminate in accepting membership. Private clubs may restrict units to its members **provided** they do not discriminate in accepting membership.

★ **Students of the post-licensing 45-hour course are instructed to do the following exercise:**

> What would you do if...
> You are a real estate licensee who is representing a buyer who wants to buy property in an exclusive golf course community. Your buyer becomes upset when he finds out that he has to be a member of the golf club to purchase the home. Your buyer, who happens to be Hispanic, claims that this is discriminatory practice.
>
> A. You explain to the owner that as long as the club does not discriminate in who they allow to join the club, then this is a legal practice.
> B. You agree with buyer and encourage them to file charges against the seller and the club.
>
> A is the correct choice. Religious organizations and private clubs may restrict units to members **provided** they do not discriminate in accepting membership

Fair Housing Act - Acts Prohibited
    (1) Refusing to rent
    (2) Quoting different terms
    (3) Discriminatory advertising
    (4) Steering
    (5) Blockbusting
    (6) Redlining
    (7) Denying membership
    (8) False statements regarding availability

Discriminatory Advertising

As clarified by the U.S. Department of Housing and Urban Development, "it is unlawful to make, print, or publish any statement, in connection with the sale or rental of a dwelling, that indicates a preference, limitation, or discrimination based on race, color, religion, gender, disability, familial status, or national origin." So even if someone appears to be exempt from the law, they cannot discriminate in the advertising.

Steering

It is unlawful to steer a group of people away or toward housing based on being a member in a protected class.

★ **Students of the post-licensing 45-hour course are instructed to do the following exercise:**

> What would you do if...
> You are a real estate licensee who while working phone duty in your office, you receive a phone call from a prospective buyer who tells you that she wants you to find her a house but that it must not be near the "wrong kind of people."
>
>   A. You tell her that she has a right to live near or not near anyone that she wants to. Therefore, it is your job to find her exactly what she is looking for and that you will be happy to assist her.
>
>   B. You explain that "there is good housing everywhere" and that only she as the buyer can decide what house to buy.
>
> B is the correct choice. Intentionally directing the buyer to or from a certain area based on who lives there would be steering and illegal.

Blockbusting
Convincing owners to sell property cheaply by scaring them that the property will lose value due to members of a protected group is moving into the neighborhood, and thus profiting by reselling at a higher price.

Redlining
When lenders and insurance companies refuse services based on an area being made up of a high concentration of a protected group.

Denying Membership
Deny anyone access to or membership in a facility or service due to being a member of a protected class when the membership is related to the sale or rental of housing – such as being able to join a multiple listing service or real estate association.

False Statements Regarding Availability
Falsely claim that housing is no longer available for inspection, sale, or rental in order to avoid selling or renting to a member of a protected class.

Housing for Older Persons Act of 1995
The Fair Housing Act was amended by defining "housing for older persons" as being exempt from the law for housing intended and operated for occupancy by persons 55 years of age or older, and--
Because of the amendment, it is legal for communities to market themselves as "55+" or "age-restricted." In order for the exemption to apply, they must maintain that 80 percent of the occupied units are occupied by at least one person who is 55 years of age or older. By letting the number fall below 80 percent, they could lose the status as an age-restricted community.

Public Law 104–76 104th Congress

Fair Housing Posters
The Fair Housing Act combined with regulation through The U.S. Department of Housing and Urban Development (HUD) requires that a Fair Housing Poster must be displayed by rental and brokerage offices and construction locations. All fair housing posters must be prominently displayed "so as to be readily apparent to all persons seeking housing accommodations or seeking to engage in residential real estate-related transactions or brokerage services." The failure to display the fair housing poster as required by this part shall be deemed prima facie evidence of a discriminatory housing practice. 24 C.F.R. § 110.30

Fair Housing Complaint Process
When Fair Housing Rights have been violated, the aggrieved person can file a complaint with HUD, the U.S. Department of Housing and Urban Development. The agency must begin to work with the complainant within 30 days. Within 10 days after receipt of a signed complaint, HUD will send the respondent notice that a fair housing complaint has been filed against him or her along with a copy of the complaint. At the same time, HUD will send the complainant an acknowledgement letter and a copy of the complaint. Within 10 days of receiving the notice, the respondent must submit to HUD an answer to the complaint.

If, after a thorough investigation, HUD finds no reasonable cause to believe that housing discrimination has occurred or is about to occur, HUD will issue a determination of "no reasonable cause" and close the case. If the investigation produces reasonable cause to believe that discrimination has occurred or is about to occur, HUD will issue a determination of "reasonable cause" and charge the respondent with violating the law. An HUD Administrative Law Judge (ALJ) will hear the case unless either party elects to have the case heard in federal civil court. Parties must elect within 20 days of receipt of the charge.

Within 30 days after either party elects to go to federal court, DOJ will commence a civil action on behalf of the aggrieved person in U.S. district court. If the court finds that a discriminatory housing practice has or is about to occur, the court can award actual and punitive damages as well as attorney's fees.

Civil Suits Filed in Federal District Court

In addition to filing a complaint with the U.S. Housing and Urban Development, a person could file a civil lawsuit in federal court. The lawsuit must be filed within two years after the discriminatory act occurred or ended, or after a conciliation agreement was breached, whichever occurs last. This lawsuit can be filed even if a complaint had been filed with HUD, provided that an Administrative Law Judge has not yet begun a hearing.

Action Taken by the Department of Justice

Under the Fair Housing Act, the Department of Justice may bring lawsuits, where there is reason to believe that a person or entity is engaged in a "pattern or practice" of discrimination. This means that there doesn't have to be a complaint made by an individual for an investigation to begin. If there is evidence of "force or threat" then the Department of Justice may also pursue criminal proceedings.

Responsibility and Liability of Real Estate Licensee

Any real estate licensee assisting in a real estate transaction IS prohibited by law from discriminating on the basis of race, color, religion, sex, handicap, familial status, or national origin. *The American with Disabilities Act of 1990 applies to real estate dealings as well as the Fair Housing Act which prohibits discrimination against individuals with disabilities.*

The Americans with Disabilities Act - An Overview
The ADA is a wide-ranging civil rights law that is intended to protect against discrimination based on disability.

The Americans with Disabilities Act (ADA) became U.S. law on July 26, 1990. **The purpose of the act is to make society more accessible to people with disabilities.** Amendments were passed to the Act in 2008 (ADAAA) to broaden the definition of disability.

Federal laws define a person with a disability as "any person who has a physical or mental impairment that substantially limits one or more major life activities; has a record of such impairment; or is regarded as having such an impairment."

Private and Public – Reasonable Accommodations
The ADA requires reasonable accommodations as necessary to suit the needs of the person with the disability. This includes changes in rules, policies, practices, or services to accommodate the person. Reasonable accommodations may be necessary in the housing itself or in the process of providing housing such as in how an application is taken.

Private and Public - Reasonable Modifications

Federal law requires that reasonable modifications must be allowed to alter housing to suit a person with a disability. This applies to private as well as public housing. However, these modifications are to be made at the resident's expense. Examples: Installing an entrance ramp, lowering the entry threshold, or installing grab bars in a bathroom.

FLORIDA REAL ESTATE 45-HOUR COURSE COMPANION

★ **Students of the post-licensing 45-hour course are instructed to do the following exercise:**

> What would you do if…
> You are a real estate licensee who is doing property management for a homeowner. You have received a request for the rental from an individual who is demanding that the owner install an entry ramp and to put in safety bars in the shower. The owner is refusing to do so.
>
> A. You inform the owner that the modifications must be allowed to be made, but that the tenant would have to pay for them – not the owner.
> B. You explain to the owner that under the law they must make reasonable modifications.
>
> A is the correct choice. Although these types of changes would be considered reasonable, the landlord would not be required to pay for the changes.

Multi-family Housing

The law further requires that "covered" housing built and ready for occupancy after March 13, 1991 must follow design requirements to ensure that housing is accessible to persons with disabilities. Per the HUD website, "these requirements apply to most public and private housing. However, there are limited exemptions for owner-occupied buildings with no more than four units, single-family housing sold or rented without the use of a broker, and housing operated by organizations and private clubs that limit occupancy to members."

Interstate Land Sales Full Disclosure Act (ILSA)

The Interstate Land Sales Full Disclosure Act was passed by Congress in 1968 to protect consumers from risk of fraud when purchasing or leasing land. Land developers must register developments of 100 or more lots with the Consumer Financial Protection Bureau (CFPB). For developments of 25 or more lots, the developer must give purchasers Property Report prior to the buyer signing the purchase agreement. The Property Report is a disclosure that details information about the subdivision. Developers who fail to comply with the disclosure requirements risk the buyers rescinding the contract.

Florida Fair Housing Law

Florida's Fair Housing Law protects the same 7 classes as the federal fair housing law. Prohibits:

- Refuse to rent or sell housing

- Falsely deny that housing is available for inspection, rental, or sale

- Refuse to make a mortgage loan

- Impose different conditions or terms on a loan

- Threaten, coerce, or intimidate any individual exercising a fair housing right

- Refuse reasonable changes to a dwelling to accommodate a disability.

The Florida Fair Housing Act makes it illegal to discriminate in the sale, rental, advertising, financing, or providing of brokerage services for housing.
- The Fair Housing Act parallels the Federal Fair Housing Act.

- The Florida laws do not add any additional covered groups or classes of people.

Chapter 760 of the Florida Statutes
Real estate licensees violate law if the licensee coerces a homeowner to sell or rent with discriminatory intent.

Florida Americans with Disabilities Accessibility Implementation Act
Passed in 1993 by Florida Statutes to adopt accessibility requirements of the Americans with Disabilities Act of 1990, Public Law No. 101-336, 42 U.S.C. Section 12101 et. seq. ADA. Florida laws. Mirrors the ADA standards and places design guideline on new construction per F.S. 553.

Florida Residential Landlord and Tenant Act - Overview of the law
Regardless of whether a rental property is being managed by a real estate brokerage property manager or the owner handling the property him or herself, there are landlord and tenant laws that must be followed per Florida Statutes Chapter 83, Part II. The purpose of Florida's landlord and tenant laws is to try to place landlords and tenants in an equitable legal basis. Landlord tenant laws apply to rental of residential dwelling units not to the renting of mobile home lots or commercial properties.

F.S. 83.40-49

Landlord must account for deposits and advance rents
When the landlord is holding the deposit without the use of a property manager, the landlord must choose one of the following methods to hold security deposits.
- Hold money in a separate non-interest-bearing Florida bank account for the benefit of tenant

- Hold money in a separate interest-bearing Florida bank account and pay the tenant at least 75% interest or 5% per year simple interest

- Post a bond for amount of security deposits and advance rents or $50,000 (whichever is less) and pay tenant 5% per year simple interest.

How the money is being kept must be disclosed to the tenant. The landlord must provide written notice to tenant within 30 days of collecting deposit as to which method was chosen.

Landlord's Obligation to Maintain Premises
Landlords must comply with the requirements of building, housing and health codes in the maintenance of property including maintenance of the roof, windows, screens, floors, steps, porches, exterior walls, foundations and structural components and keep the plumbing in reasonably good working condition.

Tenant's Obligation to Maintain Premises
Tenants are obligated to comply with all building, housing and health codes; keep the dwelling clean and sanitary; remove garbage from the dwelling in a clean and sanitary manner; keep plumbing fixtures clean, sanitary and in repair; not destroy, deface, damage, impair or remove any part of the premises or property belonging to the landlord, nor permit any person to do so; conduct him/herself, and require other persons on the premises with his/her consent to conduct themselves, in a manner that does not unreasonably disturb the tenant's neighbors or constitute a breach of the peace; and use and operate in a

reasonable manner all electrical, plumbing, sanitary, heating, ventilating, air-conditioning and other facilities and appliances, including elevators.

Landlord's Access to Premises

Tenants cannot withhold permission for a landlord to enter the premises without cause. Tenants must allow landlords to enter property to make inspections, provide services, make repairs, and to show property. The landlord may enter property at any time in case of emergency. Otherwise, they are obligated to give tenant reasonable notice (at least 24* hours—*changed in 2022 from a 12 hour notice*).

Notice to End a Lease

- Yearly Lease Termination – Either party must give notice no less than 60 days prior to the end of any annual period. This is per Florida Statute 83.57(1).

- Quarterly Lease Termination – Either party must give notice of no less than 30 days prior to the end of any quarterly period. This is per Florida Statute 83.57(2).

- Monthly Lease Termination – Either party must give notice of no less than 15 days prior to the end of any monthly period. This is per Florida Statute 83.57(3).

- Weekly Lease Termination - Either party must give notice of no less than 7 days prior to the end of any weekly period. This is per Florida Statute 83.57(4).

- A landlord may terminate a lease for nonpayment of rent with only 3 days' notice (business days excluding Saturday, Sunday, and legal holidays). This is per Florida Statute 83.56(3).

- Either party may terminate a lease if the other party is not living up to the terms of the lease (such as maintaining sanitary conditions) by giving the other Notice of the Violation and a 7-day opportunity to correct the situation. This is per Florida Statutes 83.56(2).

Vacating Premises

When landlord is holding a security deposit, the landlord must:
- Return the deposit to tenant within 15 days if no claim is to be made, or
- Send written notice by certified mail within 30 days if claim is made on the deposit.
- Tenant allowed 15 days to respond to landlord's written claim
- Disputes are handled in civil court.

Breaking a Lease Due to Condition

In order to legally vacate based on condition, the tenant/landlord must have given the other party notice to make corrections. The problem must be "truly serious, such as the lack of heat or other essential service."

Notice to Cancel Lease

A 7-day written notice of intent to cancel the lease must be provided. This notice must be given in writing and delivered personally or mailed if given by the tenant. The landlord may also choose to post the notice on the door.

Eviction in Florida:
- Notify tenant in writing (3-business-day or 7-day); After time period is up, file complaint for eviction with the courts; Tenant has 5 business days to respond to complaint; If tenant continues to occupy without responding, obtain final judgment from court; Post 24-hour notice; and Court issues writ of possession to be served by the sheriff to the tenant.

Broker Property Management
- If a broker holds the funds on behalf of the landlord, broker must abide by license law regarding escrow funds
- Deposits and advance rents are trust funds that must be deposited into the broker's escrow
- Best to open a separate escrow for property management but not required
- $5,000 broker's funds to maintain the account
- Sales associates must deliver rent and rental deposits to broker by end of next business day.

★ **Students of the post-licensing 45-hour course are instructed to do the following exercise:**

> What would you do if…
> You are a real estate licensee who has agreed to do property management for an owner. You are holding advance rent of $1,500 and $1,000 deposit from the tenant. Plus, you are holding $1,000 from the property owner just in case repairs are needed. The air conditioning unit on the property breaks down and will cost $2,500 to fix. The owner is out of the country but tells you to pay the bill from the escrow account and that she will make up the difference when she gets back the next week.
>
> A. You explain to the owner that she cannot authorize the bill to be paid with funds from the escrow account, even temporarily, as that money is being held in trust on behalf of the tenant.
> B. Since that is the only way to make the repairs, you follow the owner's direction.
>
> A is the correct choice. Use of the tenant's money would be considered conversion and is illegal.

*Effective July 1, 2022, the bill changed the time for entry for nonemergency from 12 hours to 24 hours. This is the result of the murder of Miya Marcano.

*The Supreme Court, in Bostock v. Clayton County (2020), held that prohibition because of sex covers discrimination on the basis of gender identity and sexual orientation. As such, President Biden signed an executive order, January 2021, specifying that no one may be discriminated for housing based on gender identity or sexual orientation.

14 ECOA / TILA / RESPA – IN PRACTICE

<u>Learning Terms and Phrases</u>

- ECOA Application
- Marital Status
- Public Assistance
- Qualifying Income
- Mortgage Discrimination
- Credit Denial
- Penalties for Breaking ECOA Laws
- TILA Application
- Regulation Z
- TILA Disclosures
- Triggering Terms
- Advertising of Property
- Bait and Switch
- Right of Rescission
- RESPA Application
- Dodd-Frank Act
- Consumer Booklet
- Loan Estimate
- Closing Disclosure
- Kickbacks

Learning Objectives

- Licensees should be able to correctly apply the Equal Credit Opportunity Act to real estate situations.
- Licensees should be able to apply the Truth in Lending Act when preparing real estate advertisements.
- Licensees should be able to recognize which real estate mortgages require a 3 day right of rescission.
- Licensees should be able to correctly identify how Dodd Frank affects the timing of the closing disclosure with the scheduling of a real estate closing.
- Licensees should be able to determine when a referral fee may be paid as compared to when it is an illegal kickback under RESPA.

Legalities of Mortgages

Advertising property or closing a deal with a loan brings in a host of different issues that licensees must keep in mind. This chapter deals with the Equal Credit Opportunity Act, Truth in Lending Act, and Real Estate Settlement Procedures Act. All of these acts are in place to protect the consumer.

The Equal Credit Opportunity Act (ECOA)

Laws are in place to protect consumers who apply for mortgage loans. The Equal Credit Opportunity Act (ECOA), Regulation B, prohibits discrimination in loan underwriting on the basis of:
- sex, marital status, race, religion, age, or national origin.

Plus, it prohibits discriminatory treatment of income from alimony, child support, public assistance, or part-time employment. It also prohibits inquiry about, or consideration of, childbearing plans or potential for childbearing. The Consumer Financial Protection Bureau has issued regulations under ECOA. These regulations, known as Regulation B, provide the substantive and procedural framework for fair lending.

Lenders May

When determining income to qualify someone for a mortgage, lenders may consider public assistance as income. This income is to be treated the same as any other type of income in regard to qualifying for a loan. Part-time income is also to be considered. (However, picking up a second part-time job may not count toward qualifying income to debt ratios.)

Anyone receiving social security, a pension, and/or annuities would have the amount counted toward qualifying income. Alimony, child support, and maintenance payments also are considered income. For any of the above types of income, the lender will request verification that the income will continue throughout the loan period. When a co-cosigner is needed on a loan, the co-signer need not be a spouse.

Lenders May Not

When working with a potential borrower, a lender may not discourage the person from applying or reject the loan based on race, color, religion, national origin, sex, marital status, or age, or because of income from public assistance. In practice, lenders will ask an applicant's sex, race, and national origin – however, this information is not required and may not be considered to qualify the individual for the loan. Immigration status may be an issue in that the lender will want assurance that the individual will remain in the country throughout the loan period to repay it.

The lender may not use issues such as a person's race, color, religion, national origin, sex, marital status, or age, or the fact that income from public assistance is being received to impose varying loan terms and conditions. The lender may not deny a loan based on the racial demographics of a neighborhood. The lender may not ask about future plans for having children. The lender may not require a co-signer, IF the applicant qualifies alone.

Mortgage Discrimination. November 2016. https://www.consumer.ftc.gov/articles/0188-mortgage-discrimination

When Denied Credit

A potential borrower must be informed within 30 days of whether the person has been denied or granted credit. This notice may be provided verbally, but for record keeping purposes, generally is provided in writing. Also, anyone who has been turned down for credit must be given the specific reason(s) for the denial.

Equal Credit Opportunity Act. November 2016.
https://en.wikipedia.org/wiki/Equal_Credit_Opportunity_Act

Suspicion of Failure to Comply with the ECOA

Licensees who suspect that a lender has failed to comply with the Equal Credit Opportunity Act should inform the client of the law and encourage them to report violations to appropriate government agency.

Violations should be reported to the Consumer Financial Protection Bureau. Complaints may be made at www.consumerfinance.gov or by calling 855-411-2372.

Penalties for Breaking the ECOA

Lenders who fail to follow the Equal Credit Opportunity Act can face civil liability for actual and punitive damages of up to $10,000. If it is a class action lawsuit, it could be as much as the lesser of $500,000 or 1% of the creditor's net worth.

Equal Credit Opportunity Act. November 2016.
https://en.wikipedia.org/wiki/Equal_Credit_Opportunity_Act

★ **Students of the post-licensing 45-hour course are instructed to do the following exercise:**

What would you do if…

You are a real estate licensee who has a buyer contact you about seeing a property that you have listed. The buyers really like the house and mention that because it is more than they were expecting to spend, they would need to take out a mortgage. You can't help noticing that they are quite elderly and they also mention that they are retired.

    A. You tell the buyers that they should consider a less expensive home in order to avoid applying for a loan.
    B. You let the buyers know of several lenders that they could contact to weigh out their options.

B is the correct choice. It is the buyers' right to apply for a loan the same as younger buyers.

Consumer Credit Protection Act (Truth in Lending Act)

Another act that protects borrowers is Title I of the Consumer Credit Protection Act called the Truth in Lending Act (TILA). This act was passed in 1968. The Truth in Lending Act promotes the informed use of consumer credit by requiring disclosures from lenders about loan terms and costs of the loan.

"This regulation applies to each individual or business that offers or extends credit when the credit that is being offered is subject to a finance charge or is payable by a written agreement in more than four installments; the credit is primarily for personal, family or household purposes; and the loan balance equals or exceeds $25,000.00 or is secured by an interest in real property or a dwelling."

January 2016. https://usffcu.org/TruthinLendingAct.asp

Implemented by the Federal Reserve Regulation Z

The Truth in Lending Act pairs with the Federal Reserve Regulation Z for actual implementation of the act's provisions.
- The overall goal is to inform borrowers of the true costs of a loan.

It does not regulate loan charges, but instead it requires a "uniform standard disclosure" of loan costs and charges so that the consumer can fairly shop loans by comparing one to the other.

TILA Requires Disclosure of Full Credit Costs

Specifically, TILA requires disclosure of loan terms in 4 formats:

- Finance charge
- Total amount financed
- Total amount of payments
- Annual percentage rate (APR)
  - Within 1/8 of 1%

And it requires lenders to disclose interest, discount points, servicing fees, & origination fees
- *but not title, legal, survey, appraisal, credit report, or deed preparation.*

TILA Requires Disclosure of Annual Percentage rate (APR)

Specifically, TILA requires that the full credit costs must be disclosed in the form of the Annual Percentage Rate.
- Included in the APR is the interest rate, origination fees, discount points, and other loan costs. The APR represents the Annual Cost of Credit
- By expressing all loans in terms of the APR, potential borrowers are able to compare loans and better shop the terms for a more competitive deal

Advertising Disclosures

TILA affects advertising rules. If an advertisement for credit for real estate (mortgages) contains "trigger terms", then the three specific following disclosures must also be included in the advertisement:
1. The amount or percentage of the down payment;
2. The terms of repayment; and
3. The "Annual Percentage Rate," using that term spelled out in full. If the annual percentage rate may be increased after consummation of credit transaction, that fact must be disclosed.

Triggering Terms

1. The amount of the down payment, expressed either as a percentage or as a dollar amount.
2. The amount of any payment expressed either as a percentage or as a dollar amount.
3. The period of repayment (the total time required to repay)

Any of the above are considered Triggering Terms and requires that all three disclosures must be included!

Examples of Triggering Terms
The following terms are triggering terms which would require the three disclosures mentioned:
- 25% down
- 90% financing
- Monthly payments less than $850
- 36 small payments are all you make
- 4 year loans available
- Less than $100 interest

NOT Triggering Terms
Some terms may seem like a triggering term, but not actually qualify as one and, therefore, do not require that all disclosures be made. These are vague phrases that simply "talk up" the loan terms without specifics:
- No down payment
- Easy monthly payments
- Pay weekly
- Terms to fit your budget
- 5% below are standard Rate

If in doubt, include disclosures!

TILA for Real Estate Agents
So, what does this mean for a real estate licensee?
If along with the real estate property you are advertising for sale, you also mention a triggering term, then the real estate agent is subject to TILA the same as a lender.

> # Home for Sale!
> ## Payments as low as $900 a month!
> Terms based on qualified borrower, $20,000 down, 4.25% paid over 30 years.

Sample Advertising
Making bait and switch advertising or misleading advertising is unlawful so be clear in any statements made.

"Only $850 a month for this beautiful home!"
- Because this statement is a triggering term; to include this statement, the amount of required down payment, how long the term is, and the APR must also be clearly disclosed in the advertisement.

"Easy payments available on this lovely home!"
- To include this statement, no other loan details would have to be provided. This is considered too vague to be a triggering term.

⭐ **Students of the post-licensing 45-hour course are instructed to do the following exercise:**

What would you do if...
You are a real estate licensee and you want to create a flyer to put into the listing box. You call your favorite lender and find out that with $15,000 down payment and an interest rate of 3.75%, the monthly payment would be $1,250 for a 30-year loan.

A. You want to make the flyer as attractive and simple as possible, so you only include the fact that the home would only have a $1,250 payment.
B. You include on the flyer that a qualified borrower could pay $1,250 a month – with $15,000 down at an interest rate of 3.75% paid over 30 years.

B is the correct choice. The monthly payment is a triggering term and requires that full disclosure regarding loan terms be included in the advertisement.

3 Day Right of Rescission

TILA also requires that the disclosure be made to consumers of credit, that they have a 3 day right of rescission.

In some credit transactions in which a security interest is or will be retained or acquired in a consumer's principal dwelling, each consumer whose ownership is or will be subject to the security interest has the right to rescind the transaction.

This means that the buyer can cancel the transaction!

- This 3 day right of rescission applies to home equity lines of credit, to second mortgages and to refinance loans.

- This 3 day right of rescission does NOT apply to new loans on a home the borrower did not previously own before securing the mortgage.

- It also does NOT apply to construction loans.

Notice of Right of Rescission

Lenders are required to deliver two copies of the notice of the right to rescind and one copy of the disclosure statement to each consumer entitled to rescind. The notice must be on a separate document that identifies the rescission period on the transaction and must clearly and conspicuously disclose the retention or acquisition of a security interest in the consumer's principal dwelling; the consumer's right to rescind the transaction; and how the consumer may exercise the right to rescind with a form for that purpose, designating the address of the lender's place of business.

★ **Students of the post-licensing 45-hour course are instructed to do the following exercise:**

> What would you do if...
> You represented a buyer in the sale of a home who used a loan to complete the purchase. The home closed at a title lawyer's office, funds were distributed, and keys were exchanged from the seller to the buyer. The buyer calls you the next day and tells you that he has changed his mind and is calling his lender next to invoke the 3 day right of rescission to cancel the purchase of the home.
>
> A. You encourage your buyer to have conversations with the lender and/or lawyer as you are licensed neither as a mortgage broker or an attorney and therefore think it is best to have that conversation with them. Then you tell him that you are sorry that he is feeling trepid about the purchase and you'd be happy to assist him in any way that you can in the future – including possibly reselling the home!
> B. You panic and don't cash your commission check.
>
> A is the correct choice. The 3 day right of rescission only applies to home equity loans, refinancing, or 2nd mortgages. They do not apply to a new loan on a home not previously owned by the borrower.

Real Estate Settlement Procedures Act (RESPA)

Another type of consumer protection act is the Real Estate Settlement Procedures Act (RESPA). The Real Estate Settlement Procedures Act (RESPA) was passed by Congress in 1974. It was created because various companies associated with real estate transactions such as lenders and real estate agents were often engaging in providing undisclosed kickbacks to each other which actually causes the cost of the transaction to increase for the consumer.

Dodd-Frank Act

In 2010, Congress passed the Dodd-Frank Act, which combined regulations under the Truth-in-Savings Act, the Funds Availability Act, the Equal Credit Opportunity Act and the Truth-in-Lending Act. On July 21, 2011, administration and enforcement of the Real Estate Settlement Procedures Act (RESPA) was transferred from the Department of Housing and Urban Development to the Consumer Financial Protection Bureau (CFPB). Called TILA-RESPA Integrated Disclosure Rule (TRID), it consolidated consumer protection agencies under CFPB to simplify oversight and compliance. It took the four previously required disclosures regarding credit and the costs of credit down to only two disclosures.

Loans Requiring RESPA Compliance

The Real Estate Settlement Procedures Act (RESPA) applies to most any closing involving a "standard" home mortgage loan from a financial institution or mortgage banker.

RESPA applies to all *federally related mortgage loans* for the purchase of:

- 1 to 4 family structure (including construction loans)
- Manufactured homes using proceeds of a loan
- With the loan made by a lender, creditor, or dealer
- Made by or insured by an agency of the federal government
- Made in connection with a federal housing program
- Made by and intended to be sold by a lender to FNMA, GNMA, or FHLMC
- Subject of a home equity conversion mortgage
- Made by a lender, dealer, or creditor to be used to fund an installment sales contract, land contract or contract for deed

Consumer Booklet

RESPA requires that the borrower be provided a booklet of information regarding closing costs.
- Under RESPA, a financial institution or mortgage broker is required to provide a borrower with a copy of the "special information booklet" at the time a written application is submitted or no later than 3-business days after application is received.

- If the application is denied before the end of the 3-day period, the institution does not have to supply the booklet.

Loan Estimate

Requires advanced estimates of closing costs

- RESPA also requires that no later than the third business day after the submission of a loan application, the borrower is provided with a Loan Estimate which discloses key features, costs, and risks of the mortgage loan for which the person has applied.

Closing Disclosure

Requires that the borrower be able to examine the RESPA-specified closing statement in advance of closing. A closing disclosure form must be provided to the borrower within 3-business days BEFORE the loan closing. This form details all the costs associated with the closing including lender fees, real estate agent commissions, title closing fees, APR, and prorated items between the buyer and the seller. It is designed in the same format as the loan estimate for easy comparison.

★ **Students of the post-licensing 45-hour course are instructed to do the following exercise:**

> What would you do if…
> You are representing a buyer in the sale of a home who is using a loan to complete the purchase. The closing is scheduled on March 14th. The lender had difficulty pulling the details of the loan together so the closing disclosure wasn't finalized until March 13th.
>
> A. You tell your buyer that she is so lucky that everything got done in time to close so that she didn't risk losing the house by missing the contract date!
> B. You prepare a contract addendum to request the buyer and seller to extend the closing date to March 16th.
>
> B is the correct choice. The buyer must have the closing disclosure at least 3 days prior to closing.

Kick-backs

RESPA prohibits kick-backs, also called fee-splitting or unearned fees, to a lender from vendors of closing related services.

A kickback is illegal under RESPA. A kickback is something of value given in exchange for referring a settlement service business to another person. Kickbacks are said to harm consumers by driving up the cost of transaction.

- Mortgage brokers can only pay other mortgage brokers a referral fee.

- Real Estate Licensees can only pay other real estate licensees a referral fee.

- And title companies may not pay a referral fee or give something of value in return for referring the business.

⭐ **Students of the post-licensing 45-hour course are instructed to do the following exercise:**

> What would you do if...
> You have recently launched your real estate career and you are desperate to build your business. A mortgage lender in town contacts you and welcomes you to the world of real estate. She tells you that she would be happy to refer qualified buyers to you. The only thing that she asks, is that you send her $500 after every successful closing.
>
> A. You agree.
> B. You inquire with the lender to find out if the person is also licensed as real estate licensee. If yes, you agree. However, you explain that the referral fee has to be paid by your broker to her broker and disclosed as part of the deal and not after the closing. If not, you tell the person that you would be happy to follow the arrangement – but only after a real estate license is obtained.
>
> B is the correct answer. Paying an unlicensed person, a real estate fee would be an illegal kickback.

Refer to Chapter 6, "Financing Considerations," to learn about structuring real estate deals and closings when a loan is involved.

15 AGENCY IN PRACTICE

Learning Terms and Phrases

- Law of Agency
- Fiduciary Relationship
- General Agency Applied
- Special Agency Applied
- Arm's Length Transaction
- Dual Agency Applied
- Termination of Agency
- Brokerage Disclosure Act
- Residential Sale
- Exceptions to Disclosure Requirements
- No Brokerage Relationship
- Material Facts
- Single Agency
- Obedience
- Confidentiality
- Full Disclosure
- Present All Offers
- Presumption of Transaction Brokerage
- Consent to Transition
- Designated Sales Associate

Learning Objectives

- Licensees should be able to apply the concept of fiduciary duty to the licensees' brokers in real estate transactions.
- Licensees should be able to apply concepts of agency relationships when dealing with buyers and sellers.
- Licensees should be able to apply agency disclosure rules to real estate transactions.
- Licensees should be able to balance agency duties while hosting open houses.
- Licensees should understand how to manage the duty to disclose defects in property.
- Licensees should be able to apply the duty of obedience to real estate situations.
- Licensees should be able to apply the duty to present all offers to real estate situations.
- Licensees should be able to balance single agency, transaction brokerage, and the transition back to a transaction brokerage in the practice of real estate.
- Licensees should be able to recognize when bound by agency duty when the other agent involved in a transaction works within the same brokerage.

Understanding Agency

The practice of real estate is about representing buyers and sellers. The question becomes as to what extent the licensee is legally bound to represent the parties involved in a real estate transaction. It is common for real estate licensees to be referred to as "real estate agents." This very common reference to the real estate licensee seems to imply there is some type of agency representation involved in a real estate transaction. It is imperative that a real estate licensee understands in what capacity the licensee is acting, the duties involved, and the disclosures that must be made.

Fiduciary Relationship

An agency relationship is formed when a person delegates authority to another to act in a fiduciary relationship. A fiduciary relationship is a relationship of trust and confidence between an agent and the principal. Failure to adequately tend to the duties and obligations in the relationship can result in legal consequences.

Statutory Law

Statute law is written law set down by a body of legislature. Statutes may be put into place by national or state legislatures or by local governments. Statutory laws can never be written to override a higher constitutional law.

Common Law

Common law is case law that takes shape from the decisions judges make in the courts as each judicial case is decided upon. Each decision in the courtroom is then held up as case law to mold decisions of future court cases.

Law of Agency

When a principal delegates authority to an agent to act on the principal's behalf, an agency relationship is created. A principal is the person who delegates authority to another acting in a fiduciary relationship. An agent is the person who is authorized to represent and act for principal. A fiduciary is the relationship of trust and confidence between the agent and the principal (Does not have to be a "paid" relationship.)

Types of Agents

There are three potential types of agency relationships recognized by law.
The three types of agency relationships are: Universal agent, General agent, and Special agent.

Universal Agent

A universal agent is the broadest and most comprehensive form of agency. It's considered a broad form of agency in that the agent can do a broad range of things for the principal. To have such broad powers, universal agents are commonly created via a power of attorney – with the agent becoming an attorney in fact. Know that real estate licensees do NOT act as universal agents.

General Agent

A general agent's power is much more limited than a universal agent. General agents are empowered to perform a multitude of acts associated with one area of the principal's life, such as for operation of a business. The general agent can make contracts and do things for the principal that is necessary in the normal course of ordinary business of the principal. The difference between the general agent and the universal agent is that the power of the general agent stops there. It doesn't reach into the rest of the principal's life.

Keep in mind then, that by the very definition of a general agent, real estate licensees are general agents of the employing broker. The licensee works to further the broker's real estate business. The agent prospects for new business and works directly with clients. The agent even creates contracts on behalf of the principal – the employing broker. These contracts bind the broker to the buyers and sellers as the client's agent.

Sometimes, it is the broker who acts as a general agent—but not to the licensee. When a broker is hired to be a property manager the broker is a general agent of the property owner. Property management is an ongoing activity that encompasses many tasks. Furthermore, it is the broker's duty, as a general agent to the property owner, the principal, to work in the best interest of the principal.

Special Agent

A special agent is extremely limited and has narrowly defined powers. The special agent is appointed for a specific purpose or to do something such as to handle a single business transaction. Often the activity is outside of the individual's usual course of business.

Where a real estate broker is a general agent when services are engaged for property management; the broker acts as that of a special agent when working to sell a property for a seller or assist a buyer in purchasing a property. Once that single transaction is accomplished, the agency relationship ends.

Arm's Length Transaction

A fiduciary is someone who acts in a special position of trust and confidence; the fiduciary relationship. The exact opposite of a fiduciary relationship is when someone deals with another in what is said to be an "arm's length transaction." In an arm's length transaction, each party is acting only to the benefit of themselves. It assumes that each person will strive to create the best deal for him or herself and that they are not responsible for whether the deal is equitable and fair to the other party.

Dual Agency

Because the very definition of a fiduciary relationship involves acting in a position of trust and confidence, the question becomes in real estate as to how a broker can act as a fiduciary for both a buyer and a seller at the same time. The term for this is acting as a dual agent. Because Florida legislature believes that it is impossible to fulfill fiduciary duties to two parties of the same transaction, dual agency is not allowed.

Know that when a licensee works on behalf of a broker for either a buyer or a seller the licensee does also owe fiduciary duties to the principal just as the broker does. This is because the licensee, who is a general agent of the broker, is now a subagent of the broker's principal when dealing with the broker's principal.

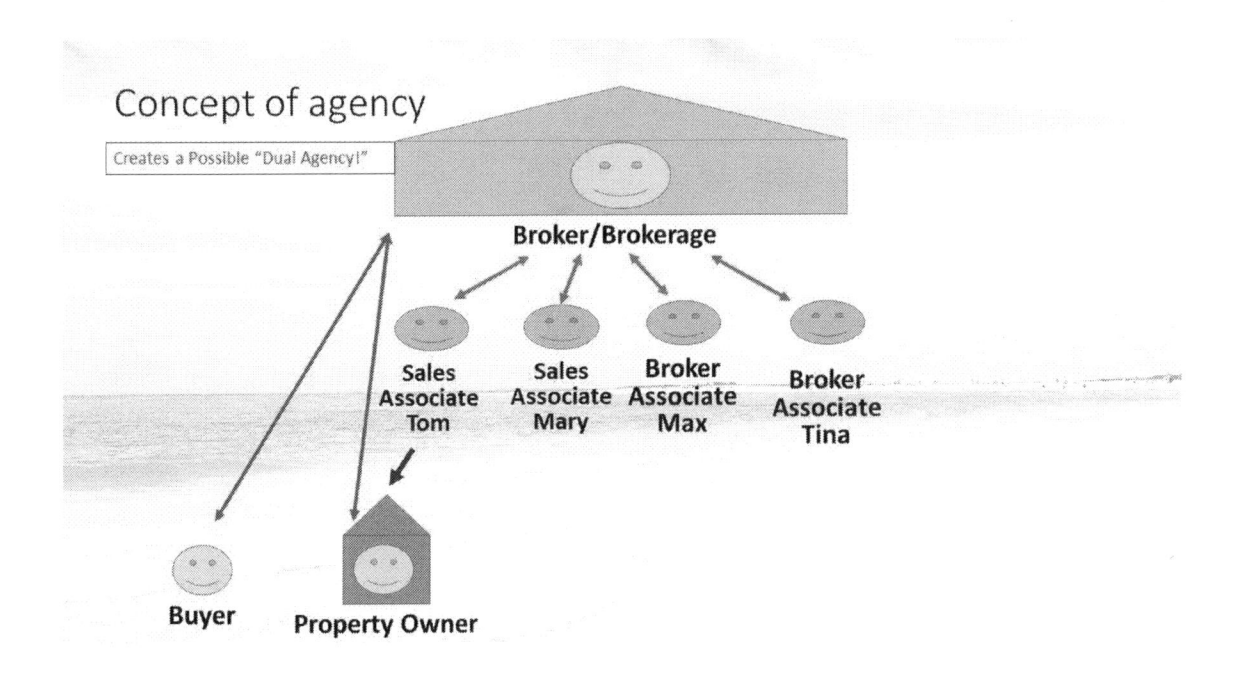

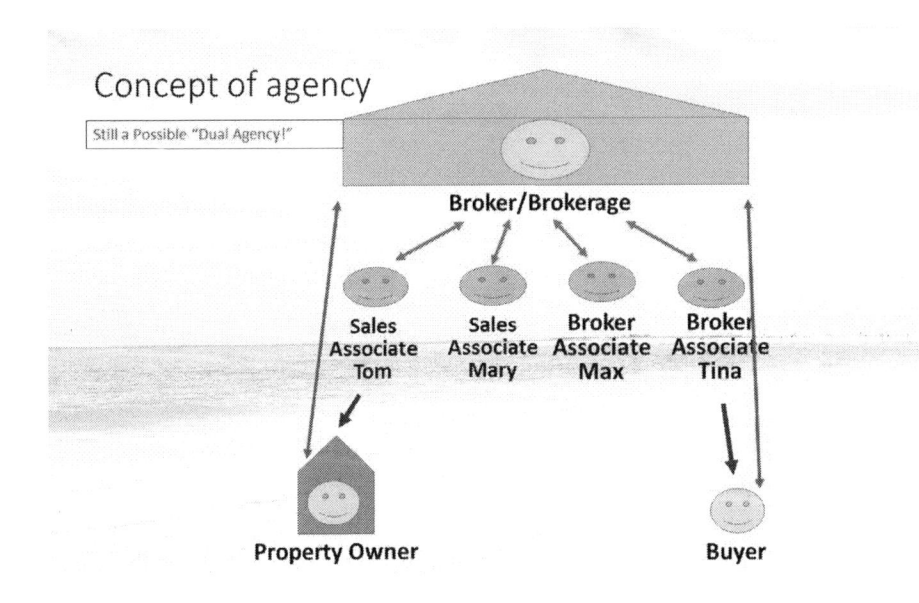

Concept of agency

Creates a Possible "Dual Agency!"

Broker/Brokerage — Sales Associate Tom, Sales Associate Mary, Broker Associate Max, Broker Associate Tina — Buyer, Property Owner

Concept of agency

Still a Possible "Dual Agency!"

Broker/Brokerage — Sales Associate Tom, Sales Associate Mary, Broker Associate Max, Broker Associate Tina — Property Owner, Buyer

Agency Compared

- The broker acts as that of a special agent when working to sell a property for a seller or assist a buyer in purchasing a property.

- When a broker is hired to be a property manager the broker is a general agent of the property owner.

- Real estate licensees are general agents of the employing broker.

- The licensee, who is a general agent of the broker, is now a subagent of the broker's principal when dealing with the broker's principal.

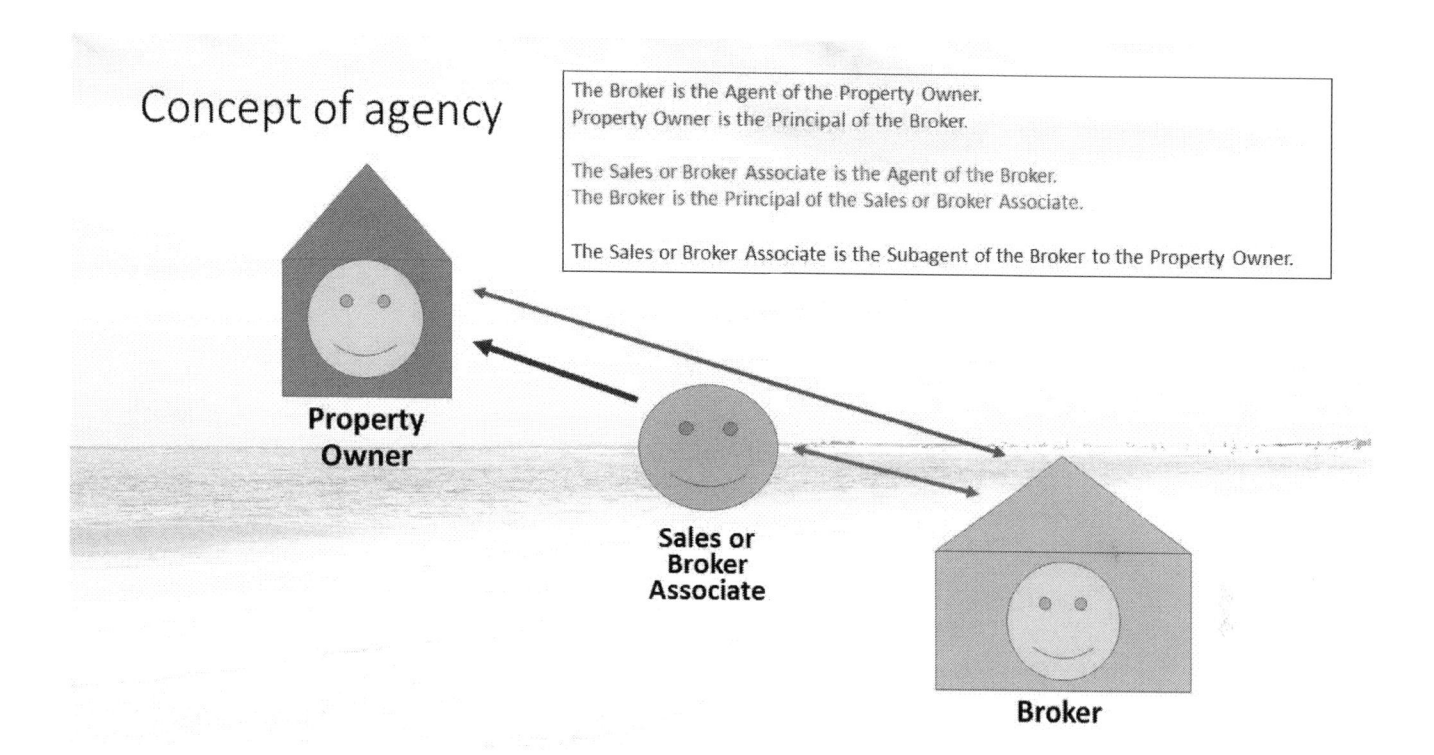

Concept of agency

The Broker is the Agent of the Property Owner.
Property Owner is the Principal of the Broker.

The Sales or Broker Associate is the Agent of the Broker.
The Broker is the Principal of the Sales or Broker Associate.

The Sales or Broker Associate is the Subagent of the Broker to the Property Owner.

Property Owner

Sales or Broker Associate

Broker

⭐ **Students of the post-licensing 45-hour course are instructed to do the following exercise:**

> What would you do if…
> You are eager to get listings and you come across an investor that you have known for years. The investor is looking for a new real estate agent to list his properties. You have known this person for years and you have evidence that the investor takes shortcuts in fixing up properties which has left buyers quite unhappy in the past. The investor wants your full loyalty as his agent.
>
> A. Eager to get rolling in real estate, you agree.
> B. You decline to work with the investor.
>
> B is the best answer. By working with the investor, not only you – but your broker becomes responsible for insufficient work done by the investor. As the general agent of the broker, you are obligated to look out for your broker's best interests.

Agency Relationships are Determined by the Broker

Real estate involves the transfer of property which is a vitally important transaction. However, the general public rarely has the knowledge to understand what is being given up when not being represented in an agency relationship. Therefore, the Florida legislature found it necessary to protect the public by imposing specific agency rules for the licensee to follow.

Part of the clarification of the statutes is based on the fact that, it is the licensee who has the advantage of knowledge of agency- it is the broker who is ultimately responsible for determining what type of agency relationship applies. If the agency relationship that the broker knows to be appropriate is somehow not acceptable to the buyer or the seller, then the broker should not proceed with working with that person as it is the broker who is held responsible by law.

Approved Agency Relationships for Property Transfer in Florida

When determining what type of relationship is most fitting for the situation, a broker in Florida has four types of legal relationships that are allowed when conducting a real estate transaction:

- Transaction Broker for buyer and/or seller

- Single Agent for EITHER a buyer or seller (not both in same transaction)

- No Brokerage Relationship (non-representation so can represent the other party either as a transaction broker, single agent, or no brokerage relationship).

- Designated Sales Associate (allowed for only certain non-residential sales transactions).

Florida Statutes 475.255

Events that Terminate an Agency Relationship

All agency relationships eventually end. There are many ways to terminate an agency relationship.

Ways to terminate an agency relationship include:
- Lapse of time: The agency relationship terminates when the time period passes that was agreed upon the formation of the relationship.

- Purpose achieved: Once the purpose is achieved that the relationship was formed to accomplish, the agency relationship is terminated.

- Mutual agreement: An agency relationship can be terminated early if both parties agree to do so.

- Certain events: An agency relationship will not continue if certain events happen such as one of the parties dying or being declared mentally incompetent or declaring bankruptcy.

- Court action: If all parties will not agree to terminate the relationship, a court action to do so may be sought.

★ **Students of the post-licensing 45-hour course are instructed to do the following exercise:**

What would you do if...
You are working with a buyer and the buyer signed a buyer broker agreement. Despite your best efforts you can't seem to find a property that satisfies the buyer. The buyer has become very aggravated and is blaming you and wants to cancel the buyer broker agreement.

A. You contact your broker to intervene with the buyer. If the buyer does not want to continue working with you after discussion with the broker, the broker could arrange to have the buyer work with another agent. If that agent finds a property for the buyer, you can be paid a referral commission from your broker.
B. You refuse to cancel the buyer broker agreement and insist on continuing to represent the buyer. After all, you worked hard for the buyer already.

A is the best answer. It is unlikely that a buyer that has decided not to work with you will. By allowing another agent to work with the buyer it is possible to still earn a partial commission which is better than completely losing the deal.

Brokerage Disclosure Act

To avoid confusion about what type of agency relationship exists, if any, licensees are subject to certain disclosure requirements. When a licensee is working with a buyer or a seller of property for the purpose of transferring ownership of the property, agency disclosure requirements must be met as outlined in the Brokerage Disclosure Act.

Florida has three types of legal relationships that are allowed when conducting a residential real estate sales transaction. The broker can work as a transaction broker for either a buyer or a seller. The broker may work as a transaction broker for both the buyer and seller in the same transaction. This type of relationship provides duties and obligations from the broker to the buyer, however, since it is not a true fiduciary relationship- dual agency is avoided. The broker may work as a single agent, which creates fiduciary obligations, but only with either a buyer or a seller and never both in the same transaction. The broker may work in a no brokerage relationship capacity, meaning the buyer or the seller is agreeing to not be represented by the broker.

In Writing

With some exceptions, in Florida, a broker is presumed to be working in the capacity of a transaction broker <u>unless a disclosure is made in writing</u> to the buyer or seller of residential property that either a single agency or a no brokerage relationship has been formed.

Notice that the rule requires that the disclosure be made in writing. It does not require that it actually be signed to create the relationship.

★ **Students of the post-licensing 45-hour course are instructed to do the following exercise:**

> What would you do if...
> You are working with a new buyer and you explain that you are going to be working in the capacity as a single agent. You present the single agency disclosure in writing to the buyer. You ask the buyer to sign the disclosure, but the buyer refuses to sign.
>
> A. You stop working with the buyer because they refused to sign the form.
> B. You write on the signature line the date that the form was presented to the buyer and write the statement "presented but buyer refused to sign."
>
> B is the correct answer. Buyers do not have to sign either the single agent or no agency agreement. However, brokers are to maintain records of agency agreements; therefore, the form should be dated and noted of presentation and refusal of client to sign*.
>
> *Check with your broker's policy, as many brokers will only work with a someone as a transaction broker who refuses to sign otherwise. It is difficult to prove that the disclosure was provided if the client refused to sign it.*

Applies to Residential Sales *Only*

This rule that the disclosure must be made applies to residential sales only. This means that if a broker is working in the capacity of a property manager, the disclosure does NOT need to be made. Disclosures do have to be made for residential sale as defined as being an improved residential property of four units or fewer, or the sale of unimproved residential property intended for use of four units or fewer, or the sale of agricultural property of 10 acres or fewer.

Exceptions to Residential Sales Disclosure Requirements

There are times that a broker is not required to make the disclosure even in a residential sales transaction. These situations include:

- When the licensee knows that a single agent or transaction broker already represents the buyer or seller.

- At a Bona fide open house or model showing.

- In unanticipated casual encounters.

- When responding to general questions of advertised property.

- While communicating about real estate services being offered.

- When selling new residential units and working for the owner/developer.

Disclosure Requirements Do Not Apply To:

Agency disclosure requirements apply to residential sales only. They do not apply, then, to the following transactions.

- If the property being sold qualifies as a non-residential property, no disclosure is required.

- If the licensee is working in the capacity to rent a property, then the licensee does not have to provide agency disclosures to either the landlord or the tenant.

- Nor do disclosures have to be made when selling property via an auction.

- Appraisal services do not require agency disclosures.

- Business opportunity sales do not require disclosures.

Note however, that licensees are still bound to the duties of agency; it is the disclosure of the duty that is exempt in these situations.

No Brokerage Relationship (Non-representation)

A seller or a buyer can choose not to be represented. A broker's assistance may be requested to facilitate a sale/purchase through such tasks as filling out a contract. However, the customer may feel confident in their own negotiation skills and not desire the assistance or representation of the broker through an agency relationship. This is perfectly acceptable. In the No Brokerage Relationship, the broker still has duties to the customer.

Duties of No Brokerage Relationship

These duties include:

- Deal honestly and fairly.

- Disclose all known facts that materially affect the value of residential property that are not readily observable to the buyer.

- Account for all funds entrusted to the licensee.

No Brokerage Relationship Disclosure

These duties must be fully described and disclosed in writing to the buyer or seller. The disclosure must be made before the showing of property to a buyer. When working with a seller, the required disclosure notice <u>may be</u> included within the listing agreement.

If it is within the listing agreement, then the disclosure must be of the same size type, or larger, as the other provisions of the document and the disclosure must be obvious in where it is placed within the listing agreement with the first sentence of the information identified in paragraph printed in uppercase bold type.

F.S. Statute 475.278 (4) (a) & (b)

⭐ **Students of the post-licensing 45-hour course are instructed to do the following exercise:**

> What would you do if...
> You were holding an open house for a seller and a prospective buyer began asking you a lot of questions not just about the house but the process of looking at other homes available for sale in the area.
>
> A. Nothing, because disclosures are not required when holding an open house.
> B. Upon offering to show the buyer other properties, (if planning to represent the buyer as a single agent rather than a transaction agent) present the single agency disclosure to the buyer.
>
> B is the best answer. Although "A" is legally correct, many agents use the duties of a single agent to help buyers understand the benefits of being represented by a buyer's agent. It may help the buyer to make a commitment to work with you.

Disclose All Known Material Facts

So, what does it mean to disclose all known facts that materially affect the value of the residential real property which are not readily observable to the buyer?

A material defect is any fact about what is wrong with a property that may have a significant and reasonable impact on the market value. The issue of whether a disclosure was made is a major source of litigation, not just against property owners, but against the broker handling the transaction. This can result in the broker and licensee being charged with misrepresentation or fraud.

Although buyers have an opportunity to have the property inspected, this duty to disclose is NEVER relieved. So, if there are hidden cracks to the structure or damage to walls or floors that are covered from sight – the broker must disclose this information. Note that "ignorance is not always bliss" as a broker may be held accountable for having "should have known!"

F.S. Statute 475.278 (4) (a) & (b)

⭐ **Students of the post-licensing 45-hour course are instructed to do the following exercise:**

> What would you do if...
> You have a house listed that you show to a prospective buyer. The buyer loves the house and enters into a contract to purchase the house. You are not aware of any material defects in the home and the buyer asks you your opinion on whether he should spend money on a house inspection.
>
> A. You tell your buyer that you always recommend a home inspection because you never know what issues there might be that are not easily observable.
> B. Ignorance is bliss. Since you don't have any knowledge that there is a problem with the home you suggest to the buyer to save money by skipping the inspection.
>
> A is the correct answer. If you advised against the inspection and a problem was later found with the home; you, your broker, and the seller could all be sued.

Authorized Brokerage Relationships

Special Emphasis
Duties in No Brokerage Relationship — *Also with Single & Transaction!*
- Account for all funds
- Dealing honestly and fairly
- Disclosure of all known facts that materially affect the value of residential real property that are not readily observable to the buyer

Single Agent Relationship

A single agent is a broker who represents, as a fiduciary, *either* the buyer or seller *but not both* in the same transaction. This applies to any agent working under the broker, as it is the broker that has the fiduciary relationship. So, this means that if one agent under a broker is working as a subagent in a single agent relationship, then another agent in the same brokerage would only be able to work with the buyer in a No Brokerage Agency capacity. The party with whom a real estate broker has entered into a single agent relationship with is called the principal.

Duties of Single Agency

The single agent disclosure must be given before, or at the time of, entering into a listing agreement or an agreement for representation or before showing the property, whichever occurs first. There are nine duties that Florida Statutes dictate must be upheld within the single agent relationship.

The first three are the same as required with a no agency relationship:
- Deal honestly and fairly.
- Disclose all known facts that materially affect the value of residential property that are not readily observable to the buyer.
- Account for all funds entrusted to the licensee.

The Other Six of the Nine Duties of Single Agency:
- Loyalty
- Confidentiality
- Obedience
- Full disclosure
- Skill, care, and diligence in the transaction
- Presenting all offers and counteroffers in a timely manner.

475.278 (b) (1)

Single Agent Relationship

So, what does the duty of confidentiality mean?

Throughout the course of a real estate transaction, the licensee will discover very personal information about the principal, which could directly hurt the principal's bargaining power if it was inadvertently revealed. The licensee is not allowed to share this information with anyone (except the broker or the other subagents within the same brokerage).

For example, if a broker in a single agency relationship with a seller discovers that the sellers are listing the property because the sellers are getting a divorce– the broker and the agents within the brokerage must keep this information private.

Sometimes, licensees will advertise a property as "Seller is highly motivated – bring all offers!" This would be unlawful as a single agent unless the seller had given permission for the wording. Furthermore, you must get the permission must be in writing!

475.278 (c) (1)

Obedience

Simply put, the licensee is to follow the instructions of the principal.
Sometimes this can create a conflict if the licensee doesn't believe that the instructions are in the best interest of the licensee. If this is the case, the licensee should share his or her opinion with the principal. However, if the principal isn't persuaded to change the instructions, then the licensee must either follow the instructions or formally end the relationship. If the request of the principal is for the licensee to do something that is unlawful, then the licensee cannot follow the principal's instructions!

475.278 (c) (1)

★ **Students of the post-licensing 45-hour course are instructed to do the following exercise:**

> What would you do if…
> You are working with a seller as a single agent. Comparable sales show that the property should be worth $500,000, but the seller wants to list the property for $400,000.
> A. You explain to the seller why you think the property is worth $500,000. When the seller insists on listing it for only $400,000, you list it for $400,000 (assuming that you believe the seller is mentally competent).
> B. You argue with the seller because not only is the seller going to lose out on the $100,000 difference – you will lose out on the difference in the commission that you earn as a percentage of the sale price.
>
> A is the correct answer. Because you are loyal to your client's interests, you would explain the value of the home. But also, because you are obedient - when the seller insists on the lower price; you would follow the seller's instructions.

Full Disclosure

The broker is required to share any and all information that may work to the benefit of the principal to know.

FLORIDA REAL ESTATE 45-HOUR COURSE COMPANION

475.278 (c) (1)

Present all Offers

A single agent is obligated to present all offers and counteroffers in a timely manner, unless the principal has previously directed the licensee otherwise *in writing*.

475.278 (c) (1)

Authorized Brokerage Relationships

Special Emphasis
Duties of a Single Agent

- Account for all funds
- Dealing honestly and fairly
- Disclosure of all known facts that materially affect the value of residential real property that are not readily observable to the buyer
- Use skill, care, and diligence in the transaction
- Presenting all offers and counteroffers in a timely manner
- Loyalty
- Obedience
- Confidentiality
- Full disclosure

Also with No Disclosure & Transaction!

Also with Transaction!

★ Students of the post-licensing 45-hour course are instructed to do the following exercise:

> What would you do if…
> You have a home listed and the seller told you not to bother him with an offer of less than $350,000. You have an agent that contacts you and gives you a verbal offer of $325,000.
>
> A. When the seller told you not to bother with offers below $350,000, you advised the seller that he must put the directive in writing or you would have to present all offers. And then when you received the offer for $325,000, you ignored it.
> B. When the seller told you not to bother with offers below $350,000, you tell the seller that although you understand that he has a price in mind that it was best to keep the seller informed of all offers. If the seller wasn't interested in an offer, it would be no problem to reject or ignore them. Because the seller agreed, when the $325,000 offer was given, you notify the seller.
>
> B is the correct answer. Although "A" is legally correct, it is not unusual for a seller to later accept an offer below an amount he or she first would have rejected.

Presumption of Transaction Broker Relationship

Per Florida Statute 475.278 (b), there is a "presumption of transaction brokerage" meaning that it shall be assumed that all licensees are operating as transaction brokers unless a single agent or no brokerage relationship is established, in writing, with a customer.

Because of the presumption, a <u>transaction broker disclosure is not required to be made in writing or otherwise</u>. A transaction broker means a broker who provides limited representation to a buyer, a seller, or both, in a real estate transaction; but does not represent either in a fiduciary capacity or as a single agent. Transaction brokers provide a limited form of non-fiduciary representation to a buyer, a seller, or both in a real estate transaction.

In a transaction broker relationship, a buyer or seller is not responsible for the acts of a licensee.

★ **Students of the post-licensing 45-hour course are instructed to do the following exercise:**

What would you do if…
You work for a broker that only authorizes you to operate as a transaction broker – never as a single agent. When you work with a buyer or seller:
  A. Do not have to present an agency disclosure since Florida law presumes that you are working as a transaction agent when no other disclosure is presented.
  B. You must present the Transition to Transaction Broker form and get a signature on the form agreeing to the relationship.

A is the correct answer. A Transition to Transaction Broker form would only be necessary had the relationship been operating as a single agent and was changing back to a transaction agent.

Limited Representation of Transaction Broker Relationship

The parties to a real estate transaction must understand that they are giving up their rights to the undivided loyalty of a licensee. This aspect of limited representation allows a licensee to facilitate a real estate transaction by assisting both the buyer and the seller, but a licensee will not work to represent one party to the detriment of the other party when acting as a transaction broker to both parties.

Duties of a Transaction Broker

There are seven duties that must be upheld.
The first three are the same as required with a no agency relationship and single agency relationship:

- Deal honestly and fairly.

- Disclose all known facts that materially affect the value of residential property that are not readily observable to the buyer.

- Account for all funds entrusted to the licensee.

Two of the Other Four Duties of Transaction Broker are the Same as with a Single Agency

- Skill, care, and diligence in the transaction
- Presenting all offers and counteroffers in a timely manner.

The remaining two duties are:
- Exercise limited confidentiality, unless waived in writing by a party
- Perform additional duties mutually agreed to with a party.

This type of relationship does not obligate the licensee to either disclosure or full confidentiality. Limited Confidentiality will prevent disclosure that the seller will accept a price less than the asking or listed price, that the buyer will pay a price greater than the price submitted in a written offer, of the motivation of any party for selling or buying property, that a seller or buyer will agree to financing terms other than those offered, or any other information expected by a party to remain confidential.

F.S. 475.278 (1)(b)

Authorized Brokerage Relationships

Special Emphasis

Duties of a Transaction Broker

- Account for all funds
- Dealing honestly and fairly
- Disclosure of all known facts that materially affect the value of residential real property that are not readily observable to the buyer
- Use skill, care, and diligence in the transaction
- Presenting all offers and counteroffers in a timely manner
- Exercise limited confidentiality, unless waived in writing by a party
- Perform additional duties as mutually agreed to

Also with No Disclosure & Single!

Also with Single Agent!

★ Students of the post-licensing 45-hour course are instructed to do the following exercise:

> What would you do if…
> You have a buyer that is very eager to buy a home that is listed by another agent in your brokerage. While walking to your office, you happen to overhear the listing agent talking with the seller of that home. You learn that the seller is behind on his mortgage and needs to sell the home fast.
>
> A. You immediately call your buyer and insist that the buyer make a low ball offer right away. After all, the seller is desperate.
> B. Tell the other agent that you accidentally overheard that the seller is eager to sell and ask if the agent has gotten written permission to disclose this motivation to a buyer in order to illicit competitive offers. When you find out that the seller wants the information kept confidential, you do not tell your buyer.
>
> B is the correct answer. It is the broker that has the fiduciary relationship with both the buyer and the seller. Both agents are acting as general agents of the broker. Therefore, the buyer's agent must hold what the seller has said in confidence.

Consent to Transition from Single Agent to Transaction Broker

Sometimes, despite having entered into a relationship as single agent with a principal, it makes sense to transition back to a transaction broker. If a single agency relationship has not been entered into, the licensee automatically would have been in a transaction broker relationship with the customer.

Once the single agent relationship has been formed, it may be changed to a transaction broker relationship at any time during the relationship between an agent and principal, provided the agent gives the transition disclosure and the principal consents to the transition in writing and with a signature before a change in the relationship.

Limited representation means that a buyer or seller is not responsible for the acts of the licensee. Additionally, parties are giving up their rights to the undivided loyalty of the licensee. This aspect of limited representation allows a licensee to facilitate a real estate transaction by assisting both the buyer and the seller, but a licensee will not work to represent one party to the detriment of the other party when acting as a transaction broker to both parties.

The procedure to do this requires that the single agent disclosure be given before, or at the time of entering into a listing agreement or an agreement for representation or before showing of property, whichever occurs first. Then, a transition disclosure is given and a secure consent (signature) from the party is obtained.

★ **Students of the post-licensing 45-hour course are instructed to do the following exercise:**

> What would you do if...
> You have a home listed and you are representing the seller as a single agent. You plan to advertise the property and also hope to be able to assist a buyer in the purchase of the home.
>
> A. At the time of listing, you present the single agency disclosure in writing to the seller. And then you also present the transition to transaction agency agreement and secure the seller's signature just in case you have the opportunity to also work with the buyer.
> B. You have the "no agency disclosures" on hand to present to a buyer just in case you get a buyer who isn't represented by another agent.
>
> A is the best answer. Although "B" isn't incorrect, many buyers are not prepared to represent themselves in a transaction so "A" is the better answer. In fact, there is a listing contract available for use for members of the Florida Association that has the Transition to Transaction Agent agreement written directly into the listing contract.

Designated Sales Associate

In residential real estate, a broker is not allowed to act as a single agent for both a buyer and a seller. To do so would create a dual agency which is illegal in Florida. However, in non-residential real estate there is a twist on this concept known as the Designated Sales Associate which is allowed per Florida Statutes. In a non-residential transaction where the buyer and seller each have assets of $1 million or more, the broker at the request of the customers, may designate sales associates to act as single agents for different customers in the same transaction.

Such designated sales associates shall have the duties of a single agent including the requirement to disclose in writing the duties of the relationship. In addition to disclosure requirements presented in reference to residential real estate, the buyer and seller, as customers, shall both sign disclosures stating that their assets meet the threshold of $1 million or more and requesting that the broker use the designated sales associate form of representation.

Florida Statutes 475.2755

Duties of Designated Sales Associate

The duties of a designated sales associate are the same as a regular single agent and must be fully described and disclosed in writing to a buyer or seller in agreements for representation include the following:

- Account for all funds

- Dealing honestly and fairly

- Disclosure of these duties must be made before or during entrance into a listing/representation agreement, or before the showing of property.

- Use skill, care, and diligence in the transaction

- Presenting all offers and counteroffers in a timely manner

- Loyalty

- Obedience

- Confidentiality
- Full disclosure

Confidentiality

In regard to the duty of confidentiality, what this rule does is that it removes the broker from having direct contact with the buyer and seller and to instead act as an advisor of the sales associates who interface with the principals. THE PURPOSE OF this provision is to allow each agent to seek advice from the broker for the benefit of the customer in regard to the transaction. Any information obtained by the broker during these discussions must be held confidential from the other sales associate and the other principal. This allows each party to equally benefit by the relationship with the sales associate and the broker without detriment to their dealings.

SECTION 4 PROPERTY MANAGEMENT

SECTION 4 PROPERTY MANAGEMENT of this course, focuses on providing property management services.

Chapters include:
  16 Property Management

Upon completion of this section, licensees should have a good grasp of how to conduct real estate property management. This includes helping investors choose properties that will bring a good rate of return as a rental property, dealing with management and rental contracts, setting rental rates, screening tenants, management rent collection, inspections, repairs, problem tenants, and financial reporting.

16 PROPERTY MANAGEMENT

Learning Terms and Phrases

- Property Manager
- Types of Property
- Attracting Landlords
- Types of Landlords
- Management Contracts
- Maximizing Profits
- Choosing Rental Property
- Setting Rental Rates
- Tenant Criteria
- Remaining Legally Compliant

- Attracting a Tenant
- Tenant Applications
- Background Checks
- Lease Agreements
- Move-Ins
- Rent Collection
- Managing Repairs
- Inspections
- Move-Outs
- Problem Tenants
- Key-Log

Learning Objectives

- Licensees should have an understanding of the different types of properties for a property manager to manage.
- Licensees should have an understanding of how to execute the various tasks required by property managers.
- Licensees should have a good understanding of the importance of documenting a property's condition prior to leasing, during leasing, and following a lease.
- Licensees should have a good grasp on the importance and process of conducting tenant background checks.
- Licensees should understand the importance of properly crafted property management agreements and lease agreements.
- Licensees should be able to correctly handle property management escrow accounts.

What is Property Management?

Whenever a property is offered for rent, property management is required to facilitate the rental process. Although property management duties may be handled by the actual owner, it is common for the property owner to hire a property manager to perform these duties for compensation.

Growth of Property Management

With an ever-increasing number of people looking to own real estate as an investment, the need for property managers continues to be on the rise. Property managers are expected to have diverse skills including being able to prepare and analyze financial documents, being able to guide a landlord in acquiring and maintaining profitable rental property, being able to interface and manage potential and existing tenants, and being able to manage legal issues.

Rental Agent or Property Manager?

Similar to hiring a real estate licensee to sell a property, a rental agent's duties end upon securing a tenant for a property. Property management, however, is more involved than just securing a tenant for the property. It involves ongoing duties such as rent collection, periodic inspections, overseeing move-ins and move-outs, and the handling of legal issues from contracts to evictions.

Real Estate License Required?

In Florida, to conduct business as a rental agent or property manager for compensation, a real estate broker license is required. Real estate sales associates and broker associates may interface with landlords and tenants on behalf of the broker – just as with real estate sales. A real estate license is not required to act as an on-site property manager for an apartment building. However, compensation must be paid as a salary and not as a commission or on a transactional basis.

Non-licensed assistants may be paid a salary for activities that do not require a real estate license. This includes activities such as collecting and recording scheduled rent payments, answering incoming phone inquiries about a property (answers must be limited to a fact sheet prepared by the broker about the property), preparing advertisements to be approved by the broker, and preparing contracts as directed by the broker.

Refer to the description of acceptable activities by non-licensed assistants posted on www.myfloridalicense.com

On-site property managers and non-licensed assistants must NEVER be paid a commission or on a transaction basis. To do so triggers the requirement for the assistant to be licensed.

Types of Property to Manage

There is a need to manage three basic types of properties: residential, commercial, and industrial. Residential real estate can be divided into single-family homes and multi-family residences. Residential real estate can further be broken down into either long-term rentals or seasonal/vacation rentals. The rentals may or may not involve furnishings. When the property is rented "turnkey", this indicates that everything is included right down to forks and towels. Due to the shorter rental period involved with seasonal/vacation rentals – this type of property management is normally more involved than with other types of property management and therefore, normally also brings in more income to the licensee conducting the property management duties.

Although multi-family residences larger than 4 units is legally defined as commercial real estate, property managers specializing in commercial real estate are generally focused on income-producing property not used as a residence. These include properties such as office buildings, shopping centers, stand-alone business properties, and gas stations. This type of property management may or may not involve the sale or lease of the business opportunity already connected with the site.

Industrial property managers focus on property connected with manufacturing or storage. As manufacturing may involve emissions and effluents, property managers working in this field require a specific knowledge base of applicable laws regarding testing for, the control of, the containment of and the elimination of these potential pollutants. Due to the complexity of each type of property management category, it is common for property managers to specialize in only one of these types of rental categories.

Attracting Residential Landlords

Working as a residential property manager involves finding properties to manage. This means that the broker/licensee must market themselves to the community to attract potential landlords. Marketing services as a property manager is similar to marketing services as a real estate sales agent. It involves prospecting for leads and then converting leads to clients. The licensee must be able to articulate the benefit of hiring the broker as a property manager.

Types of Landlords

Many homeowners unintentionally find themselves in the position of being a landlord. This includes individuals who have suddenly inherited a second property, individuals who have suddenly been transferred by their employer, and individuals who unexpectedly find an opportunity to purchase a property – when the deal is "too good to pass up." These homeowners are often eager to find help from a property manager as their unexpected ownership of the property has left them ill-prepared to deal with the aspects of managing the rental property themselves.

The absent owner is another good candidate for utilizing the services of a property manager. These include individuals who may have intentionally sought ownership of rental property along with the unintentional owner. The distinction being that these owners do not live near enough to the rental property to easily manage it on their own. In Florida, absentee owners often live in other countries. This means that the ability to reach owners from abroad is key along with having the ability to communicate with foreign speaking clients.

Real Estate Investment Trusts also are in need of property managers. These are investment groups formed by multiple investors for the purpose of acquiring real estate. This type of owner is generally looking for passive income without being involved in the day-to-day activities of property management.

Rental Management Contracts

Most property management relationships are formally created between the broker and the homeowner by the signing of a written management agreement. This contract specifies the duties of the property manager, the length of the contract, and the compensation to be paid for providing management services. As with any contract, should a dispute arise between the broker and the homeowner, the contract will act as the basis to determine compliance with the terms.

The primary purpose of the management agreement is to give the property manager the authority to secure a lessee and to oversee the maintenance and financial aspects of the property. Keep in mind, though, that without specific power of attorney being obtained, the property owner would need to approve and sign all rental agreements with the tenant.

The Statute of Frauds require that all contracts secured for more than one year must be in writing.

Job Tasks of Property Manager

As already stated, the job tasks of the property manager are far more diverse and ongoing than a rental agent. It often starts with assisting the landlord in choosing and preparing a property for purchase and rent. A rental rate will need to be determined. Tenants will need to be attracted, screened, and selected. Adherence to fair housing and disability acts will need to be maintained. Tenants will need assistance in arranging move-ins and move-outs of the property. Rents will need to be collected, managed, and reported in prepared financial disclosures. Required disclosures will need to be made. Inspections and repairs will need to be managed. Handling problems with tenants will need to be managed accordingly, such as initiating evictions.

Maximizing Profits

It is the property manager's job to ensure that the property owner is maximizing his or her return on the investment in the rental property. This often starts with guiding the client into choosing the right property to purchase and offer as a rental. It continues through choosing a rental rate that will put as much money in the owner's pocket as possible, while also attracting a tenant. The property manager will need to ensure that services provided for the property, such as security and maintenance, are adequate to preserve the value of the property while also being charged a competitive rate to the owner. Furthermore, the property manager will need to ensure that tenants are taking care of the property while it is being used.

Choosing a Property

Potential landlords will often look to the licensee to help find and analyze the potential purchase of property to be used as a rental investment.

The licensee will need to analyze market saturation levels of rentals in any area a purchase is being considered. This involves pulling data from the multiple listing service to determine how many rentals are currently on the market for rent, how long they have been sitting vacant, and how long recently rented properties remained on the market before securing tenants. From this data, the licensee should also be able to determine average rental rates for properties being considered for purchase. Keep in mind, that not all rental property is advertised in the MLS. A broader picture of the rental market may be obtained by speaking directly with property managers already working within that market area.

Analyzing the property will also involve noting the desirable property features commonly sought by renters. For example, 2 or 3 bedroom units are usually much easier to rent out than 1 bedroom properties. Location and neighborhood amenities such as community pools, school ratings, and crime statistics should also be considered.

Setting Rental Rates

The same data pulled to determine whether the property is a good investment will also be used to determine a rental rate for the property. The goal of the rental rate is to be attractive enough to secure a tenant while also maximizing the return on the investment in the property.

Analyzing Property Condition

Property owners may need to be guided in what improvements should immediately be made to the property in order to prepare it as a rental. The costs of the improvements should be weighed against possible increases in rent due to the improvements as well as general marketability of the property.

Once the property is ready to put on the market, the property manager must meticulously document the condition of the property. This involves taking photographs and videos of the property. It also involves making a property feature list, such as appliances, furnishings, window coverings, etc.

Setting Tenant Criteria

Landlords may require a minimum credit score and proof of income for prospective tenants. They may also screen for criminal background issues. Landlords may also set terms such as whether pets are allowed on the property. A decision also has to be made as to whether a deposit is required and how much the deposit would be, plus, whether first and last month's rent must be paid before moving into the property. All these requirements must be applied equally to all prospective tenants.

Remaining Fair Housing Compliant

The licensee must ensure that no fair housing laws are violated. Tenant criteria must be applied equally for all applicants. A tenant may not be turned down based on race, religion, national origin, gender, disability or familial status.

See Chapter 13, "Fair Housing Applied," for more information.

Remaining ADA Compliant

The Americans with Disabilities Act requires that both reasonable accommodations and reasonable modifications be allowed for tenants with disabilities. This includes changes in rules, policies, practices, or services to accommodate the person such as in how an application is taken. Plus, the addition of ramps, lowering thresholds, installing grab bars etc. must be allowed. This is at the expense of the tenant not the landlord.

Since a rental property should appeal to as large a population as possible, it is advisable to keep in mind the potential need for modifications while making any improvements to the property. For example, if new wiring is being run throughout the property, it may be a good idea to install outlets and switches at recommended heights for wheelchair access.

See Chapter 13, "Fair Housing Applied," for more information.

Attracting a Tenant

Attracting a tenant to a rental property is similar to attracting a buyer to a home for sale. It starts with making sure that the property looks as appealing as possible. The property should be clean and clear of any sign of previous tenants. Fresh paint may make the home more inviting. Curb appeal should be heightened with the addition of appropriate flowers, etc. The licensee may utilize property for rent signage, entry into the multiple listing service, online rental websites, and print media to market the property.

Tenant Applications

It is recommended that a formal written application be taken to screen tenants. By using a written form, licensees have a record to prove that all potential applicants are treated equally – without discrimination regarding the information that is gathered. Information should be gathered about all individuals that would be living in the home. Signed permission should be obtained before attempting to verify credit, rental history, employment, or background checks. A record should be kept of anyone who was turned down.

Tenant Background Checks

As stated, signed permission should be obtained before running a background check on a potential tenant. Should a tenant refuse to grant permission, this could be used as a basis to turn the person down as a tenant – so long as you require that all prospective tenants submit to a background check.

Due to the complexity of performing background checks, property managers are better served by utilizing an outside service to perform the check rather than trying to vet the individual him or herself. The property management agreement would specify who would carry the cost for the background check. The cost could be absorbed by the property manager, paid by the property owner, or even passed on to the applicant.

> **Students of the post-licensing 45-hour course are instructed to do the following exercise:**

> What would you do if...
> You have been hired as a property manager and are looking to secure a tenant. Someone that you have known for ten years wants to rent the home. How do you handle the background check?
>
> A. Because you have known the person so long, you decide to save on the cost of a formal background check and complete the application process without it.
> B. You explain to your friend that the background check is required by the seller and proceed as normal.
>
> B is the correct answer. Remember that as a property manager it is your duty to ensure that all procedures are followed for all applicants. Not only does this uphold your fiduciary duty to the landlord, it keeps you compliant with fair housing by treating all prospects equally.

Lease Agreement

In Florida, licensees are not allowed to draw up a lease from scratch. Instead, licensees may use fill-in-the-blank contracts that have been approved by the Florida Supreme Court. Members of the Florida Association of Realtors® can find access to forms through Forms Simplicity. As always, licensees should inquire with their brokers about forms.

Leases should clearly detail who is allowed to reside in the property. The terms of lease, such as payment amounts and dates, and when the lease expires, they must also be included. Conditions, such as whether pets are permitted, should be detailed. Also, expectations about property condition and who is obligated to what would also be specified (who pays for trash removal, utilities, minor repairs, etc.).

Lease agreements should also specify where advance rents and deposits will be held.

See Chapter 8, "Contracts," for more information.

Lead Based Paint Disclosure

Recall that a lead based paint disclosure must be made to renters as well as buyers for homes built prior to 1978. The purpose is to disclose whether knowledge of or records exist of lead based paint in the home.

Agency Disclosure

Recall that agency disclosures only must be made with residential "sales." Thus, they do not apply to leasing. However, this doesn't relieve you from duties such as accounting for all funds, disclosing any material defects that could affect residing in the property, and treating everyone honestly and fairly. Also, be mindful of creating a fiduciary relationship, which obligates you to other duties (such as loyalty and obedience) if that is not your intention!

Tenant Move-In Process

It is imperative that all lease agreements are signed and all monies are collected before allowing a tenant to move into the property. Otherwise it could require a legal eviction process to get the person back out of the property – even if money never exchanged hands!

Before turning keys over to the tenant, the property manager should escort the tenant throughout the property to verify the condition of the property. All flaws should be noted on a form and signed by the tenant. The form should also be written as an acknowledgment that the tenant is responsible for anything not noted on the form. The addition of photographs and videos time stamped immediately prior to move-in is a great tool for documenting condition.

Rent Collection Duties

Property managers must have a specific process in place for handling rent collection. Collected rent should be deposited into the broker's escrow account and never in the broker's general operating account. The property management agreement should specify when the rent will be paid from the property manager to the homeowner. When setting up these policies, allow time for "checks to clear" before having to issue funds to the property owner.

Most property managers will have, as part of the management contract, that the rent issued to the property owner will be minus the management fee. The management fee would be transferred to the broker's operating account upon the issuance of the rent to the property owner. Recall that the licensee working for the broker must be compensated directly from the broker and not diverted from these funds.

★ **Students of the post-licensing 45-hour course are instructed to do the following exercise:**

> What would you do if...
> You collect a $1,500 rent check from a tenant for a home. The management fee is $200 with 50% going to you as the licensee. How should the funds be handled?
>
> A. Immediately cash the check and take $100 as the licensee, send $1,300 to the property owner, and give your broker $100.
> B. Give your broker the entire amount to deposit into the broker's escrow funds. Then follow the release guidelines as directed within the management agreement with the property owners.
>
> B is the correct answer. Licensees may not be paid directly by clients – only by the broker.

Managing Maintenance and Repairs

It is common that upon entering a property management agreement, money is collected from the homeowner to set up a maintenance and repair fund. This becomes a type of "escrow" and should be deposited into the broker's escrow account and not the broker's general operating account. These funds are then on hand to pay for small pre-authorized repairs such as emergency plumbing issues. At no time should the tenant's advance rent and security deposit be used to pay for repairs. To do so would be illegal as "conversion" of funds. This is true even if the property owner later reimburses the cost of the repairs.

★ **Students of the post-licensing 45-hour course are instructed to do the following exercise:**

> Rental Escrow Balance Sheet
> Review the following Rental Operating Balance Sheet. The policy of this property manager is to collect from the seller $400 at a start of a rental to handle small repairs and property expenses. The broker manages 5 properties. Based on this balance sheet, determine which part is a violation in law:
>
> | Property Address | Rent Received | Owner Reserve | Management Fee | Disbursements | Owner Balance | Escrow Acct Balance |
> |---|---|---|---|---|---|---|
> | | | | | | | $2,000 |
> | 100 Tom Cat Lane | $1,000 | $400 | $150 | $ 850 to Owner | $400 | $2,000 |
> | 171 Cart Wheel Rd | $1,200 | $400 | $160 | $1,040 to Owner | $400 | $2,000 |
> | 253 Hop Scotch St | $1,400 | $400 | $170 | $1,230 to Owner | $400 | $2,000 |
> | 111 Skip Doo Ave | $1,200 | $400 | $160 | $1600 AC repair | -$160 | $1,440 |
> | 125 Dog Wag Circle | $1,100 | $400 | $165 | $935 | $400 | $1,440 |
>
> The property at 111 Skip Doo Ave had expenses that went above the reserve held for that property plus the rent collected for that property. By ending the month $160 short for that owner in the account, you are illegally using $160, which was held in trust for other property owners. That money cannot be used to cover expenses of 111 Skip Doo Ave! You have to view each property as having separate funds held only for the benefit of that property!

Conducting Periodic Inspections

The property manager will need to conduct periodic inspections of the property while the tenant is living in the home. Surprise inspections, by law, must allow for at least a 24*-hour notice. Tenants cannot withhold permission for a landlord to enter the premises without cause. Tenants must allow landlords (or property managers acting on behalf of the landlord) to enter property to make inspections, provide services, make repairs, and to show property. The landlord may enter property at any time in case of emergency.

The majority of visits, though, are planned well in advance. Property managers should have scheduled visits in place, which may often occur on a quarterly basis. During these visits, the property manager is looking to ensure that rules are being followed and that the property is being preserved. These visits are also a good opportunity to communicate whether the tenant plans to renew the lease agreement.

Overseeing Move-Outs

Just as with move-ins, property managers will need to be on hand to escort the tenant throughout the property to document the current condition of the property. Depending upon the lease agreement, the tenant may be held liable for damages. The property manager will need to make such determinations before releasing deposits. The property manager may need to assemble documentation should the issue end up in court. If the full deposit is being returned, it must be done within 15 days. If a claim is being made against the deposit, notice must be sent by certified mail to the tenant within 30 days.

Handling Problem Tenants
The two most common problems that property managers encounter is either the tenant not maintaining the property in an acceptable manner or the tenant not paying rent. Both of these issues may warrant the need to evict the tenant. In order to legally vacate based on condition, the landlord must provide a 7-day written notice to the tenant of intent to cancel the lease. This notice gives the tenant an opportunity to make corrections and avoid the eviction. This notice must be given in writing and delivered personally or mailed. The landlord may also choose to post the notice on the door. The notice need only be for three business days if the reason for eviction is for lack of payment of rent. If the tenant continues to occupy the property without responding, a final judgment from court for the eviction would need to be obtained. Upon the order, a 24-hour notice to vacate is posted on the door of the property. The final step would be the court issuing a writ of possession, which is served by the sheriff to the tenant.

Financial Reporting to Landlords
Accountability is key when it comes to property management. Thus, all property managers need to provide a financial accounting to landlords tracking how their investment is making a return.

These reports will include details about where money is held in escrow, totals, and a breakdown of expenditures.

Many licensees will be asked not only to produce these financial reports, but to interpret them and offer advice as to how earnings can be maximized.

Safety Measures
Safety in property management for tenants is always a concern. Senate Bill 898 requires employees of apartments to go through a background check by a consumer reporting agency as a condition of employment with certain offenses disqualifying someone from employment. A "key-log" must be kept of who has access to apartments. *Effective July 1, 2022, the bill changed the time for entry for nonemergency from 12 hours to 24 hours. This is the result of the murder of Miya Marcano. Chapter 83.53, F.S.

Sources and Resources

https://www.floridarealtors.org/LegalCenter/
http://realtormag.realtor.org/
www.myfloridalicense.com/
https://www.nar.realtor/
http://www.myfloridalicense.com/dbpr/servop/testing/documents/printable_lawbook.pdf

1: Business Planning

www.investopedia.com/terms/p/paretoprinciple.asp
www.forbes.com/sites/davelavinsky/2014/01/20/pareto-principle-how-to-use-it-to-dramatically-grow-your-business/
http://www.marketleader.com/blog/2009/06/13/calculate-number-of-transactions-needed-consider-current-commissions-and-average-sale-prices/
http://transaction911.com/real-estate-agents-how-to-calculate-your-sales-prospects/
https://www.thebalance.com/communication-skills-list-2063779

2: Prospecting

https://www.nar.realtor/field-guides/field-guide-to-farming-and-prospecting
http://realtormag.realtor.org/node/11779
http://fitsmallbusiness.com/real-estate-farming/

3: Managing Listing

http://www.inman.com/next/5-things-agents-must-do-before-their-next-listing-appointment/
http://bestlistingpresentation.com/2015/05/12/helpful-tips-for-listing-presentation-appointments/

4: Managing Buyers

www.rebac.net/home-buying/getting-started/descriptions-agency
https://www.redfin.com/definition/procuring-cause
http://realtormag.realtor.org/law-and-ethics/law/article/2005/11/procuring-cause-who-gets-paid

5: Objection Handling

www.websitebox.com/file/12470/MF_40_Real_Estate_Objections_Handled.pdf
http://www.comparebusinessproducts.com/briefs/how-overcome-top-three-objections-real-estate
http://changingminds.org/disciplines/sales/objection/objection_handling.htm
http://agocluytens.com/sales-techniques-objection-handling/
https://blog.hubspot.com/sales/the-5-most-common-objections-during-prospecting-and-how-to-overcome-them

6: Financing Considerations

http://www.realliving.com/pages/types-of-mortgage-loans
http://clark.com/homes-real-estate/6-options-for-buying-a-home-with-little-or-no/
http://www.bankrate.com/finance/mortgages/4-mortgages-that-require-little-money-down-1.aspx

7: Condo HOA CDD

www.floridacondohoalawblog.com/
www.myfloridalicense.com/dbpr/lsc/documents/7182010bookletwithannot.pdf
http://www.leg.state.fl.us/Statutes/index.cfm?App_mode=Display_Statute&URL=0700-0799/0718/0718.html

www.floridacondohoalawblog.com/
http://www.leg.state.fl.us/Statutes/index.cfm?App_mode=Display_Statute&URL=0700-0799/0720/0720ContentsIndex.html
https://en.wikipedia.org/wiki/Community_development_district
http://www.leg.state.fl.us/Statutes/index.cfm?App_mode=Display_Statute&URL=0100-0199/0190/0190.html
https://www.floridarealtors.org/news-media/news-articles/2023/02/florida-realtors-riders-being-revised

8: Contracts
http://aboutfloridalaw.com/2016/11/01/florida-real-estate-contract-lawsuits/
https://www.floridarealtors.org/LegalCenter/AskanAttorney/Contracts-Legal-FAQs.cfm
http://www.nolo.com/legal-encyclopedia/florida-home-sellers-disclosures-required-under-state-law.html
http://statelaws.findlaw.com/florida-law/florida-property-and-real-estate-laws.html

9: Inspections
http://www.imhomeinspector.com/Home-Inspections-Things-To-Know.html
http://www.williamsparker.com/docs/default-source/PDFs/residential-inspections-and-repairs---procedures-and-pitfalls
https://www.nar.realtor/field-guides/field-guide-to-home-inspections
http://www.realtor.com/advice/buy/what-does-a-home-inspector-look-for/
https://www.aol.com/article/2013/07/19/home-inspection-red-flags/20664859/

10: Closing
https://en.wikipedia.org/wiki/Closing_(real_estate)
www.homebuyinginstitute.com/closing.php
http://aboutfloridalaw.com/2015/06/09/big-changes-in-florida-real-estate-closings-the-hud-1-settlement-form-replaced-with-trid-form/
https://www.thebalance.com/what-are-prorations-1798778
http://www.recsfl.com/consumer-services/customary-expenses-for-florida-real-estate-closings/

11: Licensing Law – Maintaining Compliance
http://www.leg.state.fl.us/Statutes/index.cfm?App_mode=Display_Statute&URL=0400-0499/0475/0475.html
https://www.floridarealtors.org/LegalCenter/AskanAttorney/Real-Estate-License-Law-Legal-FAQs.cfm
http://www.myfloridalicense.com/dbpr/servop/testing/documents/printable_lawbook.pdf
https://www.floridarealtors.org/Education/LicensingRequirements/License-Renewal.cfm
http://www.myfloridalicense.com/dbpr/re/documents/real_estate_ed_requirements.pdf

12: Ethics and Business Practices
https://www.floridarealtors.org/LegalCenter/CodeofEthics/Index.cfm
https://www.nar.realtor/about-nar/governing-documents/the-code-of-ethics
http://www.orlandorealtors.org/news/336115/FREC-adds-ethics-requirement-to-the-license-renewal-process.htm

13: Fair Housing Applied
https://portal.hud.gov/hudportal/HUD?src=/program_offices/fair_housing_equal_opp/FHLaws/yourrights
https://www.justice.gov/crt/fair-housing-act-2
https://www.thespruce.com/florida-fair-housing-law-protected-classes-155926

http://www.leg.state.fl.us/Statutes/index.cfm/index.cfm?App_mode=Display_Statute&Search_String=&URL=0700-0799/0760/Sections/0760.23.html
https://www.whitehouse.gov/briefing-room/presidential-actions/2021/01/20/executive-order-preventing-and-combating-discrimination-on-basis-of-gender-identity-or-sexual-orientation/

14: ECOA TILA RESPA
https://en.wikipedia.org/wiki/Equal_Credit_Opportunity_Act
http://files.consumerfinance.gov/f/201306_cfpb_laws-and-regulations_ecoa-combined-june-2013.pdf
https://www.consumer.ftc.gov/articles/0347-your-equal-credit-opportunity-rights
https://www.consumerfinance.gov/f/201503_cfpb_truth-in-lending-act.pdf
https://www.consumerfinance.gov/.../what-is-a-final-truth-in-lending-disclosure.html
https://www.ftc.gov/sites/...disclosures...disclosure-forms/samplecurrentforms.pdf
https://s3.amazonaws.com/files.consumerfinance.gov/f/201503_cfpb_regulation-x-real-estate-settlement-procedures-act.pdf
https://portal.hud.gov/hudportal/HUD?src=/hudprograms/respa

15: Agency in Practice
http://www.saadlegal.com/blog/2014/07/real-estate-qa---single-agent-vs-transaction-broker.shtml
http://www.leg.state.fl.us/Statutes/index.cfm?App_mode=Display_Statute&URL=0400-0499/0475/Sections/0475.278.html
https://toughnickel.com/real-estate/The-Problem-with-Dual-Agency-in-a-Real-Estate-Transaction
https://www.nar.realtor/about-nar/governing-documents/the-code-of-ethics

16: Property Management
http://www.allpropertymanagement.com/propertylaw/property-management-law-in-florida.html
http://www.myfloridalicense.com/dbpr/pro/division/servicesthatrequirealicense_re.html
https://www.floridarealtors.org/FLRealtorMagazine/2007/March/RA0307.cfm
https://www.fox35orlando.com/news/florida-senate-to-vote-on-miyas-law-for-murdered-orlando-teen

ABOUT THE AUTHORS

Pamela Kemper is a veteran licensed Florida Real Estate Broker and Real Estate Instructor. She is the Broker of Azure Tide Realty and owns and teaches real estate courses at her school: Azure Tide Realty All Florida School of Real Estate. She also previously practiced Real Estate in Indiana and Michigan. Plus, Pamela holds a Bachelor of Arts Degree from Manchester College.

Made in United States
Orlando, FL
03 February 2025